# improv sewing

# improvsewing

## 101
### fast, fun, and
### fearless projects

by **nicole blum** and **debra immergut**

photography by alexandra grablewski

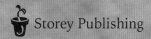

Storey Publishing

*The mission of Storey Publishing is to serve our customers by publishing practical information that encourages personal independence in harmony with the environment.*

Edited by **Deborah Balmuth and Beth Baumgartel**
Art direction and book design by **Carolyn Eckert**

Cover and interior photography by © **Alexandra Grablewski,** except for front cover (title) by Mars Vilaubi, pages 34, 36 (bottom), 40 (bottom), 49 (bottom), 101 (bottom), 108, 123 (right), 143, 145, 160, 167, 168, 189 (bottom right), 196 (bottom), 197, 229 (right), 246 (left, right), 262, 267 (top right), 272, and 287 (bottom) by Carolyn Eckert, and 100 (left) by Nicole Blum

Photo styling by **Nicole Blum**
Illustrations by © **Ryan McMenamy**
Templates by **Missy Shepler, Shepler Studios**

Indexed by **Catherine Goddard**

**Special thanks to Porches,** www.porches.com, for generously allowing us to use the inn in our photo shoots. Shot on location in the Berkshires, Massachusetts.

Storey books are available for special premium and promotional uses and for customized editions. For further information, please call 1-800-793-9396.

**Storey Publishing**
210 MASS MoCA Way
North Adams, MA 01247
*www.storey.com*

**Printed in China by R.R. Donnelley**
10 9 8 7 6 5 4 3 2 1

Library of Congress Cataloging-in-Publication Data on file

## dedication

For Jonny, Ava, and Harry — the most creative and lovely people I know. —n.b.

For my darling improv geniuses, John and Joe. —d.i.

146

72

90

# Contents

Introduction  8

1  Getting Started  10

2  Finding Your Fit  24

3  Five Basic Designs  32

4  Ruffles, Pleats, and Trims  58

5  Lines  104

6 Doodling, Sketching, and Writing 132

7 Appliqué 170

8 Stenciling 208

9 Beyond Fabric 226

10 Upcycling 242

11 Instant Gifts, Instant Gratification 274

Templates 302

Our Favorite Sources for Fabric and Specialty Supplies 312

Acknowledgments 313

Index 314

113

194

184

150

# Introduction

**This all began because we wanted to create a different kind of sewing book.**

We wanted to share our belief that creating should be about pursuing joy, not pursuing perfection.

We've called the book *Improv Sewing* because we adore the happy accidents, the trial-by-error learning, and the oh-so-sweet flashes of inspiration that can happen when you free yourself to follow your instincts.

In the pages that follow, we map out each how-to step and even use official sewing terms now and again, but it's really not about grainlines and seam allowances for us. Instead, it's about enjoying the journey as your thread travels across the fabric. Do this, and in the end, you'll have made something lovely and wonderful, because it will be made as only you, working at this moment in time, can make it.

With all that in mind, we've created over a hundred projects that allow for all kinds of improvisation. If you don't have a fabric or tool mentioned in the material list, just use what you've got. If you don't feel like hemming an edge, well, then keep it raw. Use our templates, or pencil your own. Follow our measurements to the eighth of an inch, or fudge it a little. These projects are meant to encourage all that. As you sew, know that mistakes are an important part of the process. Remember that even the project you feel like scrapping has value in what it's taught you. No home ec teacher is going to be judging your stitches; no reality-TV show judge is going to critique your cut. The only person you need to please is yourself. Keep a playful mind-set, keep at it, and soon you'll have a closet of cool custom-fit looks, a home filled with artful touches, and a life filled with friends and families who've been the happy recipients of your handmade gifts.

A few of our designs are a bit involved, but most of the projects are fast and fuss-free, because that's what fits our lives and our natures. If you similarly have more desire to create than you have time to do it, you'll be right at home here.

We're well aware that our approach is unconventional, and that's likely because neither of us has a traditional background in sewing. Nicole's grandmother didn't sew, and her mom didn't sew. She steered clear of home economics in school and had a distorted image of sewing as a really difficult process with a lot of terminology, a lot of markings that made no sense to her, and a world of books that were too technical to be interesting. She came to it as an adult with a general DIY approach to her life. Debra has been intimidated by sewing machines all her life, and in fact spent years avoiding buying one, as they seemed to promise only guilt and frustration.

And yet here we are now, women with families and careers (and sewing machines), and we are making things like crazy and loving it, and increasing the amount of beauty in our lives by large amounts. That's the feeling we wanted to share. We hope this book will be an informative and super-inspiring read, but mostly, we want it to inspire you to stop reading and start sewing.

## HOW TO USE THIS BOOK

1. **First, start with the basics.** Sure, you'll be tempted, but don't skip chapter 1 — it contains tips on fabric selection and presents some key how-tos for constructing and finishing your projects.

2. **Next, learn to sew five building blocks for your wardrobe.** Chapter 2 gives you simple instructions on taking measurements for skirts and creating homemade pattern pieces for dresses and tops. Chapter 3 shows you how to use them to sew five basic garments — a tunic, a dress, and three skirts. These are the starting point for many of the other garment projects in the book.

3. **Then, add your own style with some easy and creative embellishment techniques.** Chapters 4 through 8 each present a different method for adding texture, dimension, and style to your sewing. The chapter introductions contain helpful info and pointers on those techniques. Learn how to add ruffles or scribble-stitching to one of the five basic garments from chapter 3, or try something completely different — an appliquéd scarf, a stenciled dog bed, or a set of geometric place mats.

4. **Finally, don't forget to play around and have fun!** Chapters 9, 10, and 11 let you really cut loose, encouraging you to stitch up projects using low-stakes materials and thrift-store finds. Get tons of ideas for turning life's castoffs (cereal-box cardboard, torn t-shirts, tacky jackets) into lovely creations for everyone in your life, including yourself.

# 1
# getting started

**Whether it's gorgeously faded vintage cotton** or a fresh bolt of jersey knit, we are fabric fanatics, and we're betting you are too. We're constantly wowed by the immense array of choices that are available these days; at our local boutiques, at national retailers, and from online shops big and small, the variety is both dazzling and daunting. In preparing these projects, we dove headlong into this sea of fabric options, and we found some real pearls (as well as a few rather gnarly grains of sand but don't worry, we left those out of the book). We hope these pages will inspire you to use not only the treasures from your stash but also to experiment with some fabrics that might be new to you, like a swishy jersey, a sturdy canvas, or an upcycled leather.

The first step of every project in this book is to select and prep an appropriate fabric in a print or color that you really love. Then, once you gather the proper tools and notions (listed on the project page), you are on your way. Read on for a few pointers for happy improv adventures.

# Choose Your Fabric

For some mysterious reason, many retailers take a cavalier attitude toward organizing and displaying their beautiful fabrics. Knits in particular tend to have their fiber content and care information labeled in a haphazard fashion in the stores and on the websites. We've ordered yardage from the "cotton jersey" section of a website and then discovered that it definitely was not 100% cotton or jersey. So, when shopping in a store, be sure to check the bolt end and look closely at the fabric content information and washing instructions. If you are shopping in the virtual world, ask for swatches or contact the vendor to get specifics on any fabric that you're not sure about. If you do end up with fabric that's different from what you expected, just flip through these pages — there's bound to be something sweet you can make with it!

Most fabrics are either knitted or woven. These two fabric categories have their own characteristics and benefit from different sewing techniques. As a general rule, knitted fabrics are made from a series of connected loops that stretch, sometimes in both directions, with edges that don't fray. They are easy to sew and easy to fit, perfect for improv projects. Woven fabrics, on the other hand, are made with two sets of threads that interlace and have little or no stretch. The edges often ravel, requiring some type of edge finishing technique.

Here are our thoughts on some of the many knit and woven options out there.

## Jersey Knit

This is our favorite "everyday" fabric; it's the classic stuff of your favorite t-shirts, stretchy, soft, and deliciously comfy. Contrary to popular belief, it's not hard to work with, especially if you use the right, or most suitable, jersey for your project. It comes in many different weights and fiber blends. Jersey doesn't ravel, so a raw edge doesn't need to be hemmed — although it can be, if that's what you prefer. When shopping for jersey, look for rolled edges. They are a sign that the fabric really is a single-ply jersey (not an interlock, see page 14) and that the fabric will drape well. Jersey knits are single-sided fabrics, and appear slightly nubbier and less polished on the wrong side. The right side typically has noticeable ribs, especially when you stretch it.

Oh, and jersey has one other terrific quality: it's usually cheap! You can often find it for less than five dollars per yard. And, of course, you can harvest free jersey from old t-shirts or even those ubiquitous jersey bedsheets. So go ahead and play with jersey — no anxiety necessary!

COTTON JERSEY This fabric is our go-to choice when making casual, throw-on garments, like those dresses, tunics, shirts, and skirts that you can wear

Before cutting it, always wash jersey to preshrink it. Cotton jersey and interlock can be washed and dried as you would any t-shirt, but launder others knits according to the instructions on the fabric bolt. Press lightly and only if needed, being careful not to stretch the fabric out of shape.

**Because knitted fabrics stretch, it is important to sew with a stitch that also stretches. Most sewing machines have specific stretch stitches. If yours doesn't, you can use a zigzag stitch instead. It also helps to use a ballpoint sewing machine needle. The design of the needle allows the point to slide between the knitted loops instead of pierce them. Change the needle after about eight hours of sewing, or with every new project.**

as easily as a t-shirt and jeans. It comes in a variety of weights, from heavy to tissue-weight. It also comes blended with synthetic fibers (particularly Lycra), which is not necessarily a bad thing, especially if you really want bounce-back stretch.

**WOOL JERSEY** Elegant, slightly fuzzy, and warm, this fabric has more substance than cotton jersey, and is still very easy to stitch. Most wool jersey is smooth and soft, but be sure to rub a sample against your neck (an old knitter's trick) to make sure you like the feel of it.

**RAYON JERSEY** This fabric has a luscious drape, breathes nicely, and makes up into beautiful dresses and skirts. It's just a bit slippery, so stitching takes more patience and care. It's not the best choice for your first jersey project, but certainly okay for your third or fourth project. Rayon jersey should be washed by hand or on a gentle cycle, dried flat, and pressed with a warm (not hot) iron.

**BAMBOO/MODAL JERSEY** This ecoconscious option is springy and denser than cotton. It feels a lot like rayon jersey and is a bit slippery to work with, but we love the results. It's definitely worth experimenting with.

**SILK JERSEY** Delicate and sometimes slinky, silk fibers elevate any project into something pretty, and the added stretch in silk jersey makes it very sexy. It comes blended with several different fibers, so make sure to avoid any that look cheap and shiny.

## A Note about Solids vs. Prints

Have you noticed how the fabric design world seems to have exploded with new energy and talent lately? Browsing in our favorite stores or websites, we're instantly smitten with the yummy and incredible fabric patterns; they're all quite inspiring. And yet, as you flip through this book you'll notice that we've included relatively few of the woven cotton prints that are so ubiquitous right now. Are we just being contrary? Not at all! Instead, we hope you'll be emboldened to think of your fabric as an open canvas full of possibilities, with your stitching as your palette, and yourself as the artist. With that goal in mind, we've used prints judiciously, and instead have lavished most of our attention on exploring the amazing potential of solid colors. And by the way, solids are usually much less expensive than prints. We like that, too.

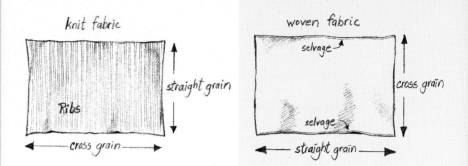

knit fabric — Ribs — straight grain — cross grain

woven fabric — selvage — cross grain — selvage — straight grain

## Tips for Working with Knits

### KNIT TIP #1: CHECK THE STRETCH DIRECTION

Especially when making clothing, it's important to be aware of the orientation of the stretch as you mark and cut your fabric. Jerseys are directional, and most have more give or stretch in a crosswise direction (double-sided knits stretch both ways). As you mark guidelines for laying out clothing patterns, always check to make sure the stretch is running across the body (from shoulder to shoulder, hip to hip). If you orient the fabric the wrong way, all the stretchy benefits of jersey will be lost and the garment won't fit right.

### KNIT TIP #2: LOOK FOR THE GRAINLINE

Throughout this book, we give guidance on grain direction. Although knit fabrics technically don't have a grainline, for our purposes, follow the vertical lines of the ribs on the fabric's right side, as you would follow the straight grainline on woven fabrics. To cut with the grain, align your scissors or rotary cutter with a rib. To cut across the grain, move your cutter straight across the ribs.

## Interlock

This flat, smooth-surfaced, double-sided knit isn't our preferred stretch cotton, but it can be used successfully for garments that don't require much drape, and for many of our gift and home decor projects. It's a staple in many large fabric stores and is often labeled or displayed with the single-ply jersey knits described above, but it's actually quite different. It does not roll at the edges and looks the same on both sides of the fabric; it's also a little heavier and denser than single-ply jersey. Because interlock doesn't have a right and wrong side, you can simply choose the side you like the best to be the right side (see Knit Tip #3 on page 15), but make sure to label it with masking tape.

## Rib Knits

These fabrics are knitted to form ribs that show on both the right and the wrong side and are very stretchy in the crosswise direction. A tight t-shirt might be made from a baby knit rib; leggings and underwear are also often made from rib knit.

## Woven Fabrics

When most of us think of fabrics, we think first of woven ones—the endlessly tempting array of patterned cottons, plus other classic fabrics like seersucker and linen. Woven fabrics come in many different weights, including light- to medium-weight,

Prep tip: Wash and dry **woven fabrics** the same way you would launder the finished garment. Press the fabric well.

Prep tip: We don't bother to wash **wool felt**; that's part of its no-fuss appeal. If a sheet is creased, mist it lightly with water, then press it with a steamy iron on low heat, covering it first with a dish towel or pressing cloth.

quilting, home-decor, and upholstery or heavyweight. (In this book, if a project requires a certain weight, it will be specified in the "What You'll Need" list.) The straight grain on woven fabric is parallel to the selvage edge, and crosswise grain threads run perpendicular to the selvage. If you cut diagonally across the threads, you'll have bias-cut fabric that will stretch more than vertical or horizontal cuts. For our projects, we suggest cutting the pattern pieces with the length positioned along the straight grain, so the garments will hang straight. If you are creating something that won't need to hang, like appliqué pieces or the

nesting boxes on page 126, then it really doesn't matter which way you cut the fabric.

## Canvas

There's a reason that, for centuries, artists have been turning to canvas. It's simply an ideal launchpad for getting creative with free-motion sketching, doodling, writing, stitched lines, and appliqué. Check the fiber content before you buy; for our projects, 100% cotton canvas or duck cloth will be perfect.

## Felt

Yes, you can buy sheets of felt at the big box store, but those felts are really meant for kids' crafts and not for a beautiful creation like yours. We strongly recommend wool felt for the projects in this book. Keep in mind that wool felt is different from felted wool, which is made at home from old wool sweaters (see page 244). You may need to order sheets of wool felt online, but it is so much nicer to work with than the usual craft variety and the colors are fantastic. Of course, felt is probably the simplest of all fabrics to use. Cut it any way you choose; it's not woven, so it won't ravel and it holds its shape perfectly.

Prep tip:

Wash **canvas** and dry it slightly, removing it from the dryer or clothesline while it's still damp and quickly pressing out the wrinkles with a hot iron. If the fabric gets all bunched up in the dryer, the creases can be tricky to remove, so a little attention will save you time later.

**KNIT TIP #3: DETERMINE THE RIGHT SIDE AND WRONG SIDE**

Sometimes it's a little challenging to orient a knit fabric; unlike printed cotton, a knit fabric often looks very similar on both sides. Here are some hints to help determine the right side:

1. The ribs that run horizontally lie on the right side. Little loops running in rows lie on the wrong side.

2. When you stretch single-ply jersey's cut edge crosswise (across the grain), the fabric will roll toward the right side.

3. Remember, interlock, rib knits, and some other double knits do not have a right or wrong side.

# Essential Tools

If you run into any trouble while sewing, blame your tools, not yourself. Beg, barter, buy, or steal yourself some suitable ones, keep them at the ready and in good repair, and you'll have eliminated a large part of the frustrations that too often keep fine sewists down.

## Sewing Machines without Fear: Part 1 // *Nicole's Advice*

If you're just dipping your toes into the world of sewing machines, then listen to me now, because I have opinions. I sewed for years on a machine my mother-in-law gave me. It felt great to sew on a machine she'd taught me how to use and that I got for free. Unfortunately, it also felt terrible to sew on that machine, because I developed a bad case of sailor's mouth whenever I used it, and because I knew it would be wrong to throw it across the room, but I had to fight to restrain myself from doing so. I finally had the sense to take it for a tune-up a few towns away, at one of those great old-fashioned shops where they really know their stuff (it's called Newman Sewing Machine and if you're in western Massachusetts, it's worth a stop). They told me it would cost about $80 to tune the machine. Instead, I walked out with a brand-new Janome Sewist 521, a just above entry-level mechanical model. I couldn't afford it at the time, but it turned out to be the best decision I'd made in a long time; in fact, it actually changed the direction of my life. I went from fearing my machine and being stymied by sewing problems to lying awake at night thinking about all the things I wanted to create. Yes, I was losing sleep, but in a good, inspiring kind of way. Flash forward, and I've now developed and sewn each and every design in this 101-project book on that basic model. Maybe a

faster stitching machine would have been helpful, but in the end, my little Sewist got the job done.

*And that is my very long-winded buildup to my following opinions:*

1. If you already have a good machine, have it tuned up and you'll be a happy camper.

2. If you have an old machine that causes you grief, or no machine at all, buy the best new one you can afford from a reputable shop that has in-house service and you'll be set for life. Cheap machines from big box stores might end up giving you big headaches later and you will have no one to help you through it. Don't feel like you have to spend a ton on digital gadgetry; although computers are fun, you don't really need them in a sewing machine unless you have big embroidery plans. Every project in this book can be completed using a basic machine with a decent selection of utility stitches. My feeling is that, without all of the computer chips and electronic gadgetry, there are fewer things to go wrong.

3. I'm not going to suggest a brand. There are many good brands and if you are lucky enough to live in an area that has a real sewing machine shop, I'm sure they would be more than happy to point you in the right direction. Do some

research online and head to the store with questions. Most likely you will be able to test sew on some machines in the showroom. The shop where I bought my machine has a one-year warranty and free one-on-one lessons; you can't beat that!

4. If you find what you want on Craigslist or eBay, check to see if you can find a local repair shop that fixes that type of machine before you buy it. And definitely bring it in for a tune-up before you start sewing with it.

## Sewing Machines without Fear: Part 2 // *Debra's Tips*

I bought my first sewing machine using advice from my friend Nicole and the nice man at the sewing machine shop. It was, as Nicole suggests above, a basic machine without a ton of bells and whistles. A few days later, I sewed my first dress using the Four-Panel Garment method (page 38) and a swishy plum-colored jersey. Eighteen months later, here I am, the coauthor of a sewing book. Come on, if I can do this, you can too!

*Here are a few more things to consider:*

1. Keep presser foot options in mind. The basic, multipurpose presser foot is perfect for most sewing needs; straight stitches and utility stitches work with this foot. It has a nice little toe and etched lines for guiding your stitches; on new machines it is often marked "A." In addition, there are feet for darning, sewing zippers and buttons, and all sorts of other tasks. New machines come with a whole set of them, and/or you can also purchase individual feet for your specific needs. Check to see which feet are included with the machine you are considering buying. There's a handy free-motion quilting foot on the market that is especially suitable for free-motion stitching, and if inspiration overcomes you while reading this book, you might want to buy one. It's totally optional, of course, and you can do any project in these pages using your machine's basic foot, but the quilting foot does allow you to see where you're going while stitching, which makes everything easier.

2. Store your owner's manual close to your sewing table and use it often. Refer to it for specifics on the correct settings and needles for different fabric types. We sometimes suggest needles or settings, but you should always test stitches on scrap fabric and follow your machine manufacturer's guidelines. We like to jot notes right in our manuals about our test results and the best settings for each fabric type we've used.

3. Stock up on extra bobbins and needles for your machine. Wind a few bobbins with white and black thread.

4. Change your needle often.

## The Other Essentials

In our project instructions, we assume you have the following basic sewing tools, so they won't appear in the "What You'll Need" lists, which focus on the fabrics, threads, and any special notions or tools.

— Rotary cutter and lots of extra blades

— Large self-healing cutting mat

— Clear quilter's ruler (we like the 24" length)

— Seam ripper

— Sharp fabric scissors (label them, and don't use them to cut paper!)

— Paper scissors

— Straight and quilting pins

— Safety pins

— Pincushion or magnetic pin dish

— Chalk (we use regular colored chalk and sharpen it with a simple pencil sharpener)

— Vanishing-ink fabric marker

— Pinking shears

— Iron and ironing board

— Tape measure

— Compass

— Kraft paper for pattern-making

# Techniques for Sewing Success

This is not a sewing manual, because there are so many great ones out there, and we recommend having a few of them close at hand. But we did want to include a few basic techniques you'll use to make the projects in this book. Be sure to refer to the chapter intros for pointers on embellishing techniques.

## Backtacking

**What it's used for:** to secure stitching at the beginning and end of stitching or seams. Unless you're basting or doing other temporary stitching, you should always backtack.

**How to do it:** At the start of each line, take a few forward stitches, then stop and sew in reverse for a few stitches, then go forward again and complete your line. At the end, repeat.

## Trimming, Notching, and Clipping

**What it's used for:** to prevent bulkiness around seamed curves and corners

**How to trim:** Where seams meet, especially at corners, cut away seam allowances at a 45-degree angle, carefully avoiding cutting the stitches. Also, if the seam allowance seems wide, trim close to the stitching.

**How to notch:** Cut out regularly spaced V-shaped notches in the seam allowance as it travels around convex curves to help the fabric lie flat.

**How to clip:** Cut regularly spaced snips in the seam allowance as it travels around concave curves to help the fabric lie flat.

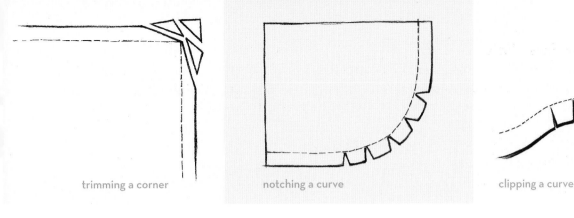

trimming a corner     notching a curve     clipping a curve

## Attaching Fold Over Elastic

**What it's used for:** to create a well-fitting waistband or cover raw edges

**What to know:** Fold over elastic has a shiny side and a dull side; it's up to you which one you want to use as the right side.

**How to do it:** For the projects in this book, always use ¾"-wide elastic. Cut a piece of elastic equal to the length of the edge you're covering (you'll end up with extra because you'll be stretching it). Trim the end so it's straight, then fold the elastic in half lengthwise. At the start of the seam, insert the raw edge of the fabric into the fold of the elastic and pinch the layers. Insert the needle near the edge of the elastic and backtack with a few zigzag stitches.

With the needle still in the fabric, pull the elastic taut about 4" from the presser foot, and zigzag stitch along the edge of the elastic. Check to make sure that the fabric edge is flush with the inside fold and that both sides of the folded elastic are caught in the stitching. Start slowly and stitch in small increments, 3" to 4" at a time, pulling the elastic but not the fabric. At the end, overlap the elastic ends by about ½" if applicable, and backtack. Trim any excess elastic.

## Double-Fold Hem

**What it's used for:** to enclose and hem an edge with machine stitching

**How to for a 1" double-fold hem:** Press the raw edge ½" to the wrong side, and then ½" again to completely enclose the raw edge. Edgestitch close to the folded edge.

**How to for a ¾" double-fold hem:** Press the raw edge ¼" to the wrong side, and then ½" and proceed as for the 1" double-fold hem.

## How to Make and Attach Binding

**What it's used for:** to finish, enclose, and decorate the raw edges of garments and other items

**What to know:** Ready-made bias tape is a neat solution, but trimming edges with custom-made binding is simple, inexpensive, and looks uniquely beautiful. All of our projects that call for homemade binding give specific measurements for cutting the strips, so be sure to follow those closely. Binding made of woven fabric should be cut on the fabric

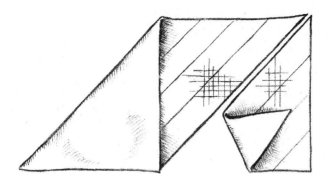

Cutting woven bias strips

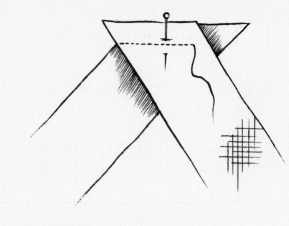

Joining bias strips for added length

bias; if it's made of jersey or other knit fabric, it can be cut on the cross grain.

**How to cut woven bias strips:** Measure and mark chalk lines at a 45-degree angle to the selvage. To find that angle, fold the fabric corner so the selvage is aligned with the cross grain. Lightly press the fold and then measure from that pressed line the desired width for the bias strip.

**How to cut knit strips for binding:** Simply cut strips so the desired width of the strips are on the straight grain, or parallel to the selvages.

**How to join strips for added length:** Sew them at an angle, as shown, aligning the seamlines, not the raw edges.

**How to press the binding:** There are several ways to press the binding. The projects in this book feature raw-edge binding and double-fold binding.

- **raw-edge binding:** Press the strip almost in half, so it is just a bit off-center and so that one side is marginally wider than the other; this makes it easier to catch both sides of the binding when it is stitched to the project edge.
- **double-fold binding:** Press the strip almost in half, so it is just a bit off-center, as for the raw-edge binding above. Open the strip and then press each long edge toward the crease. Re-press the strip in half along the original crease.

**How to attach the binding:** Insert the raw edge of the fabric between the folds of the binding and topstitch close to the inside edge of the binding (make sure the narrower edge of the binding is on top, so the stitching will easily catch the slightly wider bottom edge).

## Making Mitered Corners the Improv Way

**What it's used for:** to create neat corners where two edges or ends meet, often when you're attaching binding

**How to do it:**

1. Cut lengths of binding to match the project's two shorter edges and attach them as directed in the project.

2. Cut lengths of binding to match the project's two longer edges. Press each binding strip almost in half, with one edge about ¼" wider than the other. Unfold the strip and fold the corner edges in toward the center crease, creating pointed ends. Refold the binding along the center crease.

3. Center the binding over the remaining raw edges of the project. The corner points should hide the ends of the binding strips already sewn onto the shorter edges. Straight stitch the binding strips in place, close to the inside edges.

4. Hand-sew the binding lengths together at the corners.

**NOTE:** We used this no-fuss shortcut for mitering the edges of the Jute-Edged Throw Rug (see chapter 4, page 93) and the Reversible Loopy Bath Mat (see chapter 10, page 264) to prevent the corners from getting too bulky or bumpy.

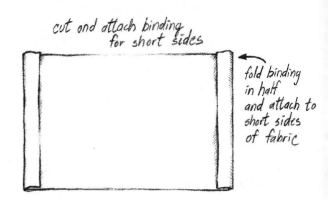

*cut and attach binding for short sides*

*fold binding in half and attach to short sides of fabric*

1. Binding the short edges

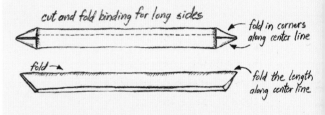

*cut and fold binding for long sides*

*fold in corners along center line*

*fold →*

*fold the length along center line*

2. Making binding for the longer edges

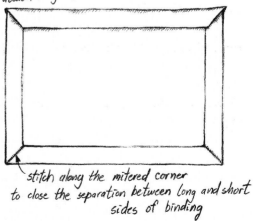

*attach long sides – sandwich the fabric between folded edges*

*stitch along the mitered corner to close the separation between long and short sides of binding*

3 & 4. Finishing longer edges and corners

# A Visual Guide to Stitches

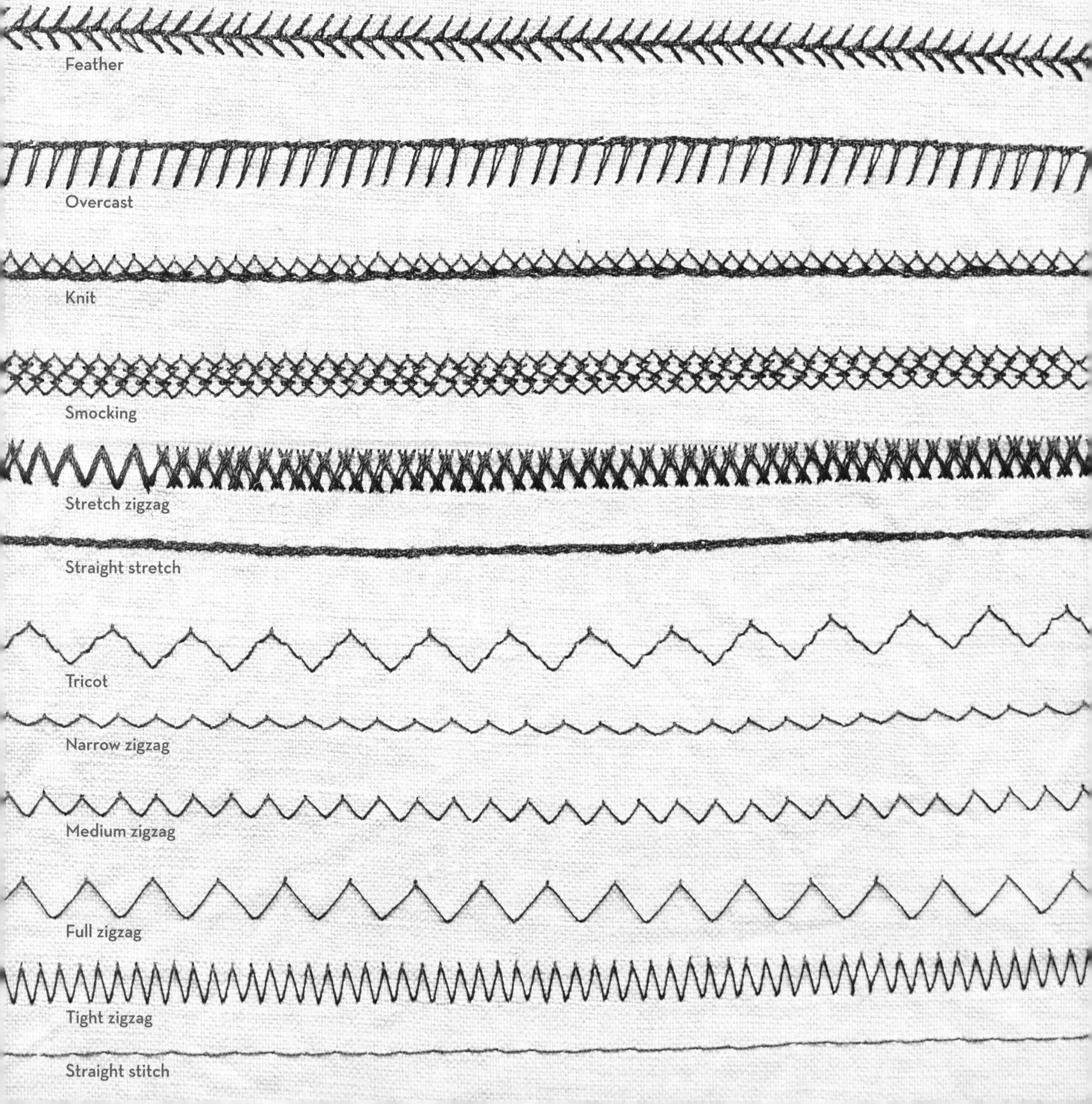

Feather

Overcast

Knit

Smocking

Stretch zigzag

Straight stretch

Tricot

Narrow zigzag

Medium zigzag

Full zigzag

Tight zigzag

Straight stitch

# Upcycling Strategies

You'll find creative ideas throughout this book for reusing textiles. It's our favorite way to get something beautiful for (almost) nothing. But, be forewarned: once you begin to turn old things into new ones, the whole world starts to look different. You touch your friend's cashmere sweater and wonder if she might be finished with it soon. Your husband's favorite t-shirt, the one with the stain, becomes a skirt for your daughter ("Sorry, Babe!").

A trip to the thrift store will become a treat-yourself outing. Yes, it can be a little stinky in there, and even if you're not the hand sanitizer type, you won't say no when your friend offers you a squirt once you're back in the car. Still, when the improv juices begin to flow, you'll be glad you braved the land of the secondhand. We've turned vintage trousers into napkins (Nicole went through a big napkin-making phase); t-shirts into skirts, tunics, dresses, and other shirts; sweaters into blankets, hats, pot holders, skirts, kids' clothing, and revamped sweaters; and men's dress shirts into pouches, produce bags, skirts, and dresses. The list is long. We used to love knitting, but the sweater section at the enormous local Salvation Army has banished that winter pastime. Someone else has already done the knitting and all we have to do is sew it into something beautiful. Plus, we never were great knitters, truth be told.

What should you be searching for? Good quality! If it is used and it still looks good, then you can count on its quality being high. Touch things and see if they are soft. Look to see if the fabric is pilled, because that won't improve with wear. If you're really not into the idea of thrifted clothes, you can certainly nab outgrown or retired items from family members and friends (they'll thank you for it!). If you do decide to hit the thrift stores, stick your finds right in the wash when you get home to give them a fresh new start. You'll be silly with happiness over how little you spent, and about the creative potential of your stash.

Tip: Chapter 10 is devoted to upcycling. It includes hints to ensure the best upcycling results as well as projects to get you started. Prepare to be amazed at what you can create from items headed for or already in the so-called junk pile.

# 2

# finding your fit

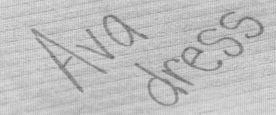

**Accurate measuring is the key to making a great-fitting garment** — though one reason we love jersey is that it is usually forgiving even if you're a teensy bit off! Take your measurements, or better yet, have a friend take them, then write the measurements down and keep them handy, so you can whip up clothing any time the spirit moves you. In fact, it's a good idea to keep a little notebook with the key measurements of family and friends; since getting measured isn't all that fun for most of us, it's nice to only have to do it once. (Of course, kids' measurements have to be updated fairly regularly!)

# Taking Measurements

Here are some basic pointers for ensuring you get the accurate measurements you need.

**Bust:** Wrap the tape measure around the chest at the fullest point, keeping the tape measure as horizontal as possible.

**Waist:** Wrap the tape measure around the body just beneath the ribs, at the torso's narrowest point. Most folks don't wear their clothes at their natural waist, but it is a good measurement to have when you are determining how much flare you want in a dress.

**Low waist:** The place where the waistband should rest, according to the wearer's preference. It might be level with or below the belly button.

**Dress/shirt/tunic length:** Stand in front of a mirror if you are measuring yourself and stand up straight. Hold one end of the tape measure at your shoulder, or the shoulder seam of your or the wearer's garment, and anchor the other end under one foot so the tape is taut. Note the measurement at the point where you'd like the garment's bottom edge to fall and remember you'll need to add length to this measurement if the garment is to be hemmed.

**Sleeve length:** Hold one end of the measuring tape at the outer end of the collarbone (this is where the shoulder seam will lie) and measure along the top of the arm to the desired sleeve length. Again you'll need to add length to this measurement if the sleeves are to be hemmed. If you're sewing with a knit fabric, simply add a little length to this measurement and trim the sleeves to the desired length after the garment is sewn.

**Skirt length:** Measure from the top of the desired waistband location to the point where you'd like the skirt's bottom edge to fall. Alternatively, use a favorite skirt with a length that you like as a guide, measuring it from the waistband to the bottom edge. Add some length to this measurement for hemming.

**Flare:** Flare is the desired width difference between the garment's waistline and the garment's bottom edge. Flare creates a nice design line and provides wearing ease for curvier parts of the body. In our designs, you will always add an equal amount of flare on each side of the center line, typically from 2" to 6" on each side.

start here for shirt/dress/tunic length

start here for sleeve length

bust

waist

low waist

tunic length (as desired)

dress length (as desired)

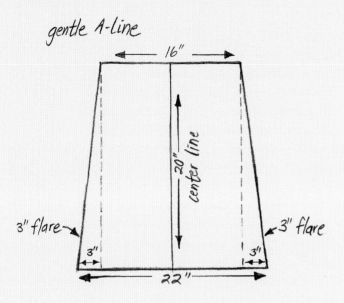

gentle A-line
16"
center line
20"
3" flare
3" flare
3"
3"
22"

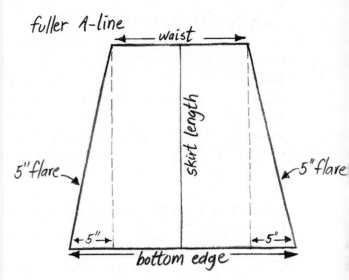

fuller A-line
waist
skirt length
5" flare
5" flare
5"
5"
bottom edge

# Making Your Own Pattern Pieces

Traditional sewing patterns are things of beauty with their rustling thin paper and all those informative and precise lines. We really like them, but we just don't like to use them! We have a "life's too short" problem with them. They're fussy. And as you may have gathered by looking at the projects in this book, we're into nonfussy. Non-fussy sewing is faster, and to us at least, it's a lot more fun.

So instead of using traditional patterns, we sew almost all of our clothing using a single set of pattern pieces, made at home by tracing a single t-shirt. Here's how it's done.

## 1. FIND A WELL-FITTING SHIRT THAT YOU'RE WILLING TO CUT UP

If you have a well-fitting shirt with a stain or tear in your drawer, sacrifice it for a good cause. Otherwise, head to a thrift or other inexpensive store and find a jersey t-shirt that makes you feel great. It should fit well across the shoulders and chest, with just the right amount of snugness. You may want to get several shirts that fit differently and feel good, and make a few different patterns. Look beyond the graphics and other design elements and just consider the fit.

Tip: When we're making a garment for a friend, we'll usually ask them what size t-shirt they wear, then find one at a thrift store or from around the house to use for making the pattern pieces.

## 2. CUT THE SHIRT APART

Press the shirt if necessary and place it right side out on the work surface. With sharp scissors, cut along the side and shoulder seams and around the arm openings, following all of the seam lines as precisely as you can; if you like, you can trim off the seam allowance afterward. (You might feel like you should use a seam ripper, but you really don't need to. It would make this a tedious process.) Cut along the seam of one sleeve so it opens flat. Remove any binding from the neckline or sleeve.

You can use the pieces of the original shirt as pattern pieces, but we suggest transferring these shapes onto sturdy brown paper. The paper patterns lie flat and are easier to label and to replace if they get lost (just remember where you stow the original fabric pieces!). The shirt's front panel will be traced to make the torso pattern piece, and the flattened sleeve will be used to make the sleeve pattern piece.

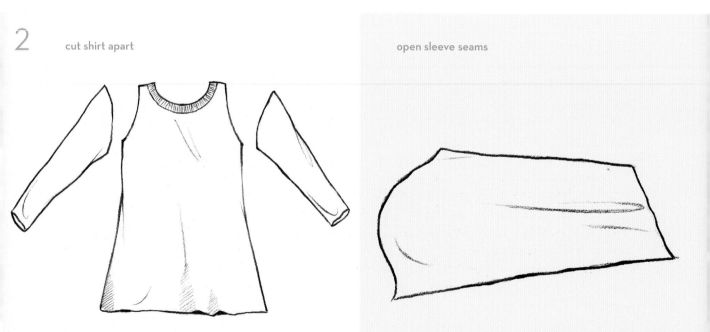

2    cut shirt apart

open sleeve seams

3

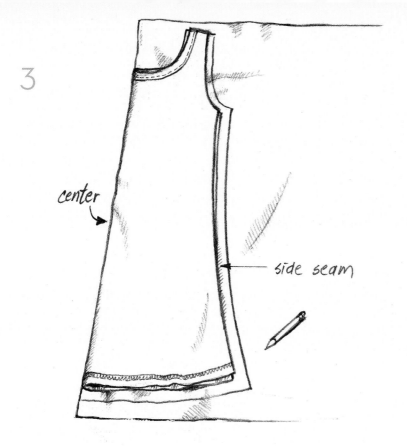

center

side seam

Tip: If you're an experienced sewist and know a lot about shirt construction, you can probably make the pattern just by tracing the shirt carefully rather than cutting it apart; if so, go for it.

## 3. TRACE THE TORSO PIECE

Cut a sheet of kraft paper, or the plain side of wrapping paper, a few inches larger all around than each of the two pieces — you can also cut open and flatten a paper grocery bag or two. Iron the paper gently to remove any creases.

**To make the torso pattern piece**, fold the front panel of the original shirt in half lengthwise and align the fold with the edge of the paper. Pat out any wrinkles until the panel is flat and aligned. Trace around it, adding ½" for the seam allowance along the armhole, shoulder, and side (don't add seam allowance to the neckline, since it will be finished in a variety of ways). Cut along the marked lines with paper scissors, and label the edges "center" and "side seam" to help you remember which is the pattern piece's center line and which is the side seam.

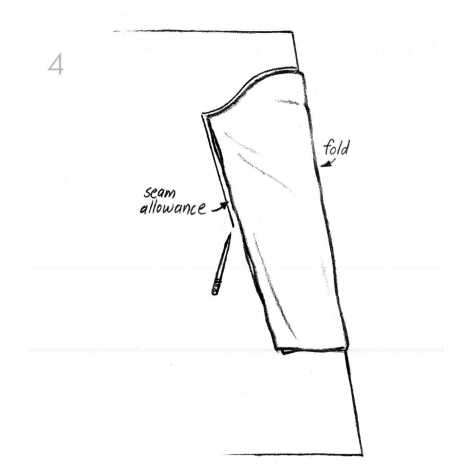

4

fold

seam
allowance

4. TRACE THE SLEEVE PATTERN PIECE

**To make the sleeve pattern piece**, fold the original sleeve piece in half lengthwise and align the fold along one edge of the paper. Trace around it, adding ½" for the seam allowance along the cap (the bell-shaped curve along the top edge of the sleeve) and down the length of the sleeve. Cut along the marked lines with paper scissors, and label the pattern piece along the sides with the words "seam" and "fold." Note the sleeve style (short, cap, long, and so on) directly on the pattern too, since you may accumulate a bunch of sleeve patterns.

# Shaping and Cutting Necklines

Your torso pattern piece will have one neckline, but you can use it to make garments with many different necklines by simply shaping the neck as you like after the dress, shirt, or tunic has been sewn together. Design a plunging V, a shallow scoop, or any neckline in between by following the same basic process.

### 1. HAVE THE WEARER TRY ON THE GARMENT

Mark the desired center front location of the V or scoop neckline. While marking this design point, it's best to wear the bra that will be worn under the garment (unless you're measuring a little girl, boy, or man, in which case, skip it).

### 2. TAKE THE SHIRT OFF AND PULL THE BACK PANELS OUT OF THE WAY

Fold the garment lengthwise down the center so the shoulder seams align.

**For a V-neck:** use a clear ruler and rotary cutter or sharp scissors to mark and cut a straight line from the start of the shoulder seam (nearest the neck) to the marked center point through both thicknesses of fabric.

**For a scoop neck:** draw a gently curved line from the start of the shoulder seam to the marked center point. Cut it with a rotary cutter.

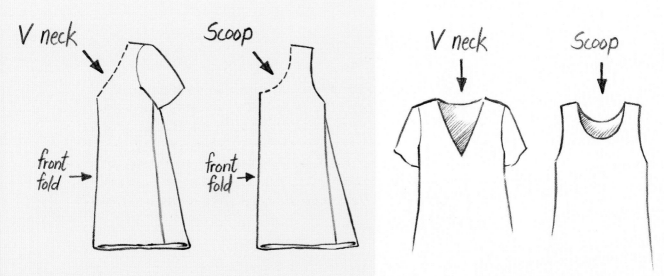

# five basic designs

**Forget any old ideas about sewing your own clothes.** Start with our five basic designs, then dive into the simple and creative embellishment techniques in the following chapters, and suddenly you'll have a whole wardrobe of dresses, skirts, shirts, and tunics, utterly and uniquely yours, made by you to fit your body, your look, and your life. Hem if you feel like it, or don't. Let the seams show, and celebrate the raw edges. Enjoy the journey and arrive looking amazing.

design #1
# The Two-Panel Garment

**The building block for a universe of shirts, tunics, and dresses,** this garment is the perfect starter project if you're new to sewing with jersey or just a bit intimidated by the idea of sewing your own clothing. We promise that you can sew yourself a new summer dress in less than an hour. After that, the choice is yours; keep your sewing sublimely simple and accessorize your new wardrobe with interesting belts or necklaces, or embellish your projects with just about any of the techniques covered in later chapters.

The how-to instructions below start with the torso pattern piece you created in chapter 2, but we'll let you in on a secret: You can just lay out a tank top with a fit you love and trace it directly onto your fabric, adding ½" at the shoulder and side seams for the seam allowance.

## what you'll need

- Torso pattern pieces to trace (see chapter 2, pages 29–30)
- 1½ yards of 60"-wide jersey fabric
- 1 spool of coordinating thread

## 1. DETERMINE THE GARMENT LENGTH

Hold one end of the measuring tape at the shoulder seam of the shirt you're wearing and step on the tape's other end to hold it taut. Note the measurement at the desired hem location.

## 2. MEASURE, MARK, AND CUT THE FIRST PANEL

Fold the fabric with the right sides together, leaving enough width to accommodate the pattern piece and the additional length and flare of the garment, as shown on page 37 (the grain will run the length of the garment). Pin the pattern piece as shown, with the fold edge of the pattern along the fabric fold.

Design tip:
Want to add sleeves
to your garment?
See Sleeves Made
Simple on page 42,
and add to garment
before stitching
side seams.

projects based on the
## two-panel garment

- Ruffled Ribbon Sundress (page 62)
- Ruched Tunic (page 65)
- Gracefully Gathered Neckline Shirt (page 68)
- Pleated Neckline Top (page 70)
- Cowl Neck Duffle (page 72)
- Shirred Empire Waist Dress (page 75)
- Leafy Ruffle Tunic (page 84)
- Keyhole T-Shirt (page 101)
- Swishy Sundress (page 128)
- Pebble Tee (page 138)
- Fiddlehead Dress (page 156)
- Wool Jumper (page 250)

# The Two-Panel Garment

Use a measuring tape and chalk to mark the following design lines directly on the fabric:

— **Bottom edge:** Measure straight down from the shoulder seam to the desired length (our garment is unhemmed, but if you'd like a hem, add ¾" and then mark). Draw a horizontal line marking the garment's bottom edge, but extend it 3" beyond the side seam of the pattern piece to add flare to the panel.*

— **Side seam and neckline:** Trace the pattern piece, extending the line of the side seam down at an angle to meet the marked end of the bottom edge.

> *The hem or bottom edge design line varies with how much flare you want. For a tunic, adding 3" on either side of the garment's center line (6" total) is average. For a roomier garment, add more. For a dress, 3½" on either side is a good starting point. (For more about flare, see chapter 2, page 26)

Remove the paper pattern. Cut along the marked lines through both thicknesses of fabric.

## 3. MARK AND CUT THE SECOND (BACK) PANEL

Refold the remaining fabric. Lay the cutout piece (still folded from cutting), flipping and rotating it to fit on the yardage. Trace around the cutout piece with chalk.

Remove the cutout piece. Cut along the marked chalk lines through both thicknesses of fabric.

## 4. JOIN THE PANELS

Align the panels with the right sides together; with a straight stretch stitch, sew at the shoulders and side seams with a ½" seam.

Turn the garment right side out. If you like, decoratively topstitch over the seams with a tricot stitch. If you allowed extra length for hemming, hem the bottom edge (see double-fold hem, page 19).

To cut a V or scoop neckline, refer to the instructions in chapter 2, page 31.

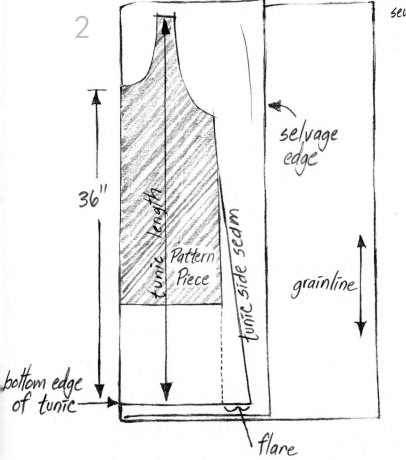

**Layout tip:** Before you trace the pattern, make sure the grain, or fine ribbing, is running from the garment's top to bottom, and the jersey's stretch is running crosswise (shoulder to shoulder). Check twice, just to be sure.

4

these edges will be pinned and sewn together

shoulder seams sew together

sleeve

2

selvage edge

36"

tunic length

Pattern Piece

tunic side seam

grainline

bottom edge of tunic

flare

**Tip:** For a more finished look, enclose the raw edges at the neckline and armholes with homemade binding (see page 19), cut either from the same color jersey or a pretty contrasting one.

## design #2
# The Four-Panel Garment

This versatile design takes the two-panel garment one step further, with a center seam that allows for an even better fit and a dose of extra design. You can stitch over that central seam with contrasting thread, hand-embroider along it with a decorative stitch, or leave the edges exposed and raw. Whatever your embellishments, the vertical line right down the middle of this design ensures a garment that elongates and flatters every body type. The four-panel garment can be a shirt, tunic, or dress, sleeveless or with sleeves of any length. Here, we start with a basic dress.

## what you'll need

- Torso and sleeve pattern pieces to trace (see chapter 2, pages 29–30)
- 1½ yards of 60"-wide jersey fabric
- 1 spool of coordinating thread

### 1. DETERMINE THE GARMENT LENGTH

Hold one end of the measuring tape at the shoulder seam of the shirt you're wearing and step on the tape's other end to hold it taut. Note the measurement at your desired length.

### 2. MEASURE, MARK, AND CUT THE FIRST (FRONT) PAIR OF PANELS

Fold the fabric in half with the right sides together and selvages aligned (the grain will run the length of the garment). Pin the pattern piece as shown on page 41, leaving space to accommodate the additional length and flare of the garment.

Use a measuring tape and chalk to mark the following design lines directly on the fabric:

— **Bottom edge:** Measure straight down from the shoulder seam to the desired length (this garment is unhemmed, but if you'd like a hem, add ¾" and then mark). Draw a horizontal line marking the bottom edge, but extend it 3½" beyond the side seam of the pattern piece to add flare to the panel.

— **Side seam and neckline:** Trace the pattern piece, extending the line of the side seam down at an angle to meet the marked end of the bottom edge.

Design tip:
Make a
four-panel
shirt, tunic,
or dress with
or without
sleeves.

projects based on the
## four-panel garment

- Ruffled Dressy Dress
  (page 78)

- Exposed Seam Tunic
  (page 86)

- Swishy Sundress
  (page 128)

- Two-Tee Dress
  (page 262)

Stitching tip:
Stop your
machine every
so often to make
sure the panels
are still aligned.

## The Four-Panel Garment

— **Center seam**: Trace the pattern piece, adding a ½" seam allowance. Extend the line down to the hemline.

Remove the paper pattern and pin the fabric layers together. Cut along the marked chalk lines through both thicknesses of fabric.

### 3. MARK AND CUT THE SECOND (BACK) PAIR OF PANELS

Lay the cutout pieces (still pinned from cutting) on the remaining fabric, flipping them as shown so the shoulders are at the opposite end of the yardage. Trace around the cutout pieces with chalk. Pat into place to remove bunching or wrinkles — don't stretch it.

Remove the cutout pieces and pin the fabric layers together. Cut along the marked chalk lines through both thicknesses of fabric.

### 4. JOIN THE PANELS

With a straight stretch stitch, sew the front panels (right sides together and still pinned from cutting) together down the center with a ½" seam.

Repeat with the remaining back panels.

With the right sides together, stitch the front and back pieces together at the shoulder seams and at the side seams (if you're adding sleeves, cut and attach them before sewing up sides, following the instructions in the next section, Sleeves Made Simple.) Turn the garment right side out.

To cut a V or scoop neckline, refer to the instructions in chapter 2, page 31.

If you like, decoratively topstitch over the seams with a zigzag stitch. If you allowed extra length for hemming, hem the bottom edge (see double-fold hem, page 19).

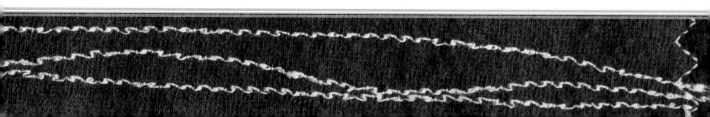

2

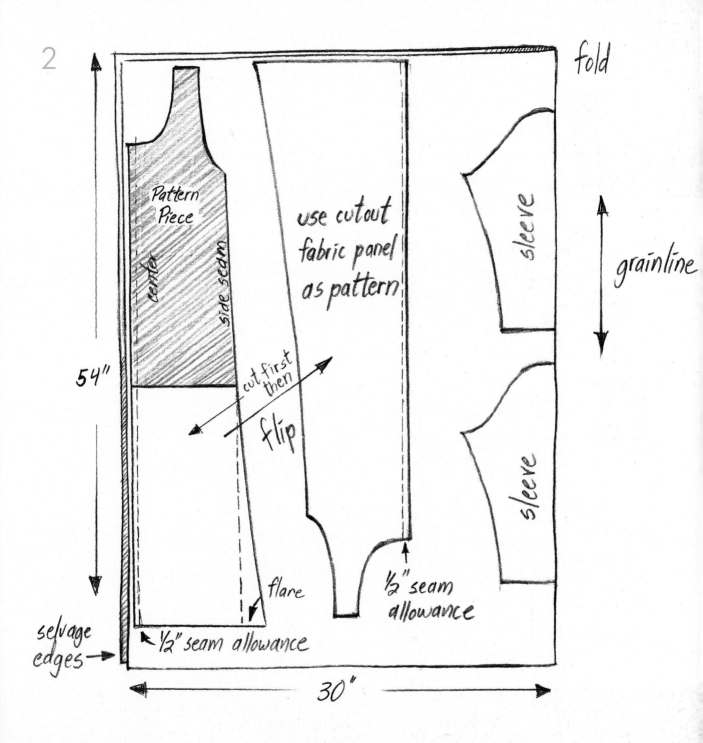

fold

Pattern
Piece

center

side seam

use cutout
fabric panel
as pattern

sleeve

grainline

54"

cut first
then

flip

sleeve

flare

½" seam
allowance

selvage
edges →

½" seam allowance

30"

# Sleeves Made Simple

**Whether you'd like short**, wrist-length, ¾-length, or cap sleeves, the process is basically the same. All you need is the sleeve pattern piece and the project fabric (see chapter 2, page 30).

## 1. MEASURE, MARK, AND CUT THE SLEEVES

Fold the fabric with the right sides together (the grain will run the length of the garment sleeve, from shoulder to the sleeve's end). Pin the pattern piece as shown with the fold edge of the pattern along the fabric fold, leaving space to accommodate the additional length and flare of the sleeve.

Trace the pattern piece with chalk, extending or shortening the sleeve length as desired (see chapter 2, page 26 on measuring for sleeve length). To change

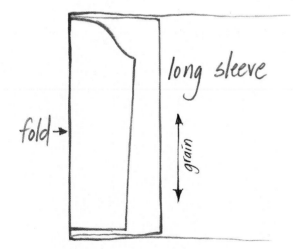

long sleeve

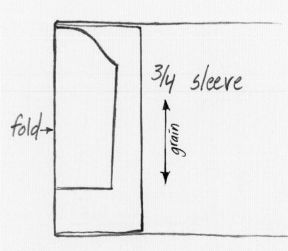

¾ sleeve

the length, use a ruler to extend the pattern's line (or eyeball it) to create a long sleeve from a short-sleeve pattern, and vice versa. Unpin the pattern and cut along the marked lines.

To cut the second sleeve, refold the fabric. Align the folded, cutout sleeve piece along the fabric fold (sleeve fold and fabric fold are aligned). Trace around it with chalk, and then cut along the lines through both thicknesses of the fabric. Mark the top center of each sleeve at its fold.

Cutting tip:
Err on the long side because you can always trim it later.

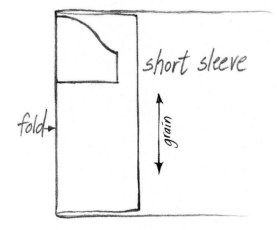

short sleeve

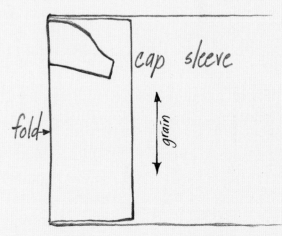

cap sleeve

## 2. ATTACH THE SLEEVES

Turn the garment wrong side out. With the right sides together, pin a sleeve in place, aligning the center mark on the sleeve with the garment shoulder seam. Add more pins, starting at the shoulder seam and proceeding along the back curve of the arm opening down to the underarm. Adjust the pieces as needed so they stay aligned, but don't stretch them out of shape. Turn the garment over and repeat, pinning along the arm opening in front from shoulder seam to underarm.

With your machine set for a straight stretch stitch, stitch a ½" seam from shoulder to underarm on the garment front, and then on the garment back.

Repeat with the remaining sleeve.

## 3. FINISH THE SLEEVES AND SIDE SEAMS

With edges aligned, pin the sleeve and side seams with the right sides together, making sure the seams at each underarm are aligned. With a straight stretch stitch and ½" seam, stitch the seams, starting at each sleeve end, across the underarms (making sure the seams lie flat), and down the side seams to the garment's bottom edge. Clip the curves within the seam allowance (see chapter 1, page 19). Hem the sleeves as desired.

Stitching tip:
If you find all these pins fussy, just use one pin at the shoulder seam.

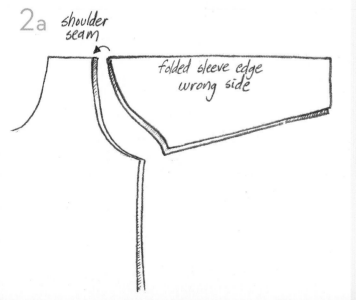

2a   shoulder seam

folded sleeve edge
wrong side

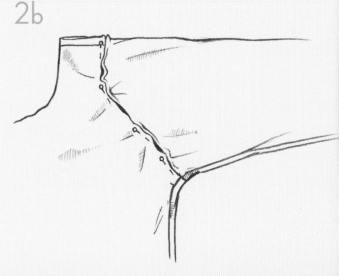

2b

3

Finishing tip:
Snip off excess thread
pieces as you go.

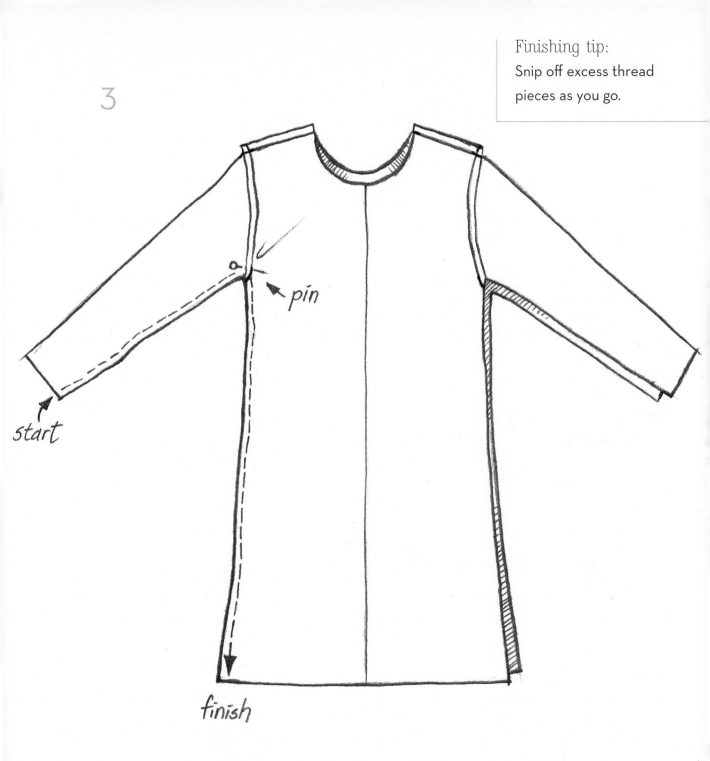

pin

start

finish

The rounded hem is barely perceptible but gives the skirt a more flattering line.

# design #3
# The Two-Panel Skirt

**Here's a flattering A-line skirt you can whip up fast.** It's pretty on its own, but we really love it as a blank slate for embellishments of just about any kind that you can dream up. For this basic skirt design, we started with a solid cotton jersey; you can use a range of other stretch fabrics or upcycle a pair of men's extra-large t-shirts into a skirt.

## 1. MEASURE, MARK, AND CUT YOUR FABRIC

Measure yourself at your preferred low waistline, pulling the measuring tape tightly around you. Next, determine the desired length (refer to page 26). We think a jersey A-line skirt is most flattering hitting just at the knee. Remember, because you're using jersey, you can leave the skirt unhemmed. If you want a hem for a more finished look, add ¾" to your length measurement.

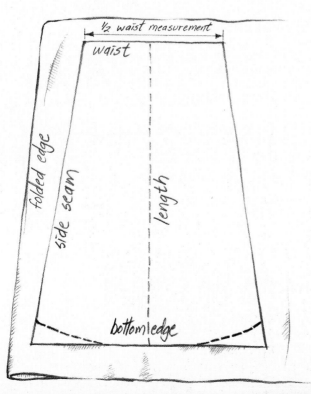

### what you'll need

- 1½ yards of 60"-wide cotton jersey

- Fold over elastic in a length equal to waist measurement

- 1 spool of coordinating thread

# The Two-Panel Skirt

projects based on the
## two-panel skirt

- Layered Hemline Skirt
  (page 88)

- Bustle Skirt (page 90)

- Reverse-Appliqué Skirt
  (page 188)

- Modern Stretch Velvet
  Skirt (page 192)

- Mod Flower Skirt
  (page 219)

With the right sides together, fold the fabric in half so it stretches horizontally (from hip to hip). Grab your chalk and mark the following design lines:

— **Waist:** Draw a straight line near the top edge of the fabric that equals half your waist measurement. Mark the center of that line.

— **Length:** Draw a line from the center marking on the waistline to the desired length.

— **Bottom edge:** Draw a line marking the skirt's bottom edge, 6" longer (3" on each side) than the waist (this gives the skirt panels 3" of flare on each side of the center line). If you want more room through the hips, increase the flare.

— **Side seams:** Draw lines connecting each end of the waistline to each end of the bottom edge. Curve the bottom edge slightly so the hemline is ½" shorter at the side seams than the center of the hemline. This gives the skirt a more even line.

Pin the fabric layers together and cut along the marked chalk lines through both thicknesses of the fabric.

## 2. ASSEMBLE THE SKIRT

With the front and back panels still pinned with the right sides together, use a straight stretch stitch to sew up the sides with a ½" seam.

Sew fold over elastic along the waistband (see chapter 1, page 19).

Leave the skirt unhemmed if you didn't add extra length when you measured and cut the fabric, or if you did add length, follow the instructions for a double-fold hem (page 19).

Design tip: Keep in mind that the wider the bottom edge is, the fuller the skirt will be. For more on flare, see chapter 2, page 26.

# design #4
# The Three-Panel Wrap Skirt

**This skirt, based on a classic wraparound design, has a breezy style all its own.** It's made with three identical panels, so the cutting portion of this project goes superfast. Since the wrap design has an adjustable waistband, you can wear it at your hip or natural waist, depending on your outfit and your mood. This design works beautifully with a cotton print or just about any other woven or knit fabric.

## 1. MEASURE, MARK, AND CUT YOUR FABRIC

Measure yourself at your actual waistline for this skirt, pulling the measuring tape tightly around you. Next, measure down from your waistline to the desired length; just above or at the knee is usually most flattering.

Fold the fabric with the right sides together and the straight grain running lengthwise. Grab your chalk and mark the following design lines:

— **Waist:** Draw a straight line near the top edge of the fabric that equals half your waist measurement. Mark the center of that line.

— **Length:** Draw a line from the center of the waistline to the desired length (add 1" if you'd like a hem along the bottom).

— **Bottom edge:** Draw a line marking the skirt's bottom edge, 4" longer (2" on each side) than the waist (this gives the skirt panels 2" of flare on each side of the center line).*

*Flare can vary according to personal preference. See page 26 for more information.

*Flare can vary according to personal preference. See page 26 for more information.

## what you'll need

- **2 yards of woven cotton fabric**

- **6 yards of double-fold ½"-wide bias tape**

- **1 spool of coordinating thread**

# The Three-Panel Wrap Skirt

projects based on the
## wrap skirt

- **Coloring Book Wrap Skirt**
  **(page 144)**
- **Rainy Day Wrap Skirt**
  **(page 221)**
- **Dress Shirt Wrap Skirt**
  **(page 266)**

— **Side seams:** Draw a line connecting the end points of the waist and bottom-edge lines.

Pin the fabric layers together and cut along the marked chalk lines through both fabric layers.

For the third panel, unfold the fabric. Lay the cutout panels on it, trace around the panels, and cut one more panel along the traced lines.

## 2. ASSEMBLE THE SKIRT

Pin two panels with the right sides together. Straight stitch them together along one side with a ½" seam. Open the panels and lay them flat. With the right sides together, pin the third panel to the unstitched side of one of the panels so the side seams align. Stitch a ½" seam. Press the seams.

If desired, pink the raw edges of the seams with pinking shears or finish them with a zigzag stitch. Press the seam allowances flat and, with the right side facing up, topstitch with a tricot stitch along the seams (see chapter 1, page 22).

## 3. HEM THE BOTTOM AND SIDE EDGES

Stitch ¾" double-fold hems along the side edges of the panels (see chapter 1, page 19).

Finish the bottom edge of the skirt with a 1" hem, stitched in place with a zigzag stitch.

## 4. ADD THE WAIST TIES

Cut 3 yards of bias tape.

With the right side facing up and the panels spread flat, pin the bias tape to encase the waist edge so that 17" of tape extends to the left of the first panel (the one you'd like to have as the outside panel on the skirt front) and approximately 44" extends beyond the last panel.

1

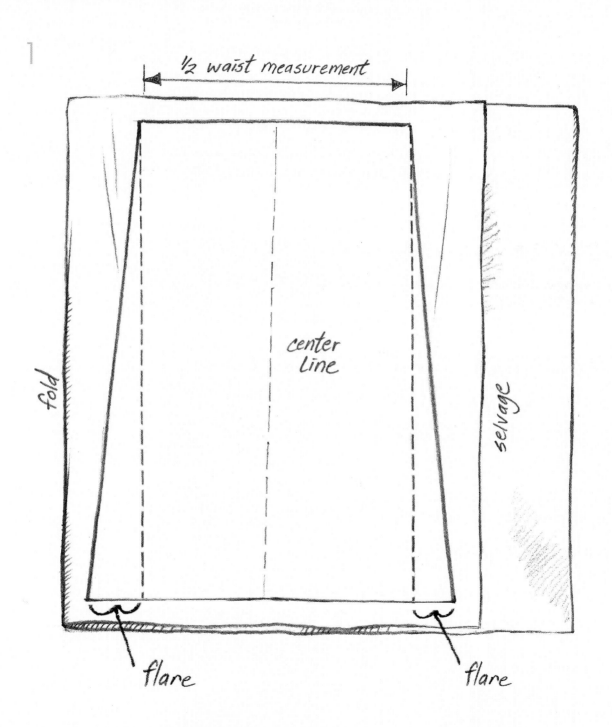

½ waist measurement

center line

fold

selvage

flare

flare

approx. 17"

enclose raw edge

approx. 44"

add vertical
buttonhole here

front
panel

4

## The Three-Panel Wrap Skirt

In one continuous seam, edgestitch with a narrow zigzag along the entire length of the bias tape, attaching the tape to the waistline and finishing the ties.

## 5. MAKE THE WAIST TIE OPENING

Following the directions for your sewing machine, sew a vertical buttonhole on the waistband at the point where the front panel meets the middle panel. The buttonhole needs to be long enough to accommodate the waist tie. Cut the buttonhole open with a seam ripper or craft knife, taking care not to cut the stitches.

Try on the skirt by threading the longer tie through the buttonhole, and tying the waist ties together. Trim the waist ties as needed and finish the ends with a narrow hem, if desired.

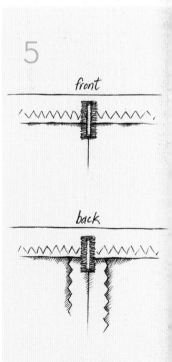

5

front

back

# design #5
# The Stretch-Panel Skirt

The term "stretch panel" may remind you of your great-grandma's era, when girdles were standard undergarb, and fabric with a bit of elasticity was consider a high-tech miracle. Now that we're writing a book that celebrates the joys of all kinds of stretchy materials, we think it's time to give this retro term new life. We've used it to describe this ingenious design, which combines the fit of a knit skirt with the fun of a woven cotton print skirt.

## what you'll need

- 1 yard of 54"- or 60"-wide woven cotton fabric*

- 1 yard of 60"-wide cotton jersey fabric

- ¾" fold over elastic (in a length equal to waist measurement)

- 1 spool of coordinating thread

  *If wearer's waist measures 30" or less, you can use 44"-wide fabric.

## 1. MEASURE, MARK, AND CUT YOUR FABRIC

Measure yourself at your preferred low waistline for this skirt, pulling the measuring tape tightly around you. Next, determine your desired length (see page 26).

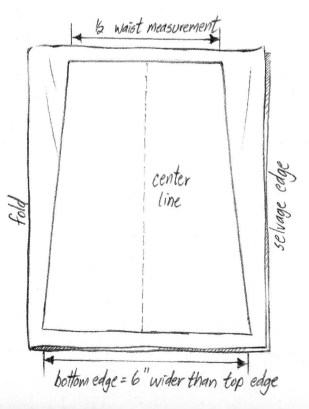

½ waist measurement

fold

center line

selvage edge

bottom edge = 6" wider than top edge

# The Stretch-Panel Skirt

Finishing tip:

If you want
a hem with a
more finished
look, add ¾"
to your length
measurement.
For another
hem idea, see
the instructions
for the Linen
Skirt with
Wavy Hemline,
page 130.

With the right sides together, fold the woven cotton fabric in half with the selvages aligned. The top edge of the skirt should be marked parallel to the cut edge (not the selvage edge) so the length of the skirt falls on the straight grain of the fabric. Grab your chalk and mark the following design lines:

— **Waist:** Draw a straight line near the top edge of the fabric that equals half your waist measurement. Mark the center of that line.

— **Length:** Mark a line from the center marking on the waistline to the desired length.

— **Bottom edge:** Draw a line marking the skirt's bottom edge, 6" longer (3" on each side) than the waist (this gives the skirt 3" of flare on each side of the center line).*

— **Side seams:** Draw a line connecting the end points of the waist and bottom-edge lines ½" above the bottom edge.

*Flare can vary according to personal preference. See page 26 for more.

side seam

2

side seam
attaching jersey strip
to front panel of skirt
right sides facing

right side
front panel

Pin the fabric layers together and cut along the chalk marked lines through both thicknesses of the fabric.

Cut two strips of jersey fabric, each 2" wide and as long as the skirt from waist to bottom edge; make sure to cut the strips so they stretch across the width. These are stretch panels, which will be sewn to the sides of the skirt.

## 2. ASSEMBLE THE SKIRT

With the right sides together, use a straight stitch to sew a jersey strip to each side of the front cotton panel with a ½" seam. Stitch the back cotton panel to the other sides of the jersey strips with the right sides together in the same manner, to complete the basic skirt assembly.

Press the seams open and on the right side, topstitch with a zigzag or tricot stitch over the side seams.

Sew fold over elastic to make the waistband (see chapter 1, page 19).

## 3. FINISH THE BOTTOM EDGE

Narrow zigzag along the bottom edge. Add more lines of stitching for a decorative hemline, if desired.

projects based on the
**stretch-panel skirt**

- **Linen Skirt with Wavy Hemline (page 130)**

Finishing tip: Instead of machine stitching, hand-embroider a decorative stitch along the seams, maybe with zigzags or cross-stitches.

3

4

# ruffles, pleats, and trims

From a
sumptuous
ruffle
to a crisp
binding,
here are a few
easy ways to add
dimension and
texture to your project.

## Making Ribbon

**What to know:** Homemade fabric ribbons lend a little pop of color or subtle texture to a garment (or an original touch to a wrapped gift!). Any light- to medium-weight fabric can be made into ribbon, and the ribbon can be any width, as long as it isn't too narrow to edgestitch.

**How to do it:** Cut strips of fabric to the desired width and length, or to the dimensions specified in the project instructions. To join strips for a longer ribbon, stitch them with the right sides together with a narrow seam and press the seam allowance to one side before finishing the edges. To finish the edges and create the ribbon, align the center mark of the presser foot with the outside fabric edge and narrow zigzag (we set our stitch width to 2) to overcast the edges. If you want the thread to be a prominent design element, use a wider and longer zigzag. Make a test sample of the zigzag to determine the width and length that best suits your needs.

## Making Ruffles

**What to know:** Ruffles start with homemade ribbon, so first follow the instructions at left. When ruffled, the ribbon will shorten, so you need to start with longer strips of fabric. How long? That depends on how full and fluffy you'd like your ruffle to be. In general, cutting a strip that measures twice the length of the area you need to cover is a safe bet. Always make a little more than you need, because after the ruffle is stitched in place, any excess can be trimmed. (If you're using jersey to make your ruffles, edgestitching is optional.)

**How to make the ruffle:** Run basting stitches down the center length of the ribbon, leaving long tails on both ends. Grasp both top threads and slide the fabric along those threads until the ribbon is ruffled as desired. Use a pin to pull both top threads to the bottom side and knot them with the bobbin thread. Snip the excess thread.

prepped ruffle strip

ruffling the ruffle

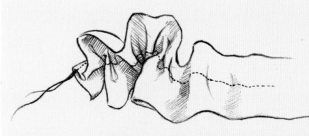

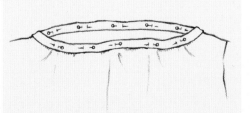

**How to attach the ruffle:** Pin the ruffle in place with the wrong side of the ruffle facing the right side of the project. Straight stitch it in place with a coordinating thread color close to the basting thread. If the basting thread is visible, remove it with a seam ripper or sharp pair of scissors after the ruffle is secured.

# Making a Binding Loop

**What to know:** This technique gives a stretchy, well-fitting finish to a rounded edge or garment opening such as a neckline, sleeve end, or hat brim. It sounds trickier than it is, and it works like a charm.

**How to do it:** Measure and mark a fabric strip or strips as required by the project (the length will generally equal the measurement of the edge to be covered minus 10 percent).

Fold the strip in half with the right sides facing, then join short edges together with a ¼" seam to make a loop. Press the seam open, then press the loop almost in half lengthwise, as for making the binding (see chapter 1, pages 19–20) with the crease just a bit off center. Pin the binding loop to encase the raw edge of the project by first aligning the seam on the loop with a seam on the garment (one of the shoulder seams if it's a neckline binding). Stretch the loop to the seam on the opposite side of the garment opening and pin it in place. Repeat to pin the loop halfway between the first two pins, then pin the rest of the binding in place, enclosing the entire edge. Stitch the binding in place, stretching it as needed and removing the pins as you go.

attaching a binding loop

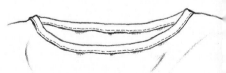

Cutting tip: When you're measuring, add a bit more flare if you like — 6" on each side is the perfect amount for a little girl who likes to twirl.

# Ruffled Ribbon Sundress

**We adore store-bought ribbon,** but we also love the improvised vibe of homemade ribbon and the fact that it is absolutely free when made from bits and pieces straight out of your stash. For this project, we used both a ruffly version and a flat one to add extra prettiness to a summer dress.

## 1. MEASURE, MARK, AND CUT YOUR FABRIC

Follow the instructions for the Two-Panel Garment (see chapter 3, page 34), through step 3, adjusting the length measurement as desired.

## 2. RUFFLE THE NECKLINE RIBBON

Plan the number and length of the decorative neckline ribbons. To cut the strips, multiply the desired finished length by 1.5 and then cut the fabric strips (for a 2" ribbon, cut a 3" strip; for a 7" ribbon, cut a 10½" strip). Ruffle the strips to make the ribbons (see page 60). We used five ½"-wide cotton strips with finished (ruffled) lengths from 2" to 7".

## 3. ATTACH THE NECKLINE RIBBON

Pin the longest ribbon to the dress so one end is at the center front of the neckline and the other end extends straight down. Narrow zigzag, in contrasting thread, directly through the center of the ruffle to attach it to the front panel. Stitch two more ruffled ribbons on either side of the center ribbon.

### what you'll need

- Torso pattern piece to trace (see chapter 2, page 29)

- 1¼ yards of jersey or stretch pique fabric

- Contrasting homemade ribbon (see page 60); about 1 yard of 1"-wide and 25" of ½"-wide

- 1 spool each of coordinating and contrasting thread

- Contrasting single-fold bias tape (store bought or homemade, see chapter 1, page 19)

## 4. ATTACH THE RIBBON HEM

Pin the unruffled 1" ribbon along the dress front panel so the ribbon extends ½" beyond the bottom of dress. Trim the ribbon ends at the side seams.

Narrow zigzag, in contrasting thread, along the top edge of the ribbon. Repeat on the dress back panel.

## 5. JOIN THE PANELS

With the right sides together, straight stretch stitch the front and back panels at the shoulders and side seams with a ½" seam. With the right side facing out, zigzag the seams with contrasting thread.

## 6. ADD THE BIAS TAPE

With coordinating thread bias tape, zigzag around the neckline and armholes, enclosing the raw edges (see chapter 1, page 19).

# Ruched Tunic

**Ruching is popular because it's so very flattering,** especially around the midriff. In making this top, you determine the amount of ruching by how tautly you pull the elastic as you sew. Fold over elastic is perfect for this project — it's soft against your skin and comes in beautiful colors, and even though it won't show on the garment's exterior, you'll know it's pretty on the inside!

## 1. MEASURE, MARK, AND CUT

Follow the instructions through step 3 for the Two-Panel Garment (see chapter 3, page 34), measuring for a tunic and adding an extra 12" in length to the front panel to allow for the ruching. After you complete the ruching, you'll trim the front and back panels to matching lengths. If you want to add sleeves to your garment, see the how-to instructions for adding sleeves on page 42.

## 2. ATTACH THE ELASTIC

With the wrong side of the front panel facing up and starting about 2" below the armhole edge, backtack in a length of fold over elastic in place. Align the edge of the elastic with the raw edge of the panel.

### what you'll need

- **Torso pattern piece to trace (see chapter 2, page 29)**

- **1 yard of 60"-wide jersey fabric**

- **1 spool of coordinating thread**

- **30" of fold over elastic**

2

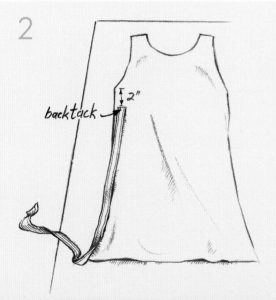

backtack → 2"

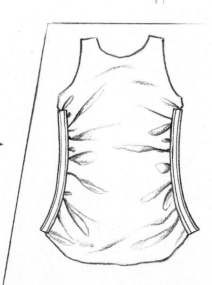

## Ruched Tunic

Using a narrow zigzag (our stitch width was 2) and working in small, approximately 3" intervals, stitch ¼" from the side edge, pulling on the elastic, but not pulling the fabric. Backtack at the end of the seam. Trim any excess elastic.

Repeat, applying an identical length of fold over elastic on the opposite side of the panel.

## 3. JOIN THE PANELS

With the right sides together and using a straight stretch stitch, join the shoulders with a ½" seam.

Align and pin the armholes to avoid shifting. Starting at the underarm, use a straight stretch stitch to sew a ½" side seam, stitching on top of the elastic ½" from the edge. Pull the front panel slightly to stretch out the ruching as you sew.

Repeat for the opposite side seam.

Turn the tunic right side out.

## 4. TRIM THE BOTTOM EDGE

Most likely, the front and back panels will be uneven, and the front will dip down at the center. Trim the bottom edge by rounding the front and back evenly, or by cutting them both straight across.

Finishing tip: It's jersey, so you can cut it any way you like and leave it like that.

# Gracefully Gathered Neckline Shirt

A gentle cluster of gathers adds a little extra prettiness to a two-panel top or any scoop-necked garment you already own. Gathers, which are basically one-edged ruffles, are easy and fun to make.

## what you'll need

- **Torso pattern piece to trace (see chapter 2, page 29)**
- **1 yard of 60"-wide jersey fabric**
- **1 spool of coordinating thread**

## 1. SEW A TWO-PANEL SHIRT

Follow the instructions for the Two-Panel Garment, adjusting the length as desired to make a shirt (see chapter 3, page 34). If you want to add sleeves to your garment, see the how-to instructions for adding sleeves in the same chapter (page 42).

## 2. MARK THE NECKLINE

With chalk, mark the front center of the neckline. Then measure and mark 1½" away from the center in both directions.

## 3. CREATE THE GATHERS

Sew a row of basting stitches between your marks, ¼" from the fabric edge, leaving long tails of thread on each end. Grasp the two top threads (leave the bobbin threads alone) and slide the fabric into gathers. Once you have pulled the threads and gathered the neckline, use a pin to pull each top thread through to the back of the garment and tie the top thread to the bobbin thread in a double knot.

## 4. FINISH THE NECKLINE

Using a straight stretch stitch, topstitch over the basting thread and gathers.

3

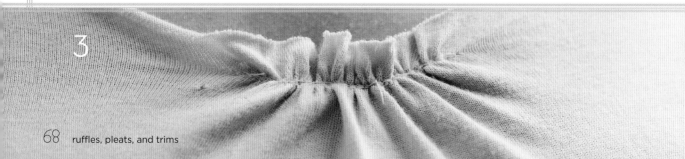

Cutting tip: Have the wearer try on the top, mark the center point, then mark the rest of the neckline lightly with chalk. That way, you'll be sure to position the neckline as desired and not make it too low-cut.

# Pleated Neckline Top

**Here's a neat way to alter a neckline** that gaps or is otherwise ill-fitting. Use it on a garment you've made from scratch, or modify one you already own. Our pleats are stitched at 1" intervals, but you can customize the spacing for a perfect fit.

## 1. SEW A TWO-PANEL SHIRT

Follow the instructions for the Two-Panel Garment, adjusting the hemline as desired to make it into a shirt (see chapter 3, page 34). If you want to add sleeves to your garment, see the how-to instructions for adding sleeves in the same chapter (page 42).

## 2. MARK THE NECKLINE

Mark the center of the front neckline with a chalk dot. Then, at 1" intervals, make three markings on both sides of the center dot as shown.

## 3. MAKE THE PLEATS

Working on the right side, fold the innermost markings (A) to meet the center point and pin the pleats in place. Fold the outermost markings (C) to meet the adjacent ones (B) and pin them in place. Baste the pleats in place close to the edge of the fabric.

## 4. FINISH THE NECKLINE

Following the instructions on page 19, make a loop of ½"-wide binding and pin it in place. Zigzag all around the binding ¼" from the edge.

## what you'll need

- **Torso pattern piece to trace (see chapter 2, page 29)**

- **1 yard of 60"-wide jersey fabric**

- **1 spool of coordinating thread**

2

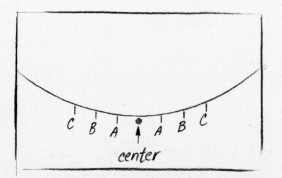

C B A ↑ A B C

center

3

# Cowl Neck Duffle

This duffle is so sleek and functional; you'll want to wear it every day. With its long cowl, you can even pull it up over your head for a more grown-up take on the beloved hoodie.

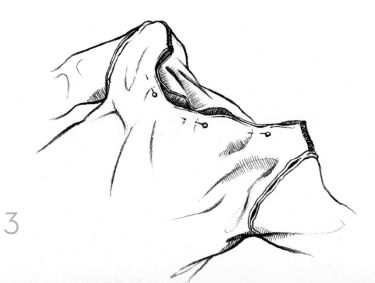

what you'll need

- **Torso pattern piece to trace (see chapter 2, page 29)**

- **Pocket template (page 311)**

- **2½ yards of knit fabric (we used a thick 2-way stretch knit fabric)**

- **1 spool of coordinating or contrasting thread**

## 1. SEW A TWO-PANEL SHIRT

Follow the instructions for The Two-Panel Garment (see chapter 3, page 34) with the following changes: add sleeves (see chapter 2, page 42) and cut a wide scoop neckline (see chapter 2, page 31).

## 2. MEASURE, CUT, AND STITCH THE COWL

Measure the entire perimeter of the neckline and add ½" to the measurement for seam allowance. Cut a rectangle of fabric that equals this measure in length × 23" wide, with the straight grain of the fabric running across the length. Straight stitch the short ends together with a ¼" seam.

## 3. ATTACH THE COWL

With the tunic inside out, slide the cowl inside the neck so the right sides are together. Pin the raw edges together, lining up the cowl's seam with a shoulder seam. Straight stitch a ½" seam around the pinned perimeter.

3

Design tip:
A wide neckline
suits a cowl
neck best
because it
allows the
encircling
drape of fabric
to highlight
your neck and
collarbones.

Design tip: Align the
top edge of the pocket with
the wearer's bellybutton.

73

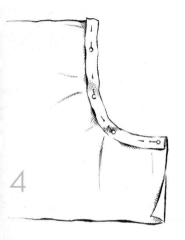

4

## 4. MAKE THE FRONT POCKET

Fold a 10" × 17" piece of fabric in half along the straight grain and pin the pocket template on the fold so the grain runs from the top to the bottom of the pocket. Trace around the template and then cut along the marked lines through both thicknesses of fabric.

To make binding for the pocket openings, cut two 1" × 8" strips along the crossgrain. Fold the strips lengthwise, just off center, with wrong sides together (see page 19 for more on making binding).

Pin the binding strips to each pocket opening so that the wider side of the folded binding is on the wrong side of the pocket and the raw edge of the pocket is encased in the binding fold.

Zigzag the edge of the binding to the pocket, overcasting the edge of the binding slightly.

Press the top, sides, and bottom edges of the pocket ½" to the wrong side and pin the pocket so it is centered on the front of the tunic.

## 5. ATTACH THE POCKET

Zigzag the pocket in place along the top, sides, and bottom (not the curved edges finished with binding). Reinforce the stitching at the corners of the pocket openings with extra backtacking.

## 6. HEM THE BOTTOM (OPTIONAL)

Depending on the fabric you have chosen for this project, you might want to hem the bottom edge. If so, trim the bottom edge so it's even all the way around, then press the cut edge under ½", and sew the hem in place with the same zigzag used for the pocket.

# Shirred Empire Waist Dress

Shirring and smocking are often associated with little girls' clothing, but this dress proves that shirring can look very sophisticated too. The empire waist also has grown-up appeal because it's flattering on just about everyone, as it accentuates the positive.

## 1. SEW A TWO-PANEL DRESS

Follow the instructions for the Two-Panel Garment (see chapter 3, page 34), adjusting the length as desired, and adding sleeves of your choice (see chapter 3, page 42).

To finish the raw edges of the dress, use a straight stretch stitch to sew three meandering lines around the neck and bottom edge. Sew two meandering lines at the bottom edge of the sleeves (for tips on decorative lines of stitching, see chapter 5, page 106).

## 2. MEASURE AND MARK THE EMPIRE WAISTLINE

Have the wearer put on the dress. Chalk mark the point where the top center of the empire waistline's shirring should lie (it's usually right at the bottom edge of the breastbone, where the ribs come together). Have the wearer take the dress off.

With the right side of the dress front facing up, measure along the side seam from the armhole to a point that is level with the waistline chalk mark. Mark that point on the side seam, then repeat on the other side. Draw a straight line across the dress front connecting the side seam and chalk markings.

## what you'll need

- Torso and sleeve pattern pieces to trace (see chapter 2, pages 29–30)

- 2 yards of wool jersey fabric

- 1 spool each of coordinating and contrasting thread

Starting at the waistline, draw two lines, each parallel to and 6" from each side seam, as shown.

## 3. SEW THE SHIRRING

Run four lines of basting at ¼" intervals across the marked shirring area. Be sure to leave long tails of thread at the beginning and end of the stitching lines, and don't backstitch.

Gently grasp the top threads and slide the fabric along them to form even gathers. With a pin, pull the top threads through to the back and knot each one to its corresponding bobbin thread.

## 4. ADD A PRETTY TOPSTITCH

Using a decorative stitch, topstitch over and between each of the four sewn lines in contrasting thread (we used four lines of featherstitch in light green thread and three lines of smocking stitch in orange thread).

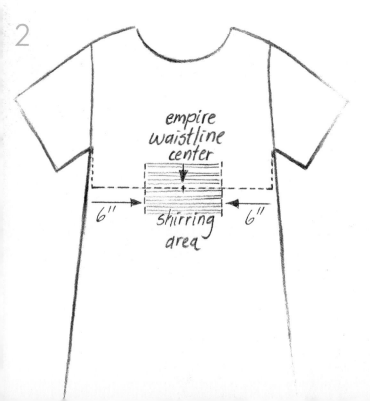

empire
waistline
center

shirring
area

6"    6"

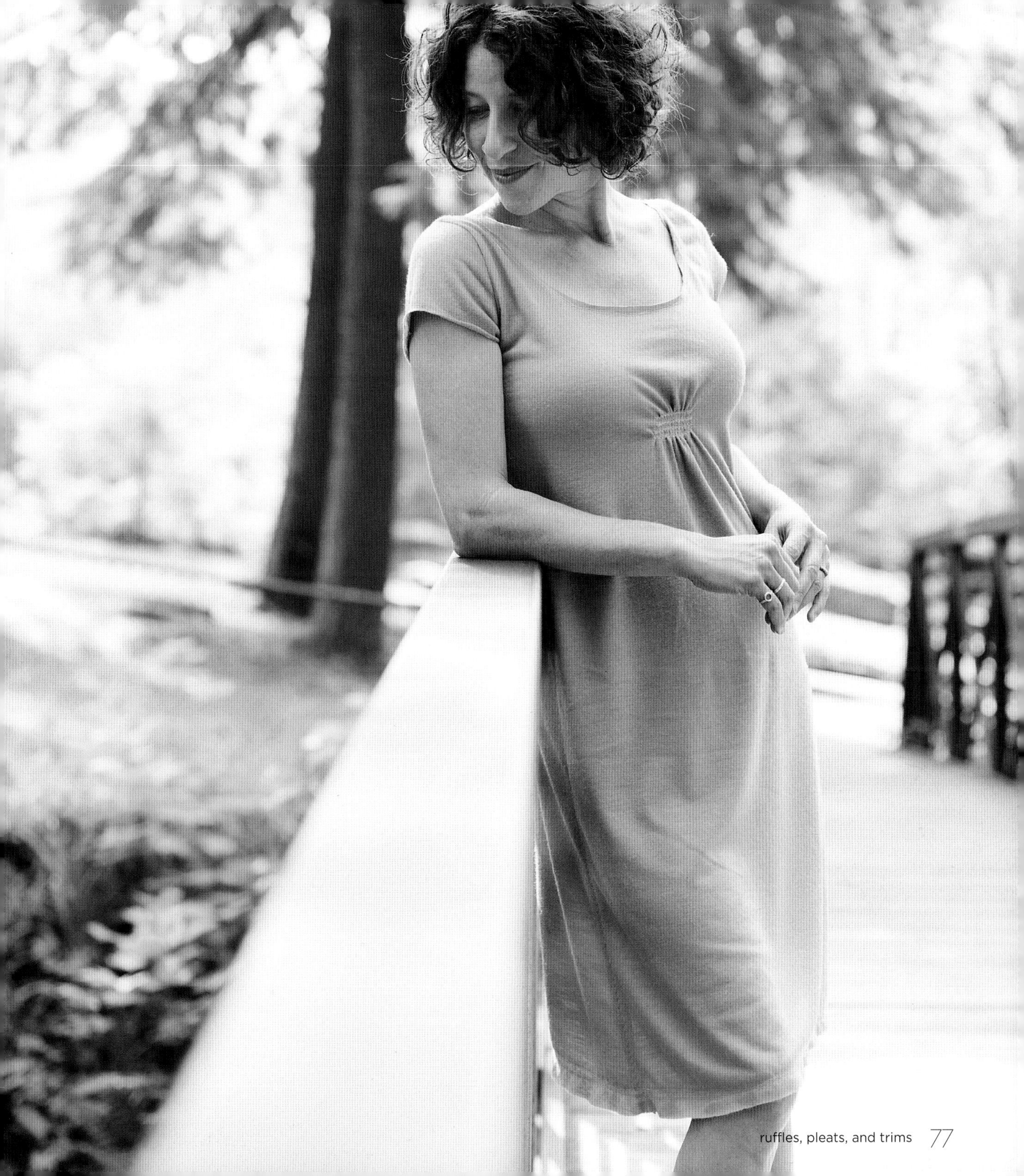

# Ruffled Dressy Dress

**Silk jersey is a joy to work with** and takes the Four-Panel Garment to new heights with its drape and smooth hand. Possibilities for embellishment are endless; think about subtle silk thread hand stitching along the seams (as shown) or a flash of beading on the sash ends.

## what you'll need

- Torso and sleeve pattern pieces to trace (see chapter 2, pages 29–30)

- 2 yards of silk jersey (54/55" wide), depending on desired length

- 1 spool of coordinating thread

## 1. SEW A FOUR-PANEL DRESS

Follow the instructions for the Four-Panel Garment, adjusting the length measurements as desired for your dress (see chapter 3, page 38).

## 2. ADD THE SLEEVES

Following the instructions in chapter 3, page 42, measure, mark, and cut short sleeves, but add an extra 1" between the fabric fold and the sleeve pattern piece (adds width to sleeve cap), to allow for a subtle puffed shoulder.

Fold the fabric sleeve in half and mark the center at the top shoulder edge. Mark a line 2" long on each side of the center marking, ¼" in from the edge. Stitch along the line with a basting stitch, leaving long thread tails at both ends.

Gently pull on the top thread and slide the fabric into gathers. With a pin, pull the top thread through to the wrong side, and then knot the top and bobbin threads together.

Attach the sleeves to the dress (see chapter 3, page 44).

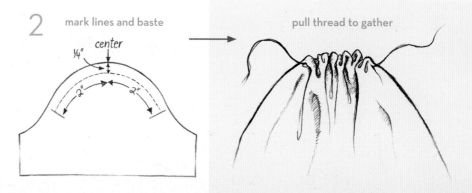

2   mark lines and baste     pull thread to gather

center
¼"
2"   2"

Stitching tip:
The gathering stitches are ¼" from the sleeve's edge and the shoulder seam will be sewn ½" from the edge, so the stitching will be hidden.

Stitching tip:
When working with silk jersey, use a fine needle (we used a 70/10 stretch needle), a slightly longer stitch length, and polyester thread. Remember to cut the pattern pieces so the straight grain of the fabric runs the length of the dress and sleeves.

### 3. MEASURE, MARK, AND CUT THE BINDING AND SASH

Working on the wrong side of fabric, measure and mark the following pieces so they will be cut out on the cross grain:

— **hemline binding (cut 2):** 1" wide × length of bottom edge from side seam to side seam + 1"

— **sash (cut 2):** 4" × 40"

— **sash loop (cut 1 or 2):** 1" × 2" (we cut 1, but if you'd like a loop on either side for symmetry's sake, cut 2)

### 4. FINISH THE HEM

Lay the dress flat. With scissors, trim the hem so that it's even and slightly rounded, ¼" higher at the side seams than at the center ones.

Straight stitch the hemline binding strips together at both ends with a ½" seam, creating a loop. Press the binding loop in half lengthwise so it is ½" wide all around.

Pin the binding so it encloses the raw edge of the hem and the seams are aligned.

Zigzag the binding in place close to the binding raw edge, taking care to catch both sides of the binding in the stitching.

### 5. MAKE THE SASH AND SASH LOOP

Sew the short edges of the sash pieces with the right sides together, making one 80"-long strip. Press one long edge 1" to the wrong side, then press the opposite edge 1½" to the wrong side. Cut the narrow end at an angle as in photo on page 81.

5

Stitch along both folded edges with a narrow zigzag (our stitch width was 2, stitch length was 1.5).

Press in both long edges of the sash loop piece, overlapping them at the center by ¼", and stitch them in place with a narrow zigzag. Turn in ¼" and hand-stitch the short edges to finish them.

To attach the sash loop, have the wearer try on the dress, tie the sash at the desired level (ours is placed under the bust to create an empire waist), and mark one side seam at the desired sash loop location. Have the wearer carefully remove the dress. With the piece folded in half to form a loop, hand-stitch the ends to the marked spot, keeping the stitches as small as possible.

Cutting tip:
Reserve enough silk for the ruffle (see step 7, page 82).

## Ruffled Dressy Dress

Stitching tip:
Don't fret if you sew over any basting stitches because they are still easy enough to remove.

### 6. CUT THE NECKLINE

Have the wearer try on the dress to mark and then cut a V neckline, following the instructions in chapter 2, page 31.

### 7. ADD THE RUFFLES

Measuring from selvage to selvage, mark and cut two 1"-wide strips, each as long as the neckline measurement plus 6". Make the strips into ruffles (see the chapter intro, page 60).

Design tip:
Always mark any
neckline wearing
the bra you (or the
wearer) are planning
to wear under the
dress. If you don't
love a V neckline,
a scooped one also
looks nice with a
ruffle.

With the right sides together and a ¼" seam, join the ruffled strips to make one long strip. Pin that seam to the center back seam at the edge of the neckline. Carefully pin the ruffle in both directions all the way around the neckline, to the front seam, and down the front as long as one or both ruffles will reach (or as long as you want them).

Straight stitch the ruffle in place next to the basting stitch. Carefully remove the basting stitches with a seam ripper. Hand stitch as desired to embellish seams and sleeves.

# Leafy Ruffle Tunic

Add texture and interest to a top with nature-inspired trimmings. The asymmetrical design makes this look modern rather than fussy.

## what you'll need

- Torso and sleeve pattern pieces to trace (see chapter 2, pages 29–30)

- 1½ yards of wool jersey fabric

- 1 spool of coordinating thread

- Embroidery floss in a coordinating or contrasting color

- Embroidery hand needle

## 1. SEW A TWO-PANEL TUNIC

Follow the instructions for the Two-Panel Garment (see chapter 3, page 34). We like this tunic with cap or short sleeves (see chapter 3, page 42).

## 2. CREATE THE LEAVES

From the same or contrasting fabric, draw and cut leaf shapes. We cut eight leaves, each measuring 4¼" × 1¾".

## 3. ATTACH THE LEAVES

Starting at the shoulder seam, lay the leaves in a line along the neckline and down the center front seam. Tuck the top of each leaf beneath the one above it. To make the embellishment look more organic, place the last two leaves randomly, at a slightly different angle from the rest.

Hand-sew the leaves in place with embroidery floss, beginning inside the shirt at the shoulder and tacking down the first leaf with an X stitch. Continue along the neckline, securing the leaves at their top edges with a running stitch.

Design tip:
We like the way
this tunic looks
sleeveless, but
feel free to add
sleeves if you
like (see chapter 3,
page 42).

# Exposed Seam Tunic

**With its hand-embroidered embellishments** and raw edges, this tunic has a real DIY style. But here's our little secret: the exposed center seams also elongate and flatter the body of the lucky wearer.

## 1. SEW A FOUR-PANEL TUNIC

Follow the instructions for the Four-Panel Garment (see chapter 3, page 38) but, in step 2, fold the fabric with the wrong sides together, and then stitch the panels with the wrong sides together.

## 2. PRESS THE EXPOSED SEAMS

Having carefully sewn the front and back panels with the wrong sides together, the raw edges of the seam allowances will be exposed. Press the seams open.

## 3. ADD THE EMBROIDERY

Knot the embroidery thread. Starting on the wrong side of the front center seam ½" below the neckline, hand-sew an X stitch at the top edge on the right side.

Continuing on the right side of the garment, hand-sew a line of running stitches down the left edge of the seam allowance, making another X stitch every so often along the center seam. At the bottom edge, make an X stitch, then sew a line of running stitches up the right edge of the opposite seam allowance back to the neckline. Knot and trim the thread on the wrong side. Repeat this seam treatment along the center back seam and side seams.

## what you'll need

- Torso pattern piece to trace (see chapter 2, page 29)
- 2 yards of jersey fabric
- Coordinating thread
- Contrasting cotton embroidery thread
- Embroidery hand needle

# Layered Hemline Skirt

**Flouncy and flirty**, this skirt is based on the two-panel skirt pattern. You can buy jersey by the yard or go thrifty and green by upcycling one or two large t-shirts. We show the skirt here with the main panel and the layered bottom piece cut from the same fabric, but you can add interest by using another color for the layered bit, or by simply using contrasting color thread.

## 1. SEW A TWO-PANEL SKIRT

Follow the instructions for the Two-Panel Skirt (page 47) through step 1. The layered hemline reduces the length by ½", which means that the skirt might end up too short for you. Add ½" to your length measurement to compensate.

## 2. MEASURE, MARK, AND CUT THE LAYER STRIPS

Measure and mark a straight line 2½" above the bottom edge of both skirt panels. Cut along the marked line. (Or cut 2½"-wide strips from contrasting color jersey).

## 3. ATTACH THE LAYER STRIPS

Pin the right side of a strip to the wrong side of the bottom edge of one panel, overlapping them by ½" (or, if you don't want to pin the layers, draw a chalk line on the panel's right side ½" from the edge, to guide you as you sew). Using a line of zigzag and a line of straight stretch stitch, topstitch the layers together ½" from the edge of the panel. Repeat for the other panel.

## 4. ASSEMBLE THE SKIRT

Pin the front and back panels with the right sides together and sew a ½" seam along each side, using a straight stretch stitch.

Sew fold over elastic along the waistband (see chapter 1, page 19).

## what you'll need

- 1½ yards of solid cotton jersey
- Fold over elastic
- 1 spool of coordinating or contrasting thread

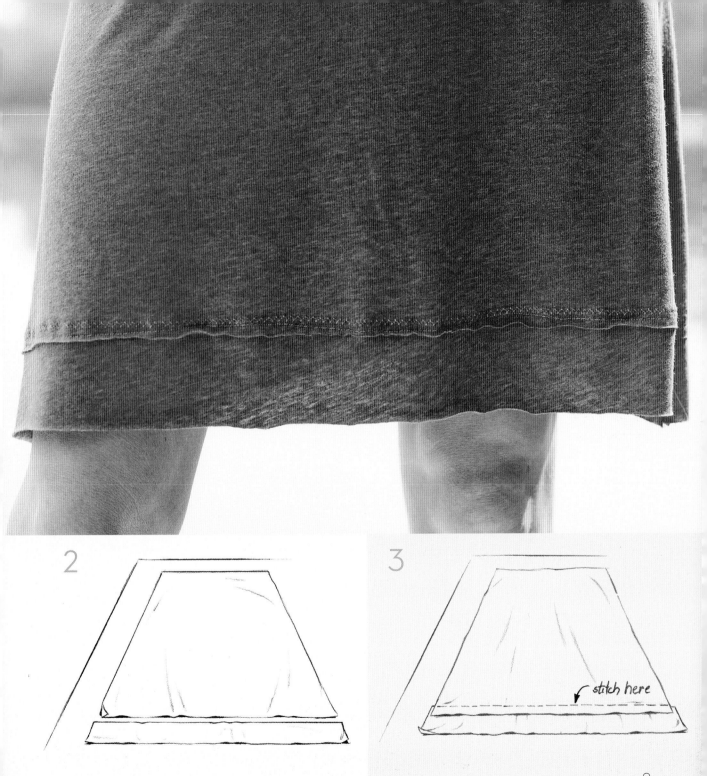

2

3

*stitch here*

**Design tip:**
Our tiers ended
2" from the bottom
edge of the skirt.
If your skirt is longer,
you can certainly
add more tiers.

# Bustle Skirt

Here's a skirt with a high adorableness factor: the front is one simple piece, but the back view is surprising and charming. For this project, choose a fine jersey, since a heavier one would likely add too much bulk to your bustle.

## 1. SEW A TWO-PANEL SKIRT

Follow the instructions through step 1 for the Two-Panel Skirt, chapter 3, page 47.

## 2. MEASURE, MARK, AND CUT THE BUSTLE TIERS

Each finished tier is 4" wide, and overlaps the tier below it by 1". Lay out the back panel with the right side up to use as a guide. From the rest of the fabric and with the straight grain running vertically, cut four strips, each 4" long and wider than the widest point (the bottom edge) of your skirt. From those four strips, measure, mark, and cut each tier as follows:

— **Tier 1** (begins at waistline)**:** Align a strip over the back panel with its top edge at the waist. Trace along the panel's side edges and cut along those marked lines.

— **Tier 2:** Align a different strip over the panel so it is positioned 3" to 7" down from the waist. Trace along the panel's side edges and cut along those marked lines.

— **Tier 3:** Align a different strip over the panel so it is positioned 6" to 10" down from the waist. Trace along the panel's side edges and cut along those marked lines.

— **Tier 4:** Align the remaining strip over the panel so it is positioned 9" to 13" down from the waist. Trace along the panel's side edges and cut along those marked lines.

### what you'll need

- **1 or 2 yards of jersey fabric (we used 1 yard to sew this little girl's version, but an adult version requires 2 yards)**
- **Fold over elastic**
- **1 spool of coordinating thread**

3

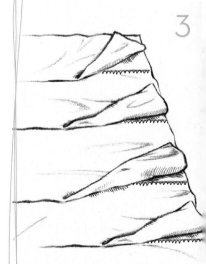

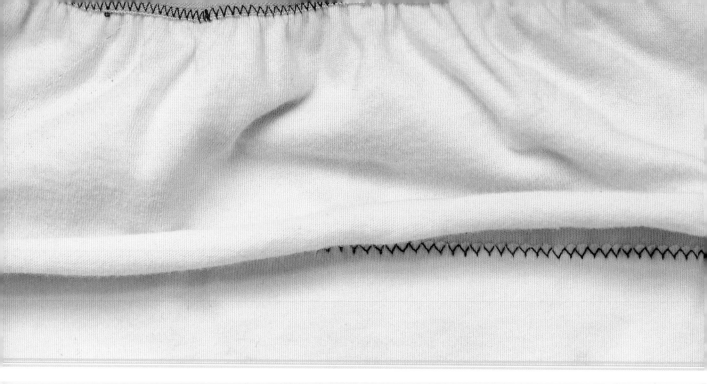

## Bustle Skirt

### 3. ATTACH THE TIERS

Draw chalk lines straight across the back panel at the locations where the tiers will be stitched to the panel. Tier 1 will be sewn to the waist, so mark the first line 3" down from the waistline for Tier 2, 6" below the waistline for Tier 3, and 9" below the waistline for the last tier.

Using a narrow zigzag, attach each tier along its marked line so the stitches are flush with the tier's raw top edge. Each tier will overlap the one below it by 1".

### 4. ASSEMBLE THE SKIRT

Smooth the tiers flat and pin the front and back panels with the right sides together, and the tiers sandwiched between them. Stitch ½" side seams with a straight stretch stitch.

Sew fold over elastic along the waistband (see chapter 1, page 19).

# Jute Edged Throw Rug

**Throw is the operative word here** — this casual floor accent can be tossed anywhere you need some color. The jute-strap binding adds texture and toughness. On a covered porch, it can be a treat for bare feet and give a homey look to a set of outdoor furniture. In cooler weather, bring it inside to warm up an entryway; don't worry about your crew's dirty shoes since this rug is fully washable.

## 1. MEASURE, MARK, AND CUT

Fold the pressed canvas in half so that the short edges meet. Press the crease, then cut one rug bottom and one rug interior layer along the fold, creating two pieces each measuring 44" × 72".

## 2. ASSEMBLE THE LAYERS

Lay out the rug bottom with the wrong side facing up. Position the interior piece over it, and then lay the rug top fabric over the two layers, with the right side facing up. Smooth the layers and pin them together with safety pins, using plenty of pins to prevent shifting.

## 3. PRESS THE JUTE STRAP AND PIN IT IN PLACE

Fold the jute strap lengthwise so that one side of the fold is about ¼" narrower than the other (see illustration on page 94). Press the crease.

## 4. MAKE THE CORNERS

Cut two 72" lengths of folded jute and pin them so they enclose the edges of the fabric layers along both long sides. Cut two 44" lengths of jute. Miter the corners as shown on page 94 and press. Pin the shorter lengths in place to enclose the fabrics' short edges.

(see illustration on page 94)

## what you'll need

- 2 yards of 44"-wide home-decor weight fabric for the rug top

- 4 yards of 44"-wide heavyweight canvas in coordinating color

- 7 yards of 3½"- or 4"-wide jute strap

- 1 spool of coordinating thread

- Extra-large safety pins

- Denim sewing machine needle

## Juted Edged Throw Rug

3

4

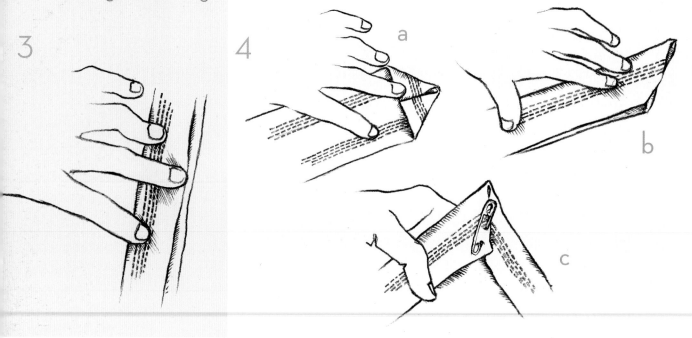

a

b

c

Layout tip: After canvas is washed, it can be very wrinkled. To get rid of the wrinkles, smooth the just-washed fabric and hang it to dry on a clothesline, if weather permits. Otherwise, take it out of the dryer when it's still a little damp and press it with a hot iron.

## 5. SEW JUTE STRAP IN PLACE

Install the denim needle and set your machine for a 2.5 straight stitch. Topstitch the jute in place, ¼" from the inside edge.

## 6. TACK THE LAYERS TOGETHER

To add extra stability to the layers of the rug, tack the layers together every 10" to 12". We used coordinating thread and free-motion stitched around some of the red flowers in the fabric pattern (this looks sweet on the rug's bottom side, too, as shown at right).

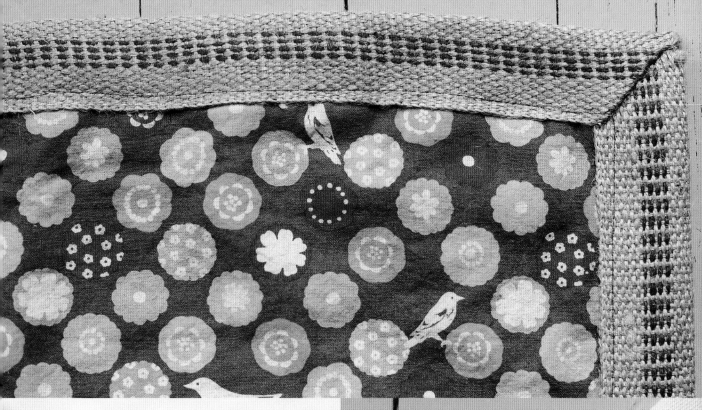

5

6

# Ruffled Wrap

The uneven hemline of this sophisticated little number looks lovely when the front is left open, and adds interest to a plain top or dress when it is tied at the waist. The simple ruffle is left with a raw edge for a more laid-back touch.

## what you'll need

- Torso pattern piece to trace (see chapter 2, page 29)
- 1 yard 58/60"-wide jersey fabric
- 1 spool of coordinating thread

## 1. MEASURE, MARK, AND CUT THE BACK PANEL

Lay the fabric right side up with the straight grain running vertically. Fold one edge toward the center so that you can fit the panel pattern piece positioned along the fabric fold. Trace the pattern piece onto the wrong side of the fabric and cut along the marked lines through both layers of fabric. Don't cut through the fold, because that's the center of the back panel. Simply unfold your fabric after cutting and it's ready to go.

## 2. MEASURE, MARK, AND CUT TWO FRONT PANELS

Fold the remaining fabric in half with the right sides together and position the panel pattern piece so the side seam is close to, but not on, the fabric fold. This will allow for ample room to draw a new shape for the center opening.

Trace the shoulder line, the armholes, and the side seam. To make the swooping design line of the front, mark a point on the fabric 5" from the bottom of the pattern piece and 7" to the right of the original center line as shown. Use a French curve or your eye to draw lines to connect this mark with the side and shoulder seams as shown. Cut along the lines through both layers of fabric.

## 3. ASSEMBLE THE WRAP

With the right sides together, pin the back to the two front pieces so the shoulder and sides are aligned. Using a straight stretch stitch, sew a ½" seam at the shoulders and sides.

## 4. ADD THE RUFFLES

Fold the remaining yardage in half with the straight grain running vertically and the right sides together. Cut two 1"-wide strips from fabric edge to fabric edge across the grain.

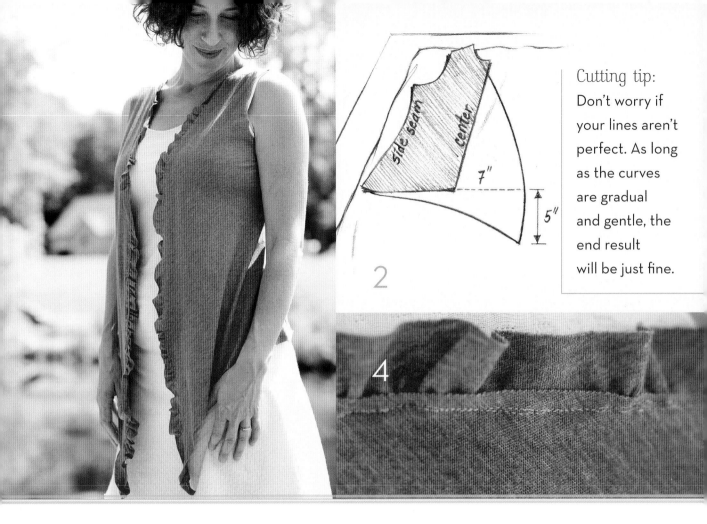

2

side seam

center

7"

5"

4

Baste ¼" from one long edge of each strip. On each strip, grasp the top thread and gently slide the fabric along the thread to make loose gathers.

Pin a ruffled strip along each edge of the front panel so that the panel overlaps the ruffle's sewn edge by ¼", extending the ruffles as desired to fit the front edge. From the right side of the panel, topstitch with a straight stitch about ⅛" from the edge (as shown in photo above). This leaves the front panel's raw edges exposed to add even more fullness and texture.

ruffles, pleats, and trims

# Ribbon Trimmed Tote

**With just a small amount of fabric** or even a remnant, you can stitch up a smart bag suitable for a million uses. Vary the fabrics and don't worry if the trimming edges fray — that's part of the tote's gypsy appeal.

## 1. MEASURE, MARK, AND CUT YOUR FABRIC

Measure and mark the following pieces directly onto the wrong side of your fabric and then cut them out:

— **lining:** 16" × 28"

— **exterior:** 16" × 28"

— **handle:** 2" × 25" (cut 2 from each fabric)

— **ribbon trim:** 1" × 32" wide (cut 3 from the exterior fabric)

## 2. SEW THE LINING

Fold the fabric with the right sides together, so the folded piece measures 16" × 14". Cut the folded edge open. Using a straight stitch, sew ½" seams along the bottom and side edges. Trim the bottom corners and press the seams open.

## 3. EDGE AND ATTACH THE RIBBONS

Make ribbons from the three ribbon strips following the instructions in the chapter intro (page 60).

Pin one ribbon to the right side of the exterior piece, straight across the longer edge, 1" from the top edge. Straight stitch through the center of the ribbon to attach it to the bag front. Repeat to attach the remaining ribbons, each parallel and adjacent to the one above it.

## 4. MAKE THE EXTERIOR

Fold the exterior fabric in half, with the right sides (the beribboned sides) together. Cut the folded edge open. Straight stitch ½" seams at the sides and bottom and press the seam allowances flat. Turn right side out.

### what you'll need

○ **½ yard of exterior fabric (we used a home-decor weight fabric)**

○ **½ yard of lining fabric (we used a woven cotton)**

○ **1 spool of contrasting thread**

interior piece
inside out

↓

slides into

↓

exterior piece
right side out

## 5. ASSEMBLE THE TOTE

With wrong side out, slide the lining piece inside the exterior piece so the wrong sides are together (as shown on left). Fold and press the top edges of the exterior and lining ¾" toward the lining side and zigzag the raw edges together (this will join the lining and the exterior).

## 6. MAKE THE STRAPS

Pair each exterior fabric strap with a lining fabric strap with the wrong sides together.

Zigzag each pair together along both long edges.

Starting and ending 1" from the ends, press the straps in half with the lining sides together to create a fold in the handle.

Zigzag the long edges together (across from the fold), leaving 1" at each end unstitched so the straps can be attached to the bag.

## 7. ATTACH THE STRAPS

Pin a strap on each side of the exterior so the strap ends are about 1" from each side seam with the ends tucked beneath the uppermost ribbon. Zigzag the ends in place (this seam will be concealed by the ribbon), then straight stitch the straps to the top edges of the tote.

# Keyhole T-Shirt

**This simple little shirt gets its creative spark** from contrasting homemade binding decoratively stitched at the neck. This project is great for practicing this handy trimming technique, which is used throughout the book. If you're an experienced sewist, you'll find this a fast and fun way to add an unusual look to your t-shirt wardrobe. We used contrasting thread for extra flair, but a coordinating color would look sleek and polished.

## 1. SEW A TWO-PANEL SHIRT

Follow the instructions for the Two-Panel Garment (see chapter 3, page 34). We like this shirt with long or ¾-length sleeves (see chapter 3, page 42). Add ½" to the length of the front and back panels and sleeves for hemming.

## 2. CUT THE NECKLINE

Cut a scoop neckline (see chapter 2, page 31).

On one side, cut a 2" slit from the neckline into the body of the shirt in a spot where it won't reveal a bra strap (the slit shown is 4½" from the shoulder seam). Open the slit a bit more by cutting its sides into shallow half-moon curves.

## 3. MEASURE, MARK, AND CUT THE BINDING

To determine the correct length for the neckline binding, measure the circumference of the neckline (disregard the keyhole for the moment), then subtract 10% because the binding needs to be a bit smaller than the neckline opening in order to lie flat.

- Torso and sleeve pattern pieces to trace (see chapter 2, pages 29 and 30)

- 1 yard of wool or cotton jersey

- ¼ yard of contrasting jersey for the binding

- 1 spool each of coordinating and contrasting thread

- Small button

## Keyhole T-Shirt

Measure the circumference of the keyhole opening next.

Place the contrasting fabric wrong side up, then measure, mark, and cut the following pieces on the cross grain of the fabric:

— **neckline binding:** 1" × neckline measurement

— **keyhole binding:** 1" × keyhole measurement + 2"

### 4. BIND THE KEYHOLE

Prepare the keyhole binding, following the instructions for making a binding loop strip (without joining the short edges) on page 61. Pin the strip so it encloses the keyhole's raw edges. Zigzag the binding in place close to the raw edge of the binding. Cut off any excess binding so the ends are flush with the neckline edge.

### 5. BIND THE NECKLINE

Make a binding loop and attach it around the neckline, following the instructions on page 61. Zigzag the binding in place close to the raw edge of the binding.

### 6. FINISH THE SHIRT

Hand-sew a decorative button onto the neckline binding at the point where the keyhole and the neckline meet.

Press under ½" double-fold hems (see chapter 1, page 19) along the sleeve openings and the bottom edge. Zigzag the hems with contrast color thread.

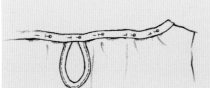

Cutting tip:
Just eyeball these
cuts, or, if you'd
rather, trace the
curve of a jar
or container lid.

5 lines

**Using thread and lines of decorative stitching as a design element** is a cheap thrill. Since you most likely already have a machine that's capable of sewing a variety of straight and zigzag stitches, all you need to do is decide which thread colors to use. After that, you simply play with the stitch length and width. Before you know it, you've added your own improv design element to any project.

## Stitching Straight Lines

**What to know:** Your machine is cleverly designed to sew in straight lines. Just don't pull on the fabric; guide it gently, using the edge of the presser foot or markings on the throat plate to help. If your line of stitching seems to be going off course, take your foot off the pedal. Your machine will stop stitching instantly. Simply readjust and begin again. Sew slowly and when you feel comfortable with your machine, you can speed up.

**How to do it:** Check your machine settings, including the tension, presser foot pressure, and stitch length and width before stitching (refer to your sewing machine manual for help). It helps to make a practice line of stitching on scrap fabric to make sure the stitch looks good. Check to see that the feed dogs are fully engaged before beginning. Most of the time, you'll want to backtack at the start and end of each stitching line (see page 18). Use your hands to guide the fabric. Typically it is easy to stitch parallel lines with exact intervals of ⅛" or ¼" between them by using the edges of the foot, the toes, or the marks on the machine as a guide.

## Stitching Meandering or Wavy Lines

**What to know:** Meandering or wavy lines might look random, but creating them takes a bit of thought and a bit of practice. Try stitching on scrap fabric until you get the hang of it. You determine how much to bend and shape the lines and whether or not you want them to cross. There are no real rules. Playing around with the stitching will be totally fun as well as a great warm-up for some free-motion techniques explained in the next chapter.

**How to do it:** Set a stitch length between 2 and 2.5, depending on the weight and texture of the fabric and the amount of contrast you want (make a scrap fabric test first). Gently guide your fabric, stitching gradual, rhythmic curved lines.

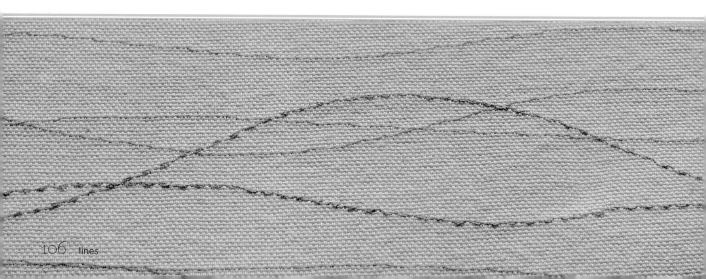

# Pretty Pillowcase

Once you've whipped up your first pillowcase, you'll quickly realize that certain items aren't worth buying when they can be made at home with very little time and effort. Create a set from a favorite fabric, or repurpose an old white top sheet, which will be silky soft after many washings, providing the perfect blank canvas for stitching decorative lines.

## 1. MEASURE, MARK, AND CUT

Fold the fabric in half with the right sides together and selvages aligned. Mark and measure the following piece, then cut along the lines through both thicknesses of fabric (do not cut along the fold):

— **pillowcase:** 19" × 34"

## 2. HEM AND STITCH THE LINES

Unfold the fabric. Along one 38" edge, press under ½", and then press under another 3½". Stitch the hem close to the inside folded edge with contrasting thread, then add meandering lines and decorative utility stitches.

## 3. CLOSE THE SEAMS

Fold the fabric in half with the right sides facing, bringing the short edges together. Using a straight stitch, sew a ½" seam along the raw edges to close the case. Finish the seam allowances with an overcast stitch such as a zigzag. Turn the pillowcase right side out.

what you'll need

- **1 yard of cotton fabric (woven or jersey)**
- **1 spool of contrasting thread**

Stitching tip: Keep your decorative stitching along the short, open edges of the pillowcase and away from the center where your head will rest while sleeping; otherwise, the texture of the stitches might be annoying.

# Meandering Cardigan

**As a layer to toss on over a dress or t-shirt**, this piece is as easy to wear as it is to make. Use a short- or long-sleeve tee that you've never really loved, or even one that has become a tiny bit too small. Either way, you'll find it deserves renewed respect once it's dressed up with a sophisticated stitched edge.

what you'll need

○ **Tissue or regular weight t-shirt**

○ **1 spool of contrasting thread**

○ **30" length of silky ribbon or tape (we used rayon seam tape)**

## 1. CUT THE SHIRT

Fold the t-shirt in half at the center of the front panel with the back panel pulled out of the way and the neck and side seams aligned as shown. Use sharp scissors to cut along the fold, right through the center front.

## 2. ATTACH THE RIBBON TIES

Cut the ribbon into two 15" lengths. Knot one end of each piece of ribbon and fold the opposite ends ½" to the wrong side. Pin the folded ribbon ends to the t-shirt at the inside top corners of the opening so the ribbons extend toward each other. Trim any excess ribbon beneath the knots.

## 3. STITCH THE LINES

Using a straight stitch, topstitch a meandering line from a bottom corner of the front opening, up the front, over the ribbon's folded end, around the back neckline, over the second ribbon, and back down the opposite side to the bottom. Repeat, to sew five or six closely spaced lines (see page 106 for sewing wavy lines).

> [UNTITLED]
>
> I worked on this story all last year out of school. It was my big project and I typed and typed and typed until was over 100 pages long. This story was kind of a landmark for me, since I moved from Sorrel to an unfinished novel. However, I chose to stop working on this. I moved on to my current work Irontongue and Ashwin, mainly because I disliked the main character, Kalina.
>
> Main Characters
>
> Kalina: Narrorator of the story, protagonist.
>
> Sachio: Supporting character. I ended up liking him a lot better than Kalina.
>
> Chantarai: Acolyte of Lord Namiro, antagonist. I also think she's more interesting than Kalina.
>
> Lord Namiro: Antagonist. Ruler of Kasairyu, one of the countries in Suddara, where it takes place.

# Personalized Project Folder

**Sew your own office supplies?** Why not? Whether you use this folder for business, school, or pleasure (we use it to stow inspirational pictures for future sewing projects), it makes getting organized a lot more fun. Plus, with its cardboard-stiffened covers, it's a great place to experiment with different types of stitched lines. Spin the dial on your machine for a little sewing roulette — there's no wrong way to decorate this one.

## 1. MEASURE, MARK, AND CUT

Measure and mark the folder cover, 18" × 36", directly on the wrong side of the fabric. Cut it out.

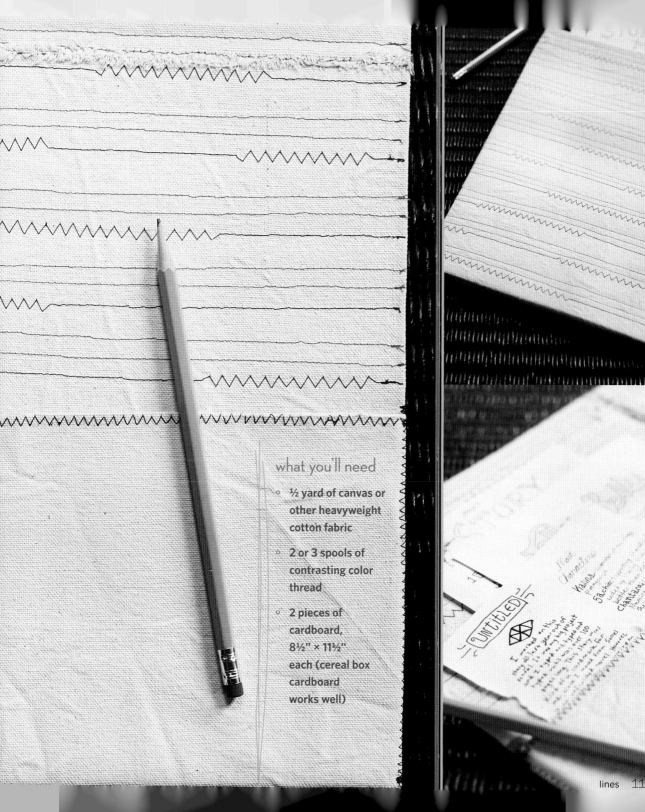

what you'll need

- ½ yard of canvas or other heavyweight cotton fabric

- 2 or 3 spools of contrasting color thread

- 2 pieces of cardboard, 8½" × 11½" each (cereal box cardboard works well)

# Personalized Project Folder

## 2. MARK, FOLD, AND PRESS

Mark foldlines on the wrong side of the fabric as follows:

— 9" in from both sides

— 18" in from both sides (center)

— ½" down from top edge

— 6" up from bottom edge

Fold along the lines and press well to set the folds.

## 3. LINE THE FOLDER

Unfold the bottom edge. Slide the cardboard pieces under the top pressed edge and position them next to each other at each side of the center crease. Fold the sides of the fabric over so they meet, and overlap slightly, at the center crease and cover the cardboard. Pin the top edge in place to secure the layers together, and pin the bottom layers of fabric together. The cardboard does not extend below the bottom pressed foldline.

## 4. ADD THE DECORATIVE STITCHED LINES

With the right side of the folder facing up and the cardboard in place, topstitch decorative lines across the fabric, sewing through all the layers and the cardboard. Vary the thread colors and types of stitches as you like. The sample shows thread sewn in straight stitch lines and livened up with random zigzags. Be sure to sew one of the decorative lines close to the upper edge to secure the folded top hem.

## 5. FINISH THE POCKET

Zigzag close to the bottom edge through both layers of fabric to create the top edge of the pocket. Fold the pocket up along the pressed foldline and sew both sides of the pocket closed with an overcast zigzag stitch.

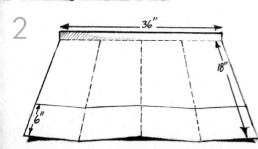

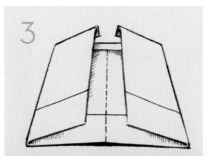

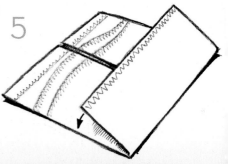

# Super-Jersey Neckerchief

**Scouts and sailors wear neckerchiefs** to give their uniforms jaunty flair.
You should wear them for the same reason. As an alternative to a necklace,
this quick-to-sew project looks beautiful with a scooped neckline top, and
it can also be used in your hair as a band or tie.

## 1. MAKE SUPER-JERSEY

Align the fabric pieces with the wrong sides together. Stitch parallel lines
in a variety of stitches, ¼" apart along the length of the fabric.

## 2. FINISH THE NECKERCHIEF

With scissors or a rotary cutter, gently taper the fabric at each end.

what you'll need

○ **Two 6" × 32" pieces
of wool or cotton
jersey (or a mix,
including silk), cut
on cross grain**

○ **1 spool of
contrasting thread**

Stitching tip: This is a great project for playing with different
stitches. Experiment with your machine to make an interesting
mix of lines.

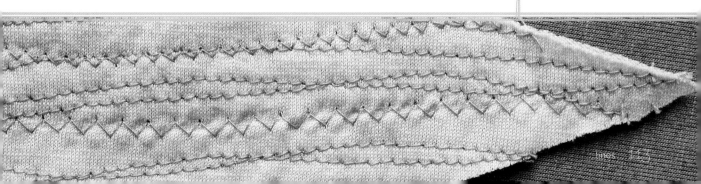

# Ribbon Headband

Tame your tresses with an accessory that's all your own. We used sturdy store-bought ribbon, but you can take the improv impulse a step further and create your own ribbon from a print or solid fabric (see chapter 4, page 60 for more on making ribbon).

## what you'll need

- Headband template (see page 302)

- 12" × 2½" piece of cotton velvet

- 60" of ⅝"-wide plush or velvet ribbon

- 1 spool of coordinating thread

- 7" of fold over elastic

## 1. MARK AND CUT THE FABRIC

Fold the fabric in half with the right sides together and trace the template onto it. Cut along the lines through both thicknesses of fabric.

## 2. CUT THE RIBBON

Pin a length of ribbon along the center of the headband from one end to the other end. Pin two more lengths of ribbon on either side of the center one, spacing them about ¼" apart. Trim the ends at an angle to align with the edges of the headband.

## 3. ATTACH THE RIBBONS

Straight stitch along both edges of all five ribbons to secure them to the headband. Finish the cut edges of the headband fabric by zigzag stitching all around.

## 4. ATTACH THE ELASTIC

Zigzag one end of the elastic to the narrow end of the headband. Have the wearer try the headband on, then mark and trim the elastic so it will fit comfortably, adding ½" for overlap. Secure the opposite end with a zigzag stitch.

# Border-Stitched Linen Place Mats

**Linen is a classic fabric choice** for table place mats and is easy to find in a gorgeous range of colors. Here we give natural linen a casual spin with a little fringe around the edges.

## 1. MEASURE, MARK, AND CUT

Fold the washed and pressed linen in half with the right sides together so the selvages meet. Mark two 12" × 18" rectangles on the wrong side of the fabric, then cut along the marked lines through both fabric layers (you'll end up with four place mat pieces).

## 2. STITCH THE LINES

Straight stitch a line ¼" from each edge. Starting ½" in from one of the stitched corners, straight stitch a second set of lines inside the first set. With a contrast thread color, straight stitch a third set of lines between the first two sets.

## 3. ADD THE LAST DETAILS

With contrast thread, straight stitch a small (approximately ¾") square at each corner. Pull a few threads along the edges to create the fringe.

### what you'll need

- ½ yard of 52"-wide linen (makes 4 place mats)
- 2 spools of contrasting thread colors

Design tip: Have some extra linen? Make a set of border-stitched napkins to match.

# Line-Quilted Blankie

**Give your favorite baby a plush tummy-time spot** with this quick blanket, whipped up from a soft bedsheet. We like to make it playful by mixing up the sheet and thread colors, and by sewing the sheets before they've been washed to create a puckered texture.

## 1. MEASURE, MARK, AND CUT

One at a time, lay out the sheet and batting with the wrong side facing up, and then measure, mark, and cut the following:

— **quilt front:** 68" × 90"

— **quilt back:** 63" × 85"

— **batting:** 63" × 85"

## 2. STACK AND PIN THE LAYERS

On the floor, lay out the quilt front, with the wrong side facing up. Center the batting over it. Then lay the quilt back, with the right side facing up, on top of the batting. There should be a 2½" margin of the wrong side of the quilt front showing all around.

Starting in the center, pin the layers together, using rows of safety pins spaced about 10" apart. Continue pinning toward the edges, smoothing the layers as you go.

### what you'll need

- 1 new twin-size flat sheet*

- 64" × 85" piece of cotton batting

- 2 or 3 spools of contrasting thread (we used 3 colors)

- Large safety pins

*Do not wash the sheet (washing after stitching will create a nice puckered look), but do press it. A few minutes in the dryer may help remove any deep creases caused by the packaging.

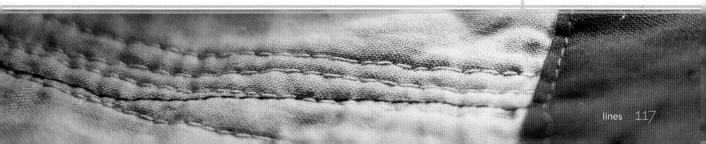

Stitching tip:
If you're using more than one thread color, it's definitely easiest to stitch all the lines in the first color before switching to the next. You will have to shift around the quilt more, but the end effect is worth it.

## 3. STITCH THE LINES

On the quilt back, use a vanishing ink pen to draw vertical lines (parallel to the long edges) at 6" intervals.

Starting at the center of the quilt and using a straight stitch (our stitch length was 3), sew a grouping of 2 to 4 straight or meandering lines along each marked guideline.

## 4. FINISH THE EDGES

With the wrong side of the quilt up, press and pin the front edges ½" to the wrong side and then another 2" to enclose the quilt's raw edges. Miter the corners as shown below, and pin them. Fold the adjoining edges to align with the corner point and pin.

Using a straight stitch, topstitch ⅛" and again ¼" from the hem edges all around, securing the hem in place. To secure the corner folds, hand-sew the mitered edges in place.

Wash and gently dry the quilt.

Design tip: After you've made this baby quilt, try a grown-up version using two full-size sheets.

4

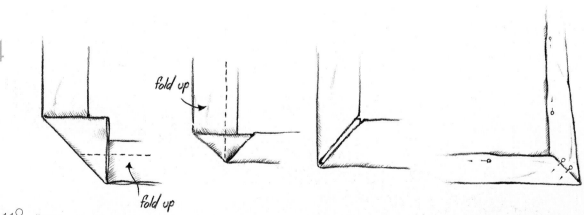

fold up

fold up

# Super-Jersey Lingerie Bag

In this project, you create a cushy new fabric by stitching the front and back panels of an old t-shirt together. The process is fun; the end result is substantial enough for travel, and beautiful too.

## 1. MEASURE, MARK, AND CUT

Lay the t-shirt right side up. Measure and mark a 13" × 17" rectangle on the front. Cut along the lines, through both the front and back of the shirt.

## 2. MAKE THE SUPER-JERSEY

With the fabric pieces still layered, straight stitch slightly wavy lines at narrow intervals across the width. Leave the top edge unstitched, as it rolls nicely.

Other pieces of fabric can be topstitched directly on the super-jersey for texture and color. We topstitched two narrow strips parallel to and ½" below the top edge.

## 3. STITCH THE SIDE SEAMS

With the right side up, measure and mark 7" from the bottom edge of the fabric. Fold the bottom edge up to this mark to create the pouch, leaving 3" extending beyond the double layers to form the flap. Using a knit stitch, sew the side seams with a ½" seam allowance.

Turn the pouch right side out. Press the top and side edges of the flap ½" to the wrong side and zigzag them in place.

## 4. ADD THE BUTTON

Measure and mark the center of the flap and make a buttonhole at the marking to fit the button. With embroidery thread hand-sew the button onto the top layer of the pocket so it aligns with the buttonhole.

what you'll need

- **T-shirt**
- **1 spool of thread***
- **Button**
- **Embroidery thread and needle**

*We like to use a thread and fabric in the same color family for this project; it adds a subtle texture without too much contrast. On the other hand, white thread against a bold color looks fabulous too.

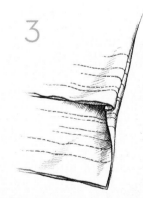

3

# Fabric Photo Frame

**Experiment with different stitched lines** and create a lovely frame to show off your loved ones. If you like, adjust the measurements to fit a piece of glass recycled from a thrifted (but less than attractive) frame.

## what you'll need

- ¼ **yard of canvas**
- ¼ **yard of linen**
- **2 or 3 spools of contrasting colors of thread**
- **4½" square piece of glass (optional)**

## 1. MEASURE, MARK, AND CUT

Lay out both fabrics with the wrong sides facing up. Measure, mark, and cut out the following pieces:

*Cut from the linen:*

— **exterior:** 5" square

— **hanging loop:** ½" × 2"

*Cut from the canvas:*

— **backing (cut 2):** 5" square

## 2. MEASURE, MARK, AND CUT THE WINDOWS

Pin the exterior square on top of one backing square with the wrong sides together. Measure and mark a 3" square window in the center, then cut through both thicknesses of fabric.

## 3. STITCH THE FRAME

Using a stretch zigzag, edgestitch around the perimeter of the window, securing the canvas to the linen. Make more stitched lines to create concentric squares around the window in a mix of decorative stitches, changing thread colors as desired. It is fine to come back and stitch between lines of the other colors, and even to stitch over previous stitches. This will add texture, heft, and brightness to the fabric.

## 4. ATTACH THE LOOP TO THE BACKING

Fold the hanging-loop strip in half, aligning the short edges. Using a zigzag stitch, secure the loop's edges to the wrong side of the remaining backing piece at the top center edge.

## 5. FINISH THE FRAME

Align the frame and the backing pieces with the wrong sides together. Using a stretch zigzag, overcast the sides and bottom edges to join the frame and backing (do not stitch the top edge). Slide in the piece of glass if desired and add a nice little photo.

Cutting tip:
The canvas will act as a stabilizer and give some weight to the thin linen.

# Stitched Lamp Shade

**Light up your life by adding a little custom stitchery** to a plain lamp shade cover. We use a loose-weave fabric for this project; linen is especially nice. Or try a subtle white-on-white striped fabric, which would look fun livened up with colorful stitched lines.

## what you'll need

- Approximately ½ yard of woven cotton fabric (depends on lamp shade circumference)
- Lamp shade to cover
- 1 spool of contrasting thread
- Embroidery thread
- Darning needle (thick gauge)
- Fabric Mod Podge
- Foam brush

## 1. MEASURE, MARK, AND CUT

*For a cylindrical lamp shade:*
Measure the shade's circumference and its height from bottom to top rim. Add ½" to the circumference. Lay the fabric right side up, then mark and cut it to match these measurements.

*For a tapered lamp shade:*
Lay the fabric right side up. Place the lamp shade on it near one end. Make a mark on the shade where it meets the fabric (this is the starting and ending point). Hold your pencil or chalk's point to the fabric, firmly resting it against the shade's lower rim, then roll the lamp shade across the fabric, marking where the shade hits the fabric as you go (you will be drawing an arc). Stop when you get to the starting point marked on the shade. Return the shade back to the original end of the fabric and repeat, resting the pencil against the shade's top rim. You will have created two parallel arcs. Using a ruler, mark lines at each end to connect the two parallel arc lines. Cut along your marked lines.

## 2. SEW THE LINES

Mark Xs randomly around the fabric. Using a straight stretch stitch and contrasting thread, sew over the marked lines.

## 3. ATTACH THE FABRIC

Press one short edge of the lampshade fabric ½" to the wrong side.

Brush Mod Podge over a 3"-wide swath on the wrong side of the lamp shade fabric, starting near the unfolded edge. Position the fabric over the old lamp shade, aligning the top and bottom edges of the fabric with the rims.

Press the unfolded short end of the fabric onto the sticky area, then brush more Mod Podge over it. Repeat, turning the shade and working on 3" at a time, smoothing any bubbles or creases as you go. When you reach the fabric's folded edge, secure it by brushing it with more Mod Podge and pressing it flat against the shade.

With the embroidery floss and darning needle, hand-sew a running stitch through the fabric and shade, just beneath the top rim and just above the bottom rim. Hand-sew a line of small Xs over the seam.

# Nesting Boxes

Corral and contain jewelry, notions, coins, or collections with these nifty catchalls. A heavyweight canvas is the ideal material for this project, since it helps the boxes become stand-up citizens. We like the geometric look of webbed lines for this set, but this project is ideal for any kind of sewn embellishment.

## what you'll need

○ 1¼ yards of heavyweight canvas

○ 1 spool of contrasting thread

○ Sharp pencil

Stitching tip:
The more stitched lines you add, the more structure your box will have. The amount shown here adds up to a fine, sturdy little container.

## 1. MEASURE, MARK, AND CUT

With the fabric right side up, measure, mark, and cut the following pieces:

— **small box:** 6" square

— **medium box:** 8" square

— **large box:** 10" square

## 2. CREATE THE SIDES

Mark four guidelines on the right side of the fabric squares for folding and pressing the box creases as follows:

— **small box:** 1½" from edges

— **medium box:** 2" from edges

— **large box:** 2½" from edges

Cut a straight line from each corner to the point where the guidelines intersect.

## 3. STITCH THE LINES

Working on one box at a time and using a straight stretch stitch, stitch along the marked guidelines to form an inner square. This square marks the bottom edges of the box. Straight stretch stitch additional lines for embellishment and added structure.

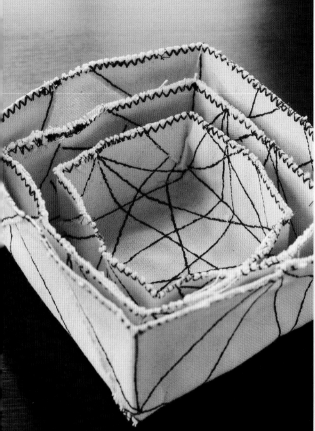

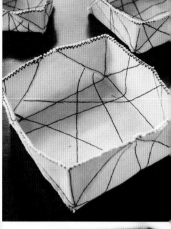

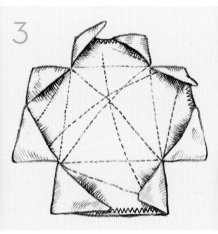

## 4. ASSEMBLE THE BOX

Fold and press the corner flaps in at the marked guidelines. Fold and press the sides in at the stitched-over guidelines. Pull up the corners, pinning one flap toward the inside of the box and one toward the outside.

Using a stretch zigzag, stitch a line around the top edges of the box. This will secure all of the corner flaps into place.

With a straight stitch, sew diagonal lines to create a V shape at each corner, aligned with the flap edges.

Finally, stitch a vertical line along each corner crease.

Finishing tip:
For symmetry's sake, fold the box so that on two opposite sides the flaps lie against the exterior, while on the other two sides, the flaps lie against the interior.

# Swishy Sundress

A swishy lightweight jersey makes up into a cool summer gown. The stitched lines at the empire waist are both graphic and functional, adding interesting detail and shape at the same time. The amount of yardage required depends on the desired length of your finished frock; consider a maxi length for a stylish variation.

## what you'll need

- Torso pattern piece to trace (see chapter 2, page 29)
- 1½ to 2 yards of lightweight jersey fabric (we recommend a bamboo/Lycra blend)
- 1 spool of contrasting thread

## 1. SEW A TWO-PANEL DRESS

Follow the instructions for the Two-Panel Garment (chapter 3, page 34), adjusting the length to make a dress instead of a tunic.

## 2. FINISH THE EDGES

Using an overcast stitch, edgestitch along the raw edges of the neckline, armholes, and bottom.

## 3. STITCH THE LINES

Have the wearer put on the dress. Mark the desired location for the top center of the empire waistline shirring (it's usually right at the bottom edge of the breastbone, where the ribs come together). Have the wearer remove the dress and lay it out with the right side facing up.

Using your mark as a guide, draw a line from side seam to side seam at the marked level.

Using a straight stretch stitch, sew along the guideline. With the edge of the presser foot as a guide, stitch six more parallel lines at ¼" intervals below the first line (our waist stitching is 1½" from top to bottom stitching line).

# Linen Skirt with Wavy Hemline

**Linen always looks elegant**, and thanks to our breezy stretch panel design, it needn't be complicated to sew up a quick linen skirt. Set against the fabric's sumptuous texture, a mix of stitched lines really stands out as a finishing touch.

## 1. MEASURE, MARK, AND CUT

Follow the instructions for the Stretch-Panel Skirt (chapter 3, page 54). Add 1" to the skirt length for a double-fold hem.

## 2. STITCH THE LINES

Press a 1" double-fold hem (see chapter 1, page 19) at the bottom edge of the skirt. Using a straight stitch and contrasting thread, topstitch the hem in place with four or five wavy lines.

### what you'll need

- **1 yard of solid color linen**
- **1 yard of coordinating solid color cotton jersey**
- **1 spool of coordinating thread**
- **Fold over elastic (a length equal to waist measurement)**
- **1 or 2 spools of contrasting thread**

# 6 doodling, sketching, and writing

# Free-motion stitching is the

essential technique used to make most of these designs, and "free" is the operative word here and throughout this book. Feel free to loosen the pressure, feel free to skip the fussy details, feel free to leave an edge raw or roughed up. And, as outlined in this chapter, feel free to scribble on your fabric, write on it, and sketch your visions and dreams. Most importantly, forget about perfection; instead, free yourself to have fun.

# Doodling with Thread

**What to know:** Doodling or scribbling with thread is a great way to explore free-motion stitching; it requires removing or reducing the presser foot pressure, and moving the fabric with your hands in any and every direction. It is important to have a good grip on the fabric so it can be manipulated as desired; this means that free-motion drawing can be tricky on really small pieces of fabric (though not impossible).

**How to do it:** Set the presser foot pressure to 0 (or install a specialty presser foot) and use a straight stitch (our stitch length is usually set on 1.5 to 2 for this technique). Grip the fabric with both hands and guide the fabric back and forth to create lots and lots of loops and circles.

For the boldest, most consistent stitches, keep the needle moving very fast, but move your hands and the fabric slowly. Stop every once in a while with the needle in the fabric to readjust your hands. If you lose your grip on the fabric, stop the machine but make sure to start up again with the needle in the fabric. Extra care needs to be taken as you get close to the fabric edge, since your hands are close to the machine mechanism.

# Sketching with Thread

**What to know:** A whole world of sewing opens up when you master drawing with thread. We like to use a sharp pencil, chalk, or vanishing ink pen to sketch some guidelines on the fabric before stitching. Come up with your own motifs, use templates (including those found in this book), or just improvise and design as you sew. Sketching with thread works best on non-stretch fabric, unless you want a textured effect (like the puckered look of our Doodled Scarf, page 136); if not, apply a stabilizer to support stretchy fabrics before you start stitching.

**How to do it:** Different line styles call for different approaches.

**Outlines:** When stitching the drawing's main lines, sew slowly. Manipulate the fabric gently

## a few supplies

There are a few supplies that make drawing with thread easier. First, it is a good idea to stabilize the back of the fabric under any free-motion stitching. There are many different stabilizers, and you can even use fusible interfacing; they all act to hold the fabric flat and support the stitches. It is helpful, though not necessary, to use a free-motion or darning presser foot. They hold the fabric against the throat plate without moving the fabric. You can also work with an appliqué foot or a spring-loaded embroidery foot. And of course, you might want to consider using some of the lustrous rayon, metallic, and silk threads that come in so many wonderful colors.

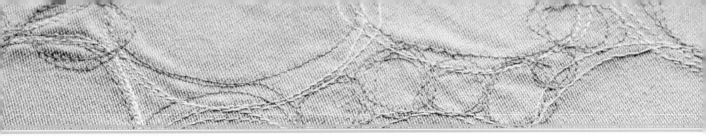

to negotiate curves. Stop often, checking your needle placement. At the point where lines intersect, stop sewing with the needle down, lift the presser foot, and turn the fabric, making sure that the stitches are always going forward to keep the lines clean and sharp. For bolder outlines, sew over the same lines two or three times. As a general rule, set your presser foot pressure to 2 for stitching gradual curves or right angles where you will stop and lift the foot to turn the fabric. This medium pressure helps keep the lines looking tidy but makes it easier to move the fabric. If the lines are small and tightly spaced, then decreasing the pressure to 0 or 1 would be better, giving you more control of the fabric.

**Scribbly areas:** Set your presser foot pressure to 0 (we set our stitch length at 2). Get a good grip on the fabric on either side of the presser foot. Increase your stitching speed so you're sewing quite fast, and manipulate the fabric by pulling it where you want the stitches to go, in tiny circles as in the pupils of a bird's eye, or back and forth for zigzagging scribbles as in a monster's hair. You can also use this technique to fill a shape with color.

# Writing with Thread

**What to know:** Since letters have curved and straight parts, you can use a combo of techniques to stitch them. Mark your guidelines first, and don't worry if your first few attempts look like a second-grader's handwriting; that's part of the charm.

**How to do it:** On large letters, use full presser foot pressure and a straight stretch stitch. On small letters, set your presser foot pressure to 1 or 2 and use a straight stitch with a stitch length of about 1.5. At sharp turns, leave the needle in the fabric, lift the foot, turn the fabric, put the foot down again, and continue stitching. The curve of most letters is gradual enough to follow while gently moving the fabric to keep the stitches on your guidelines. Take your time, but when you're stitching, keep the needle moving fast.

## stitch settings

**For doodling, set your machine for straight stitch or straight stretch stitch. The former is easier to use, but the latter gives a nice bold line. If your design requires you to move the fabric around a lot, it will be a little trickier to use the straight stretch stitch; since it goes backward as well as forward, you may end up with little stitches going this way and that, especially when you've made curving turns. Use it when you have simple lines to follow, and try to end your lines on a backward moving stitch; otherwise, you may get more stray stitches than you like.**

# Doodled Scarf

Stitching free-motion circles on jersey will make the fabric pucker a bit, lending it lots of interesting texture. For comfort's sake, keep the doodling on the ends of the scarf and leave the central portion unadorned.

## what you'll need

- ¼ yard of wool jersey (at least 52" wide)

- 1 spool of contrasting thread

## 1. MEASURE, MARK, AND CUT

Cut a rectangular piece of fabric that measures 6" × 52", cutting across the grain (see tip at right).

## 2. SKETCH YOUR DESIGN

Before you start doodling, read the techniques intro on page 134, and practice on a scrap of the project fabric.

With a contrast color thread and a straight stitch (our stitch length was 2), use the free-motion doodling technique to stitch a pebble design on the two ends of the scarf, leaving a margin of ½" at all edges and extending the thread doodles 6" to 8" up from the bottom edge of the scarf.

Tip: Trying these techniques are kind of like trying a new sport: you'll have fun right from the start, but you'll have even more fun as you practice and get better. Do plenty of test-stitching on swatches of your project fabric before you begin, and give yourself plenty of permission to mess up.

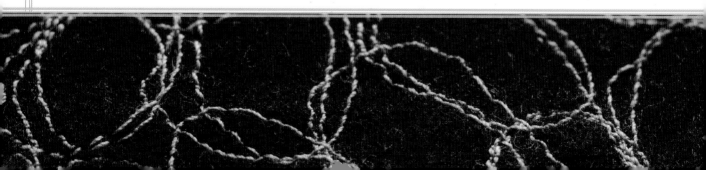

**Cutting tip:**

In the course of doodling, the shirt may become shorter in length, and if you doodle on only one part of the shirt, the bottom hem line may become a bit uneven. To avoid ending up with a shirt length problem, cut your shirt a little longer than the desired finished length, then trim the bottom edge once you are done doodling.

# Pebble Tee

This project takes the Doodled Scarf (page 136) one step further by applying the pebble design to a shirt. The textured surface is fascinating and flattering, and the stitching is just plain fun to do. Here, we stitched up a tee based on our Two-Panel Garment design, but this technique also works wonders on any plain old store-bought t-shirt.

## 1. SEW A TWO-PANEL SHIRT

Follow the instructions for the Two-Panel Garment, adding sleeves, if desired (see chapter 3, pages 34 and 42).

## 2. DOODLE THE DESIGN

Decide whether you want to doodle across the entire shirt front or just in one area. If you decide to stitch just in one area, mark borders.

Before you start free-motion stitching, read the techniques intro on page 134, and practice on a scrap of jersey.

With contrasting thread and a straight stitch (our stitch length was 2), doodle a pebble design. Continue until the desired area is filled.

### what you'll need

- Torso pattern piece to trace (see chapter 2, page 29)

- 1 yard of jersey fabric

- 1 spool of contrasting thread

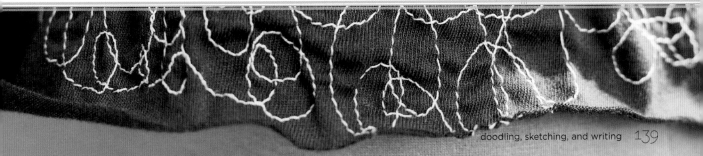

# Cutout Throw Pillow

**Remember how much fun it was to scribble?** This project lets you go crazy with lines in a way you probably haven't done since you were a kid. Embellishing the pillow's front panel (under the felt layer) is a great way to get a feel for moving your fabric under the sewing machine needle, perfect prep for the sketching projects in this chapter. Plus, we love the simple envelope closure on the pillow back, and the soft felt overlay that tops it off.

## what you'll need

- ½ yard of solid woven cotton fabric
- 17" square of wool felt*
- 1 spool of contrasting thread
- Embroidery thread and embroidery needle
- 16" square pillow form
- Template for petal (page 302)

  * *Purl Soho* (see Our Favorite Sources for Fabric and Specialty Supplies) sells precut 18" squares of wool felt in a slew of colors.

## 1. MEASURE, MARK, AND CUT

With the woven fabric and the felt right side up, measure, mark, and cut the following pieces:

*From the fabric:*

— **front panel:** 17" square

— **small back panel:** 17" × 10"

— **large back panel:** 17" × 12"

*From the felt:*

— **felt panel:** 17" square

## 2. SCRIBBLE THE LINES

Before you start free-motion stitching, read the chapter intro, page 134, and practice on a scrap of the project fabric. Decrease the pressure on your presser foot to 0. Using a straight stitch (our stitch length was 2), stitch scribbled lines, randomly moving the fabric under the needle until the entire piece is embellished to your liking.

## 3. CUT THE FELT

Fold the felt square in half, and then in half again. Trace the crescent-shaped petal template, using a vanishing ink pen or chalk, along each of the two folded edges as shown. Cut along the marked lines.

## 4. HEM THE BACK PANELS

On each of the back panel pieces, press one long edge ½" to the wrong side and then 1" again to make a double-fold hem (leave the remaining edges unhemmed). Topstitch ¾" from the edge to secure the hem.

## 5. ASSEMBLE THE PILLOWCASE

Stack the pieces in the following order:

1. Scribbled woven fabric panel, right side up

2. Cut felt square, right side up

3. Back panels, wrong side up

Pin the stacked fabrics together, overlapping the hemmed edges of the back panels so the outside edges align with the other pieces. Straight stitch a ½" seam around all four edges. Clip the seam allowance at the corners, being careful not to snip the stitching. Finish the raw edges with a zigzag stitch to prevent fraying in the wash. Turn the pillow cover right side out.

## 6. FINISH THE PILLOW

With embroidery thread, hand-sew a large X stitch in the center of the felt overlay to secure the felt to the scribbled fabric. Add a few more X stitches on the overlay as desired to decorate and further secure the two pieces. Hand-sew a running stitch around the ends of all the petal shapes. Insert the pillow form into the back opening.

**Stitching tip:**

For consistent, even length stitches, move the fabric a little more slowly when making loops and turns, but keep the needle moving quickly.

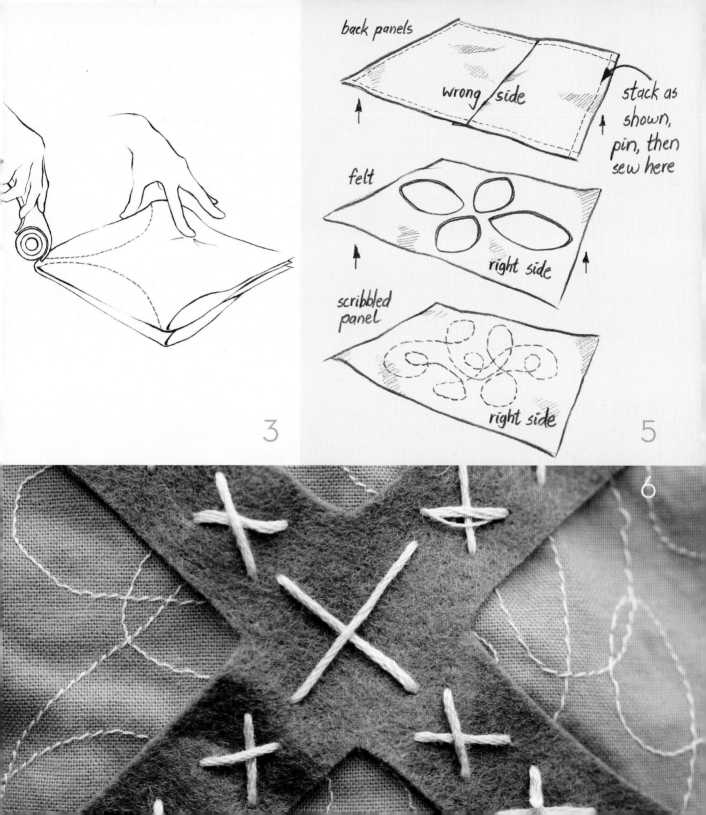

back panels

wrong side

stack as shown, pin, then sew here

felt

right side

scribbled panel

right side

3

5

6

# Coloring Book Wrap Skirt

**Creating this skirt evokes the simple pleasures** of putting crayons to paper. Embellishing a print gives it a whole new look, whether you stitch a few simple details or really layer on hue and texture. And keep in mind one of our guiding principles: it's entirely fine to color outside the lines.

## 1. MAKE THE SKIRT

Follow the instructions for the Three-Panel Wrap Skirt (see chapter 3, page 49).

## 2. ADD SKETCHED DETAILS

Before you start, read the techniques intro on page 134 and practice on a scrap of your print fabric. Load your machine with contrasting thread and embellish the designs in the fabric print of the skirt:

— **Add curves and squiggles** to fill in space by setting the foot-pressure dial to 0 and using free-motion doodling.

— **Add blocks of color** inside the shapes by free-motion doodling or stitching closely spaced or crosshatched lines.

— **Zigzag** along the shape outlines.

— **Add words** or other details with straight stretch stitches.

### what you'll need

○ **2 yards of woven cotton print fabric with a simple, large-scale black-and-white print**

○ **6 yards of cotton ribbon or bias tape**

○ **1 spool of thread to match the skirt fabric**

○ **1 to 3 spools of contrasting thread**

# Line Art Lunchbox Napkin

**If you're new to drawing with your sewing machine**, hone your skills with this low-stakes, ultracheap project (you don't even have to buy fabric if you have an old white bedsheet to cut up). This reusable napkin will make its owner proud in two ways: he or she gets to show off artwork and reduce lunchtime trash at the same time.

## what you'll need

- **10" square of Birdseye cotton, glassware toweling, or other absorbent woven cotton fabric**
- **1 to 3 spools of contrasting thread**

## 1. CREATE THE DRAWING

Tape the fabric taut to the table. With a vanishing ink pen or chalk, draw a simple design, either centered or in one corner, leaving at least a ¾" margin on all sides for the hem.

## 2. DRAW WITH THREAD

Before you start drawing, read the techniques intro, page 134, and practice on a scrap of the project fabric. Set your presser foot pressure to 2; this allows you to manipulate your fabric easily but still follow the drawn lines. Using a straight stitch with the stitch length set at 1, stitch along the drawn guidelines.

## 3. HEM THE NAPKIN

Press the edges of the napkin ¼" to the wrong side, and then ¼" again to make a ½" double-fold hem. Using contrasting thread and a narrow zigzag (our stitch width was 3 and stitch length 2.5), topstitch the hem in place, leaving the needle down and turning the fabric at the corners.

**Stitching tip:** It will make it easier for the sewist if the drawing isn't itty-bitty, so guide the artist accordingly. For a younger child, frame the target area with tape to help him or her understand where and how big to draw the artwork.

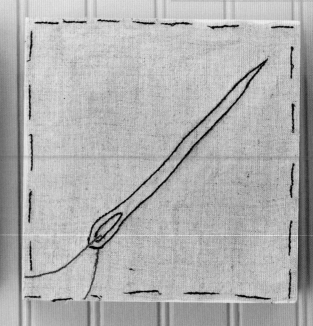

## design variations

Mount your artwork on a thick wood block and stand it on a shelf. //// Mount your artwork on cardboard and frame it. //// Mount your artwork on a pre-stretched canvas. //// Mount several sewn swatches on a single large board. //// Mount artwork on three small panels hinged together to make a stand-up triptych.

# Wall Art

**Great painters create their masterpieces on canvas,** and that's no accident. There's something about fabric that's way more eloquent and eternal than paper. Sew a small, simple design on linen or canvas, mount it on a panel of wood, and suddenly you've created something your grandkid's grandkid will hang on a wall and admire.

## 1. MEASURE, MARK, AND CUT

With a vanishing pen or chalk, trace around the wood panel on the right side of the fabric. Measure and mark cutting lines at least 3" bigger all around than the traced outline, then cut along the lines.

## 2. SKETCH YOUR DESIGN

Before you start sketching, read the techniques intro, page 134, and practice on a scrap of the project fabric.

Draw your design on the right side of the fabric. Free-motion stitch over and around the lines one or more times.

If you like, add a stitched border before trimming the fabric to fit the mounting board. Stitch the border just inside the traced lines from step 1 that marked the perimeter of the mounting board.

## 3. MOUNT YOUR ARTWORK

Trim the fabric to the desired size. Brush Mod Podge on the mounting panel and lay the fabric over it with the wrong side down, smoothing out any wrinkles or bumps. Brush a topcoat of Mod Podge over the entire front side of the fabric and panel and allow it to dry thoroughly.

## what you'll need

- Linen, canvas, or other plain fabric (amount depends on size of art)
- 1 to 3 spools of contrasting thread
- Wood panel for mounting (we used ½"-thick board; dimensions depend on size of art)
- Fabric Mod Podge
- Foam brush

Cutting tip: These curtains are left unhemmed because the selvage provides a narrow fringed finish. Stitched lines add weight to the bottom edge, and the sides are stitched to minimize (while still allowing) fraying.

# Sketched Window Sheers

**These airy window panels,** with their dainty stitched lines on gossamer-thin fabric, seem to fill a room with soft breezes and sunlight even on a gloomy day. Sew up a pair in the time it takes to buy sheers from the big box store, or if you already own the store-bought version, take them down and embellish them!

## 1. MEASURE, MARK, AND CUT

To make two curtain panels, each measuring 26" long × 18" wide, fold the fabric in half lengthwise, with the right sides together and the selvages aligned. Press the fold lightly to crease it, then open it and cut along the crease.

## 2. STITCH ALONG THE EDGES

Straight stitch four lines parallel to the bottom edge, ⅛" apart, starting ¼" from the bottom edge.

Change to the second thread color and stitch three lines between the original four stitched lines.

Use one of the contrasting threads to straight stitch a single line along both sides of each panel, ¼" in from the raw edges.

## what you'll need

- ½ yard of 52"-wide voile fabric (selvage edges still attached)*

- 2 spools of contrasting color thread

- Buttons

- Embroidery floss and embroidery needle

- Template (page 305), optional

- Fine-tipped pencil

  *Each finished curtain panel measures 26" long × 18" wide. If your windows are larger, purchase more fabric and piece it as necessary for the desired size panels.

## 3. MAKE THE ROD CASING

Press the top edge of each panel ½" to the wrong side and then again 1½" to the wrong side.

Stitch two straight lines, parallel to the top folded edge, 1¼" and 1½" down from the top edge to make the casing for the curtain rod.

## 4. SKETCH YOUR DESIGN

Draw your design on paper or use the template provided. Once you are happy with the design, lay one of the panels over it and lightly trace it with a fine-tipped pencil. Repeat with the other panel.

With the presser foot pressure set to 0, straight stitch (our stitch length was 1.5) up one of the design lines, turn around, and stitch back down. Continue to stitch all of the design lines, particularly the leaves in the template design, in this manner.

If the design has round or curved shapes, such as flowers at the end of the straight lines on the template design, use the free-motion doodling technique (see the chapter intro, page 134).

Hand-sew buttons as desired to highlight areas of the design. If you used the template, hand-sew a button on each of the round flower shapes, or skip drawing the flowers and simply add the buttons.

3

4

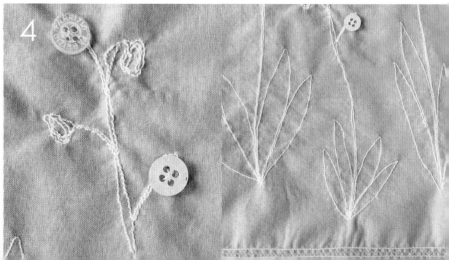

# Travel Art Kit

Pack a sketchpad and some drawing tools in this sweet book, and you'll be ready whenever inspiration strikes. Black thread not only provides the strongest contrast to the fabric print, but it also evokes the bold lines of a pencil or charcoal sketch. The idea for this design came from our inspired and inspiring friend Catherine, who gave Nicole's kids a couple of fabulous hand-sewn art kits for Christmas one year.

## 1. MEASURE, MARK, AND CUT

Measure and mark the following pieces on the right side of the fabric, and then cut them out:

— **exterior:** 10½" × 18½"

— **interior:** 8½" × 17½"

— **pencil pocket:** 4¼" × 8"

— **strap closure:** 1½" × 5"

## 2. SKETCH YOUR DESIGN

Fold the exterior piece in half with the wrong sides together and the short edges aligned. With the fabric pencil or pen, write the word "draw" down the right half of the fabric as shown in photo above.

Install the heavier denim needle in the sewing machine. Unfold the exterior piece and with the presser foot pressure set to 1, straight stitch to trace the outline of the lettering. Then, set the presser foot pressure to 0 and fill in the lettering with a narrow zigzag.

## 3. MAKE AND ATTACH THE POCKET

Fold the interior piece in half with the right sides together and short edges aligned. Press a crease to mark the center.

## what you'll need

- ½ yard of heavy canvas fabric (we used ¼ yard each of two complementary fabrics)

- 1 spool of contrasting thread (preferably black)

- 1¼" piece of ¾"-wide sew-on Velcro

- Fabric marking pen or pencil

- Denim sewing machine needle

- Craft knife

Open the interior piece and lay it out with the right side facing up. Pin the pocket piece with the right side up to the right of the fold line, ¾" from the bottom and right edges.

Draw vertical lines every 1" across the width of the pocket, starting and ending 1" from each side.

To secure the pocket to the interior piece, zigzag along the side and bottom edges.

Topstitch along the pencil lines with a straight stretch stitch, securely backtacking at both ends.

## 4. MAKE THE PAPER SLOT ON THE INTERIOR PIECE

To the left of the center crease, draw a line ½" below the top edge that starts ½" from the left edge, and ends ½" from the crease. Using your machine's manual buttonhole foot, stitch an elongated buttonhole centered on the marked line. With a craft knife, slowly cut it open, being careful not to cut through the stitches.

## 5. ATTACH THE STRAP

With the right side facing up, pin the strap piece to the right side of the exterior as shown, centered along the left edge. Zigzag around all the edges, attaching the strap to the exterior piece and overcasting the raw edges of the strap.

Attach the loop side of the Velcro to the wrong side of the strap end with a straight stitch around the edges.

Stitch the hook side of the Velcro to the right side of the exterior piece, ½" from the edge, so it aligns with the Velcro on the strap.

## 6. FINISH THE EDGES

Pin the exterior and interior pieces with the wrong sides together. The exterior piece will extend beyond the edges of the interior piece by ½" on the sides and by 1" on the top and bottom.

To enclose the raw edges of the interior piece, press the side edges of the exterior piece ¼" to the wrong side and then a generous ¼" again to cover the raw edges. Straight stitch close to the folded edges.

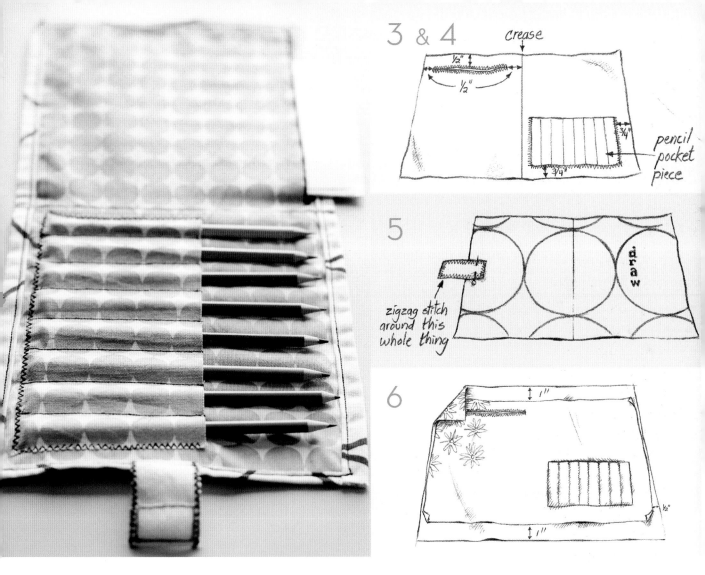

**3 & 4**

crease

½"

½"

¾"

¾"

pencil
pocket
piece

**5**

draw

zigzag stitch
around this
whole thing

**6**

1"

1"

½"

Press the top and bottom edges of the exterior piece ½" to the wrong side and then a generous ½" again to cover the interior piece's raw edges. Straight stitch close to the folded edges.

Straight stretch stitch down the center of the book, over the pressed crease.

Finishing tip:
The stitched line down the center crease adds bold definition and keeps the contents of the paper slot in place.

# Fiddlehead Dress

**Nature is always the first place to turn for inspiring designs.** We based this one on the ferns that sprout in profusion around the foundations of Debra's house each spring. We added this motif to the two-panel dress with cap sleeves, a forgiving summer solution for staying cool while not baring all.

## 1. SEW A TWO-PANEL DRESS

Follow the instructions for the Two-Panel Garment (chapter 3, page 34). The appropriate amount of flare for the dress ranges from 3" to 5" on both sides, depending on the desired fit — the flare shown here is 4". Add cap sleeves (see chapter 3, page 42).

## 2. SKETCH YOUR DESIGN

Following the manufacturer's instructions, press the stabilizer to the wrong side of the area you'd like to embellish.

Transfer the fern design by aligning the template over the carbon paper, and positioning them both on the dress at the desired location (with the carbon side of the paper facing the fabric). Draw over the template lines with a pencil to transfer the design.

Before stitching your design, read the techniques intro (page 134) and practice on a scrap of the project fabric.

Using a straight stretch stitch and with the presser foot pressure set at 1, stitch over the lines (if you're using our fiddlehead design, start sewing at the bottom of each fern). With your fingers firmly pressing the stabilized fabric, turn the fabric while the needle is moving to make the curves. You may need to stop and adjust your hold on the fabric every few inches. When stitching, get the needle going fast for a nice even stitch appearance.

When you're finished stitching, carefully tear away the stabilizer.

## what you'll need

- Torso pattern piece to trace (see chapter 2, page 29)

- 1½ yards of jersey fabric (we used a rayon jersey)

- 1 spool of contrasting thread

- Fusible tear-away stabilizer

- Fern template (page 304)

- Dressmaker's carbon paper and pencil

Stitching tip:
This isn't free-motion
drawing (which is tricky
on this slinky fabric
even with stabilizer);
rather, you're simply
lowering the presser
foot pressure so you
can turn the fabric
on the big curves.

# Tubular Sundress

**This simple tube of fabric** is finished with shoulder straps and machine sketching, allowing you show off your shoulders and your artistic talents at the same time. Its two-panel construction is similar to the Two-Panel Garment (chapter 3, page 34) but with a little less flare and a little more bare.

## 1. DETERMINE YOUR FIT

With a measuring tape, take the following measurements:

— **chest:** snug around your body, under your arms where the top band of the dress will lie

— **waist level:** from underarm to waist

— **length:** underarm to desired hemline (hold the measuring tape at your armpit while stepping on the other end to hold it taut, then note where you'd like the hem to fall)

## 2. MEASURE, MARK, AND CUT

Fold the jersey with the right sides together and the straight grain running the length of the dress. Measure, mark, and then cut the following lines through both layers of fabric:

*Dress:*

— **top edge:** Subtract 2" from the chest measurement, then divide the result in half. Center this line on the fabric.

— **sides:** Starting at each end of the top edge, draw vertical lines equal to the length measurement. Along these lines, make a mark at the waist level.

— **bottom edge:** Draw a line connecting the sides, and extending 2½" beyond them on either side so the bottom edge is 5" longer than the top edge.

— **flare:** Connect each end of the bottom edge line with the waist point. When cutting out the fabric, follow these flared design lines.

### what you'll need

- 1¼ yards of cotton jersey
- Fusible tear-away or wash-away stabilizer
- 1 spool each of coordinating and contrasting thread
- 2 decorative buttons

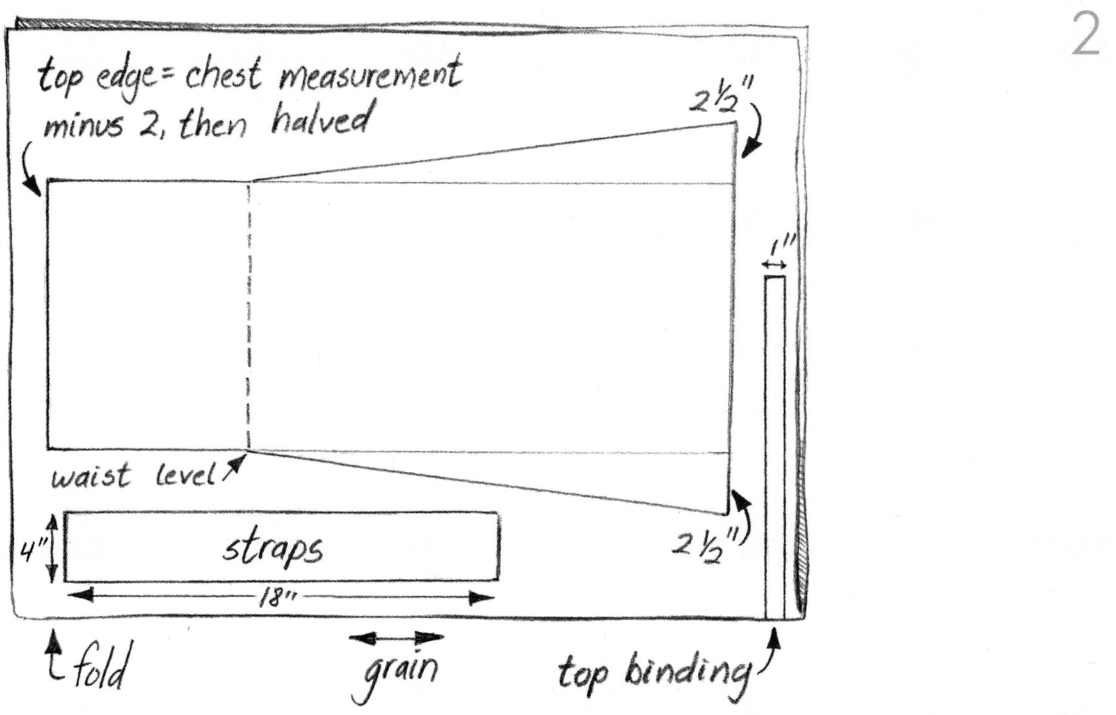

top edge = chest measurement minus 2, then halved

2½"

1"

waist level ↗

4"

straps

18"

2½"

↕ fold

grain

top binding ↗

*Also mark and cut the following:*

— **top binding:** 1" × 2" smaller than the top edge measurement (cut on the cross grain)

— **straps (cut 2):** 4" × 18" (cut with the straight grain)

## 3. SEW THE SIDE SEAMS

Straight stretch stitch the side seams with ½" seam allowance.

## 4. ATTACH THE TOP BINDING

Following the instructions in the chapter 4 intro, page 61, use the binding to make a binding loop, joining the ends with a ½" seam.

Pin the binding to the top edge of the dress. Using a small zigzag (we set our stitch width at 3), edgestitch the binding to the dress.

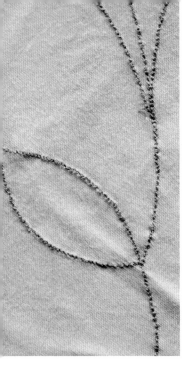

## Tubular Sundress

### 5. MAKE THE STRAPS

Fold one strap in half lengthwise and press. Edgestitch both sides with a zigzag. Press the strap so the seam is in the center and can be positioned on the underside of the strap, when the strap is sewn in place. Repeat for the other strap.

### 6. FIT THE STRAPS

Have the wearer put the dress on and pin one end of a strap in the desired location on the front of the dress with 1" extending beyond the top edge of the dress. Pin the opposite end of the strap inside the dress in the back (if you are wearing the dress, it's helpful to have a friend to do this), making sure it hugs the shoulder snugly.

Remove the dress. Measure the distance between the side seam and the strap, and use the measurement to pin the second strap in place on the dress's opposite side.

With the dress right side out, topstitch each strap in place. Trim away any excess strap length and finish the strap with a zigzag.

Sew decorative buttons onto the front of the straps at the point where they meet the binding.

### 7. SKETCH YOUR DESIGN

Cut a piece of stabilizer a little bigger than the area you'd like to decorate. Following the manufacturer's instructions, fuse it on the wrong side of the dress at the desired location.

With chalk or a vanishing fabric pen, freehand draw a leaf and bud design (ours extends from the front of the dress to the back).

Straight stretch stitch (our stitch length was 2 to 2.5) along the lines using the Sketching with Thread technique (see page 134).

Stitch twice over the leaves and buds, and a few more times over the stem.

Tear away the stabilizer, and then wash the garment to remove any bits and pieces caught between the stitches.

**Stitching tip:**
The stabilizer gives the fabric a bit of added structure, making it easier to draw.

Cutting tip: Feel free to adjust the flare to your liking. For a looser fit, try a bottom edge that's 8" wider than the top edge. Want to go slinky? Omit the flare and make a totally straight tube if you like dresses that accentuate your curves. If you're lucky, your backside is bigger than the rest of your measurements, so a dress that fits your hips will get pretty snug around your butt, but if you've got it, flaunt it!

# Birds in Flight Headboard

**An embroidered headboard sounds impossibly luxurious,** something found only in Spanish palaces or yachts docked in Dubai. But when you realize that you're basically just adding decorative stitching to fabric and stapling it to a backing, you'll want to stitch one up for your home, castle, or maybe even your yacht!

## what you'll need

- **2 yards of home-decor weight fabric***

- **1 spool of contrasting thread**

- **24" × 60" piece of 2"-thick upholstery foam***

- **2 yards of cotton batting***

- **24" × 60" sheet of ⅝"-thick plywood***

- **Hanging hardware (see note on page 164)**

- **Staple gun and staples**

- **Swallow template (page 310)**

- **Dressmaker's carbon paper and pencil**

  *The measurements and material require-ments are for a queen-size headboard.

## 1. MEASURE, MARK, AND CUT

Measure and mark the following pieces on the wrong side of the fabric and batting and cut them out:

— **cover:** 36" × 66" (mark the longer measurement along the fabric selvage)

— **batting:** 36" × 66"

## 2. SKETCH YOUR DESIGN

Draw lines 6" in from each raw edge to mark where the fabric wraps around to the back of the headboard. With a vanishing ink pen or chalk, trace the template as desired, within the marked lines. Before sketching your design, read over the techniques intro (page 134) and practice on a scrap of the project fabric.

Using a straight stretch stitch and with the presser foot pressure set to 2, stitch along the design lines.

— **To turn sharp corners,** stop with the needle down, lift the presser foot, and turn the fabric.

— **To stitch curves,** as on the back of the wings, grasp the fabric on either side of the presser foot and control its movements, so the needle follows the line, with the needle moving fast. Try not to stop until the stitching reaches the end of the line.

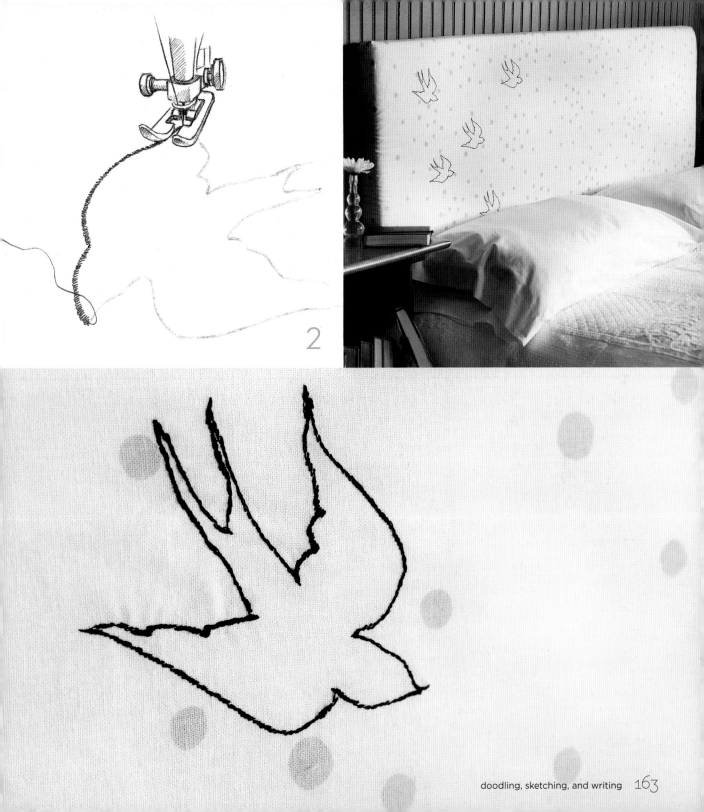

## 3. ASSEMBLE THE HEADBOARD

Place the foam on top of the plywood. Center the batting on top of the foam; it will extend 6" beyond the foam on all sides. Then, place the fabric, right side facing up, on the batting; it will also extend 6" beyond the foam and wood on all sides.

Wrap the batting and fabric around the foam and plywood on one long side, smooth it and then staple it to the plywood, starting at the center and moving out toward the corners. Repeat along the opposite long side, pulling the fabric taut before stapling.

Repeat along the short edges, making neat corners by tucking and folding the fabric over the already stapled fabric. Smooth, tighten, and staple anywhere the fabric seems loose.

## 4. ATTACH HANGING HARDWARE

Hang the headboard securely using the appropriate hardware for your wall.

Finishing tip:
The back won't look finished, but happily, it will be against a wall!

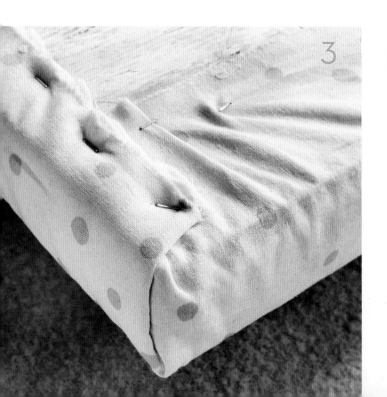

3

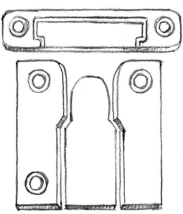

HARDWARE NOTE: We like these adjustable flush-mount hanger brackets, which we found for less than five dollars online. One piece is screwed into the back of the headboard, and its mate is screwed into the wall at a stud. The parts slide together, and you can use a few of them along the back for a very strong and stable mount.

Stitching tip: Remember, each straight stretch stitch is actually three tiny stitches, two forward and one back. Try to end each line on a backward stitch. This will make for cleaner lines without rogue backward stitches.

Stitching tip: Placing lightweight paper between the presser foot and the oilcloth keeps the foot from sticking. Use your seam ripper to help scratch away any paper left next to or in the stitches.

# Potluck Dish Cover

Nix the plastic wrap and sew a couple of these covers instead — they can be whipped up in the time it takes your lasagna to bake. You'll feel better about not producing more trash, and you'll be able walk into your next potluck party knowing that your casserole or salad bowl is outfitted just as gorgeously as you are.

## 1. MEASURE, MARK, AND CUT

With the wrong side of the fabric facing up, position your dish, pan, or bowl upside down in the center and trace around it. (Obviously, you'll want to do this step before making your culinary creation.) Measure and mark a line 1½" bigger all around than the traced line (a compass is the best tool if you're drawing a circle). Cut along the larger marked line.

## 2. SKETCH THE DESIGN

Draw your lettering and any other design elements on a lightweight piece of paper (tissue paper works especially well). Position the paper with the sketched design over the right side of the fabric.

Using a straight stitch and free-motion techniques (see page 134), topstitch over your design, through both the paper and the fabric. Tear away the paper.

## 3. ADD THE ELASTIC

Fold the elastic over the edge of the fabric. Using a zigzag stitch, sew it all around the edge of the circle, pulling the elastic as taut as possible. (see chapter 1, page 19 for fold over elastic instructions).

what you'll need

- ½ to ¾ yard of oilcloth (any width will do as long as it fits your container)

- 1 spool of contrasting thread

- Tissue or tracing paper

- Fold over elastic

# Happy Home Memo Board

**Every household needs a place to tack up invitations,** shopping lists, reminders, and love notes. That's why this board makes a terrific gift, especially when it's customized with a name or address.

## what you'll need

- 18" × 32" piece of Homasote board (or desired size)
- 1 yard of 44/45"-wide fabric (or enough fabric to cut a piece 2" bigger than the board on all sides)
- 1 spool of contrasting thread
- Staple gun and staples
- Picture-hanging hardware

## 1. MARK THE FABRIC

Center the board on the right side of the fabric and trace around it with chalk, then set the board aside. Use chalk to draw guidelines for planning your words. Remember that 2" on all sides will be wrapped to the back of the board, so avoid the edges. Mark your lettering within the guidelines.

## 2. SKETCH THE DESIGN

Using a straight stretch stitch and the free-motion writing technique (see page 135), stitch along the marked design lines in contrasting thread, turning where necessary with the needle down to hold the fabric in place.

## 3. ASSEMBLE THE MEMO BOARD

Center the board on the wrong side of the stitched fabric. Working on the long sides first, fold the fabric up and over the board and staple it in the center as shown in the illustration. Repeat on the two short sides. Then, staple the rest of the way around the board. Trim any excess fabric from the corners if necessary.

Finishing tip: If you like, add cup hooks to the bottom edge for hanging keys. Use picture-hanging hardware to display the board.

From afar, the flowers look stitched, but they're actually part of the fabric's pre-printed design.

# 7 appliqué

**Appliqué has transformative powers.** It can turn a simple piece of solid fabric into a thing of beauty that commands attention and shows just how darn creative you are. As a textile art, appliqué has been around forever, but our more modern approach is perfect for people (like us) who want a pop of color or texture without the hours spent, the perfect little stitches, and the poked fingers. After all, most of us are not ladies-in-waiting with a ton of time to spend sitting in the parlor. With that in mind, here are our thoughts on appliqué for busy people.

## Raw-Edge Appliqué

The least fussy approach to applying fabric;
the edges fray a little, giving the appliqué a soft
appearance. The look of raw-edge appliqués
actually improves with washing, though now and
then you may need to snip a thread or two.

## Stitched-Edge Appliqué

If you want a more finished look, your machine
has utility stitches that are great for stitching
appliqués in place, like the good old zigzag or any
overcast stitch. Working around the perimeter
of the appliqué piece, allowing the stitches to
overcast the edges, will seal the edges under the
stitches and create a defined border.

## Cutting Appliqué Pieces

Draw the appliqué pieces on the wrong side of the
fabric with chalk, a fine-tipped pencil, or a fabric
marker to provide good cutting lines. Keep in mind
that the fabric will be flipped for application, so if
the appliqué is asymmetrical, you'll need to draw
the mirror image on the back of the fabric. If it's
easier, use a vanishing ink pen and draw the shape
on the front of the fabric. The grain of the fabric
doesn't matter, although if you're using a print
fabric, you may want to note which way the print
is running, or plan the appliqué to incorporate your
favorite part of the print design. Be sure to have
nice sharp scissors for cutting the shapes.

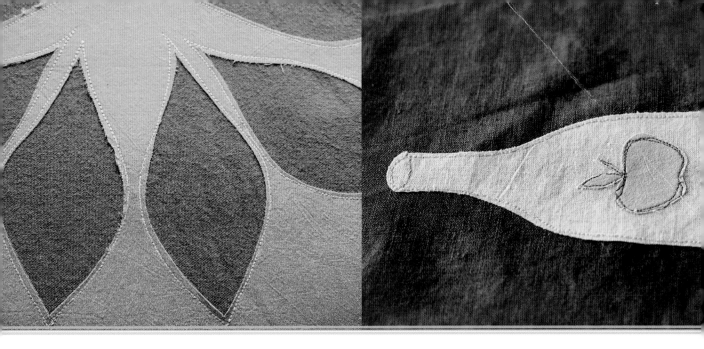

## Reverse-Appliqué

It's pretty magical to cut a window of fabric away on a shirt or skirt to reveal another fabric underneath. And truthfully, reverse-appliqué is really quite simple. You sketch a design onto the right side of the main project fabric and stitch another, contrasting fabric behind it, either with hand stitches or by machine. With the underlying fabric swatch in place, the fabric within the stitched lines can be cut away, and, voilà — reverse-appliqué! Try it with an underlay of patterned fabric, doodled fabric, contrasting fabric, or whatever seems to be a good partner to the top layer. It really looks impressive, and you don't have to tell anyone how easy it is. It can be our little secret.

## Fusible Web

Paper-backed fusible web is an indispensible appliqué aid. It provides heft and stability to appliqué pieces, and you can draw on the paper for a good defined cutting line. Following the manufacturer's instructions, fuse the web side to the back of the appliqué fabric before drawing and cutting the appliqué shapes. Then draw the shapes on the paper side of the webbing and cut them. Remove the paper backing and fuse the web-backed appliqué piece to the base fabric. The web holds the appliqué in place so it doesn't shift during stitching — and who can argue with that? The only downside is that you need to buy it, and if you are like us, you probably don't love to spend money if you don't have to. Nicole generally limits her use of fusible web to things that have intricate cuts; the more basic shapes she simply pins in place.

# Little Star Mittens

Everything looks adorable made from felted wool, so here's a simple appliqué project made from that irresistible material. We design our mittens extra long for tuck-ability, which keeps wrists warm and dry on the chilliest days.

## what you'll need

- Felted wool sweater (see page 244)
- Contrasting felted wool scrap for appliqué
- 1 spool of coordinating thread
- Star template (page 303)
- Pencil and paper

## 1. DRAFT THE PATTERN PIECE

Have the wearer place his or her hand flat on a piece of paper, with fingers slightly spread. Trace around the hand as shown, leaving about a ¼" margin on all sides. Cut along the lines.

## 2. MEASURE, MARK, AND CUT

Fold the fabric in half with the wrong sides together and the grain running vertically (from mitten top to bottom). Pin the pattern piece in place, trace it, and cut along the lines through both thicknesses of fabric. Flip the pattern and repeat to make its mate; be sure to reverse the pattern or you will end up with four identical mitten panels.

## 3. MAKE AND ATTACH THE APPLIQUÉ

Pin the star template (page 303) on the contrasting scrap, trace it, and cut along the lines. Repeat to cut a second appliqué.

Lay out two mitten pieces with the right side up and with the thumbs facing each other. Pin an appliqué on each piece and zigzag the appliqués in place (our stitch width setting was 3; stitch length was 2).

## 4. STITCH THE MITTENS

For each mitten, pin an appliquéd and unadorned piece with the right sides together (appliqué facing in) and the raw edges aligned. Straight stitch the pieces together with a ¼" seam, leaving the wrist ends open. Backtack at the beginning and end of the seam (at the wrists). Trim away the corners of the seam allowances at the wrist and carefully clip the curved seam allowances. Turn the mittens right side out.

A narrow seam allowance is used here because it wouldn't be comfy to have a lot of bulky fabric inside the mitten. Set your stitch length on the short side (we set ours at 2) to make the seams strong and draftproof.

Cutting tip:
We made a pair of mittens for a child using sleeves from an old sweater — the sleeves are already folded with the grain running correctly. Convenient!

Design tip:
You can use this same technique with just two layers of solid felt, cutting shapes from the top layer to reveal the contrasting color beneath.

# Eyeglass Case

This fast and fab project is the ideal way to use that pretty printed swatch you've been saving. Find one or two felt colors that complement it, and in less than an hour you'll have a lovely spot to stash your shades or reading glasses. We highly recommend searching out wool felt for this project (see page 312 for sourcing) — it's dyed in much nicer colors than regular craft felt, and it'll hold up better, too.

## 1. STACK THE LAYERS

Sandwich the cotton print square between the two felt pieces, with the right side of the print facing the exterior felt piece. The extra ½" of the interior felt piece should extend beyond the top edge; the other edges should align.

## 2. SECURE THE LAYERS

To create a neat top edge for the case opening, fold the extra ½" of the interior felt piece over the other two layers and press. Sew it in place with a narrow zigzag.

## 3. CREATE THE CUT-AWAY SHAPES

With chalk or a vanishing ink fabric pen, mark three 1½" squares on the right side of the exterior felt square. Straight stretch stitch around the markings. To reveal the print fabric underneath, pinch the layers apart inside the squares and use sharp-tip scissors to carefully snip away the top layer of felt, leaving a ⅛" margin of felt inside the stitching.

## 4. STITCH THE SIDES

Fold the layered fabric in half with the right (exterior) sides together. Straight stitch a ½" seam on the side and bottom edges. Trim the corner seam allowance as needed. With a small needle and thread, hand-stitch the sew-on snap inside the opening, being careful to stitch only through the interior fabric so your stitches won't show. Turn the case right side out.

### what you'll need

- 8" × 8½" piece of felt for the interior
- 8" square of felt for the exterior
- 8" square of cotton print fabric
- 1 spool of coordinating thread
- Sharp-tip embroidery scissors
- Sew-on snap

# Stacked Dot Scarf

**Piling up fabric shapes brings the art of appliqué to a whole new level.** This geometric scarf almost demands improvisation as you layer different fabrics and thread colors, giving your piece a bright boldness or a muted elegance.

## what you'll need

- 2 yards of wool or cotton jersey (any width over 7" will do)
- Wool and cotton jersey scraps
- Variety of contrasting threads

## 1. MEASURE, MARK, AND CUT

Fold the fabric in half and with the wrong side of the fabric facing up, measure, mark, and cut a strip 7" × 36" (when the fabric is unfolded it will be 72" long).

## 2. MAKE THE APPLIQUÉS

Draw sets of graduated-size circles on the jersey scraps, using lids, cups, and buttons as templates. Layer the circles and pin them in place on the scarf (steer clear of the central section that wraps around your neck) with long straight pins.

## 3. STITCH THE APPLIQUÉS

Using a straight stretch stitch, sew an X across each stack of circles, being sure to backtack at both ends.

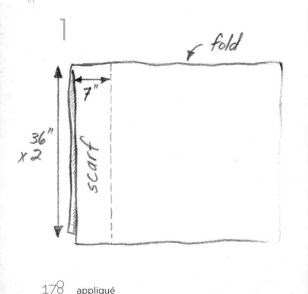

1

fold

7"

36" x 2

scarf

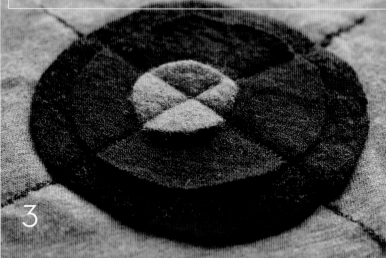

Design tip: Mix the appliqué colors as you wish, or make them all the same color for a subtler look.

3

Have some old tees on hand? Instead of using yardage, cut as many 7"-wide strips as you can from the shirts and sew the ends together with fun and decorative seaming to make one long strip. Try stitching them together with ½" seam allowances, pressing the seams open and using contrasting thread and different utility stitches to sew the seam allowances down. Alternatively, grab a needle and some embroidery thread and cross-stitch along the seams. Then use the leftover scraps to make layered appliqués.

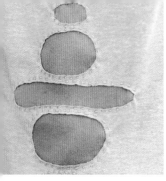

# Cairn Reverse-Appliqué Tee

**This formerly bland shirt gets a boost of style** from a hand-sewn reverse-appliqué. This technique can be adapted for any simple design; we chose a pile of rocks, called a cairn, inspired by the creations Nicole's family likes to build when walking along the creeks and rivers near their home.

## what you'll need

- T-shirt to embellish
- Contrasting jersey scraps
- Contrasting embroidery thread
- Embroidery needle
- Cairn template (page 303)

## 1. MARK YOUR DESIGN

Lay out the t-shirt with the right side facing up; smooth or iron it as needed. Pin the template in place and trace it with a vanishing ink pen or chalk.

## 2. PREP THE REVERSE-APPLIQUÉ

Cut a contrasting jersey scrap that is 1" larger all around than the marked design. Turn the shirt inside out. Pin the right side of the scrap to the wrong side of the shirt, covering the area to be appliquéd.

## 3. STITCH THE OUTLINE

Turn the shirt right side out. Bring a knotted length of embroidery thread about as long as your arm from the wrong side of the shirt to the right side on one of the marked guidelines. Working on the right side, hand-sew a running stitch along the marked guidelines. Tie off with a knot inside the shirt.

## 4. CUT AND REVEAL

Pinch the fabric inside each stitched shape to separate the layers and carefully cut away the top layer (the t-shirt fabric), leaving a ¼" border inside the stitched lines, to reveal the reverse-appliqué.

Turn the shirt wrong side out and remove the pins. Trim away any excess fabric from the reverse-appliqué piece, leaving a ¼" to ½" border outside the stitched lines as shown at right.

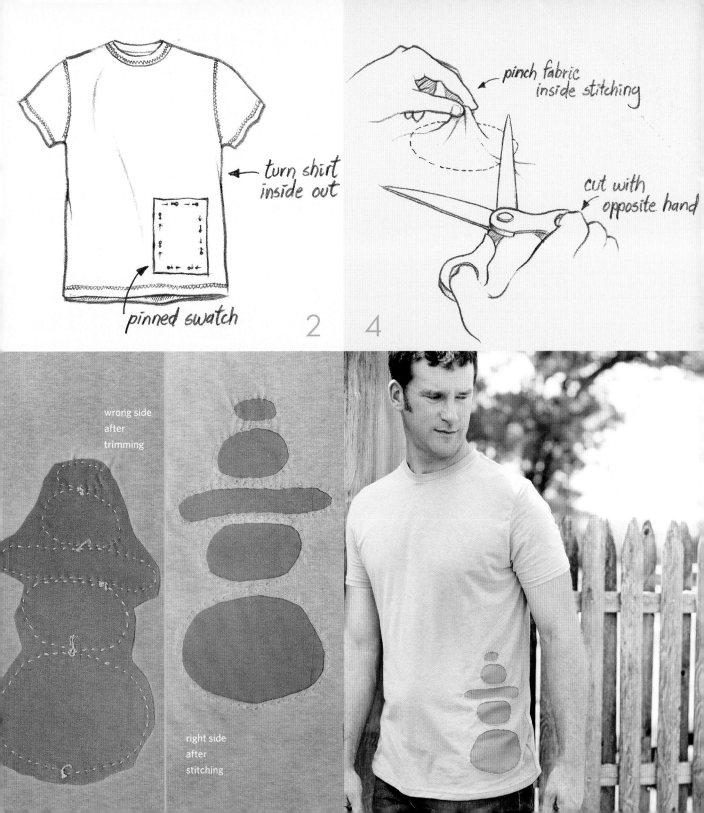

turn shirt
inside out

pinned swatch

2

pinch fabric
inside stitching

cut with
opposite hand

4

wrong side
after
trimming

right side
after
stitching

Design tip:
For a guy's hoodie, replace the velvet ribbon with strips of jersey in his favorite colors.

# Ribbon-Appliqué Embellished Hoodie

**Hooded sweatshirts are basically a uniform** in our neck of the woods. The hardiest New Englanders even wear them as winter coats and summer cover-ups — and they wear them all spring and fall, too. Yes, we're a little sick of them. Still, they are so comfy and so convenient to throw on and take off that we know we'll never kick the habit. Instead, we decided to do a little creative application of velvet ribbon and transform this workaday item into something lovely.

## 1. DESIGN THE RIBBON APPLIQUÉ

Lay out the zipped hoodie with the front side facing up. Arrange the ribbon; we cut the ribbon lengths in pairs and arranged them in a symmetrical design on both sides of the zipper. Pin the ribbons in place.

## 2. SEW IT IN PLACE

Using a narrow zigzag (our stitch width was 2; stitch length was 1.5), edgestitch all the way around each piece of ribbon with coordinating thread.

## 3. ADD THREAD EMBELLISHMENT

Stitch large zigzags of contrasting threads over the ends of the ribbons using a straight stitch; to do this, start near the end of each ribbon and stitch a line off the edge, then run the machine in reverse, then release and stitch forward. Avoid getting too close to the zipper. Repeat to cover each ribbon end with stitching, using one hand to support the fabric and the other to assist on the backstitching.

### what you'll need

- Zip-front hoodie

- Velvet ribbon in a variety of widths and colors (we used 20" of blue, 16" of light pink, 20" of plum, and 7" of fuchsia)

- Coordinating thread for each ribbon

- Contrasting thread for thread embellishment

# Appliquéd Journal

**Small journals like this one are perfect** to tuck into your purse. Use it to jot down ideas for your sewing projects, shopping lists, or poems. It's easy to make fabric covers for any size book or journal using this method.

## 1. MEASURE, MARK, AND CUT

With the right side of the fabric facing up, measure, mark, and cut the following pieces:

— **cover from main fabric:** 6½" × 9½"

— **strap closure from main or contrasting fabric:** 4" × ¾"

## 2. HEM THE TOP AND BOTTOM EDGES

Fold the cover in half with the wrong sides together and short edges aligned. Press the crease. Open the fabric. Press both long edges a scant ½" to the wrong side. Zigzag the folded edges in place (our stitch width was set to 3; stitch length 1).

## 3. STITCH THE SIDES

Zigzag along the remaining (short) edges to finish them. Press the edges 1" to the wrong side and then open them so the piece is flat. Mark the center of the left edge at the crease for strap placement.

## 4. STITCH THE STRAP

Narrow zigzag around all the sides of the strap closure piece.

## 5. ATTACH THE STRAP AND SNAP

Pin the wrong side of the strap on the right side of the cover at the strap placement marking (from step 3). Using a straight stitch, sew the strap in place with a rectangle, as shown.

## what you'll need

- 3½" × 5½" bound journal
- ¼ yard of woven cotton fabric
- Contrasting fabric scraps
- 1 spool of coordinating thread
- Paper-backed fusible web
- ⁷⁄₁₆" pearl snap and hammer
- Pencil template (page 302)

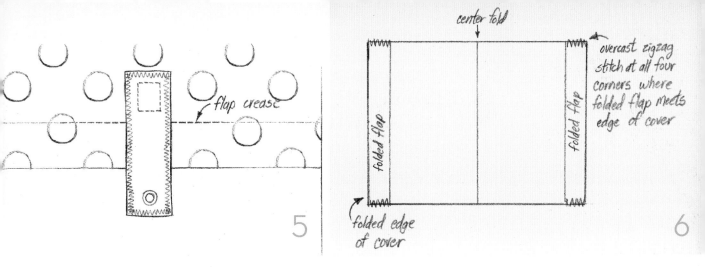

5

6

Attach the snap's decorative top piece to the strap as directed by the manufacturer. Attach its corresponding bottom piece to the front cover.

## 6. SECURE THE SIDE FLAPS

Fold the flaps to the wrong side at the creases. Zigzag the edges of the flaps to the top and bottom edges of the cover as shown.

## 7. MAKE AND STITCH THE APPLIQUÉ

Iron fusible web to the back of the appliqué scrap. Trace the template onto the web's paper backing and cut it out. Remove the paper backing and fuse the appliqué in place on the front cover. Make sure the appliqué does not lie near the side flaps or you won't be able to slide the journal into the cover.

Edgestitch around the appliqué and add details within it, using a variety of stitches as desired. We used a mix of narrow and wide zigzags and straight stretch stitch to define the edges of the pencil and create details.

Tuck the front and back covers of the journal into the side flaps.

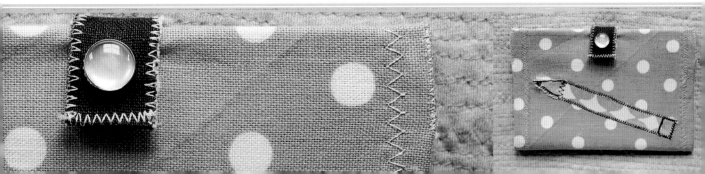

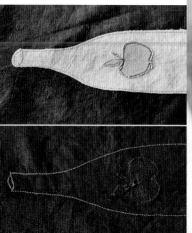

# Cider Season Table Runner

**Nicole's property is dotted with thousands of apple trees,** and her family presses and bottles their own hard cider in the fall. Inspired by this seasonal ritual, this fabulous table runner blends the art of appliqué and the fun of thread drawing with intoxicating results.

## 1. MAKE THE APPLIQUÉS

Press the appliqué fabrics. Following the manufacturer's instructions, fuse the paper-backed fusible web to the wrong side of the appliqué fabrics. On the larger piece, trace as many bottle templates as desired on the web's paper backing (we traced a total of six bottles and six apples). Repeat with the apple templates and second appliqué fabric. Cut out the appliqués on the traced lines.

## 2. FUSE THE WEB

Remove the paper backing from the bottle appliqués and lay them out as desired on the right side of the runner fabric (we positioned three bottles on each end). Press the appliqués in place as instructed by the web manufacturer. Remove the paper backing from the apple appliqués and position them on top of the bottles. Fuse them in place.

## 3. STITCH THE APPLIQUÉS

Use the Sketching with Thread technique (page 134) to stitch the bottle and apple appliqués in place, ⅛" from all the edges (our presser foot pressure was 0 and stitch length was 2). If you want, rough up the edge of the appliqués with a nailbrush.

## 4. FINISH THE RUNNER

Press the long raw edges ½" to the wrong side and trim the corners. The selvages will serve as the finished short edges. With a feather stitch (or any other decorative utility stitch you like), sew a border ½" in from the edges, all around the runner, catching the folded-under hems in the stitching.

## what you'll need

- ½ yard of linen (at least 56" wide) for runner, selvages left on

- ⅓ yard of contrasting linen for bottle appliqués

- ⅛ yard of another contrasting linen for apple appliqués

- 2 or 3 spools of contrasting color thread

- Paper-backed fusible web

- Bottle and apple templates (page 305)

# Reverse-Appliqué Skirt

**Pull this skirt on and you're ready for anything** from work to a date night. It's versatile, beautiful, comfortable, and really fun to make — which is great, because once your friends see it, they'll beg you to make one for them. You can use sleek stretch wool jersey, or piece a look together from roomy upcycled t-shirts.

## 1. STITCH A TWO-PANEL SKIRT

Follow the instructions in step 1 to measure, mark, and cut the fabric for the Two-Panel Skirt (chapter 3, page 46).

## 2. ATTACH THE APPLIQUÉ

Press or pat out any wrinkles. Trace the appliqué template onto the front panel, as desired.

Pin the right side of the contrasting jersey to the wrong side of the skirt panel, underneath the traced appliqué design. With embroidery thread, hand-sew a running stitch along the chalk lines. When you're done stitching, trim away the excess contrasting jersey from the back, around the stitching.

## 3. ASSEMBLE THE SKIRT

Pin the front and back panels with the right sides together. Using a straight stretch stitch and coordinating thread, sew ½" seams. Press the seams.

Turn the skirt right side out and, if you like, topstitch over both seams with contrasting thread and a tricot stitch (or any decorative stretch stitch).

If you choose to hem the skirt, press and then stitch the hem in place using coordinating thread and a zigzag stitch.

Sew fold over elastic along the waistband (see chapter 1, page 19).

## 4. CUT THE REVEAL

With the skirt right side out, pinch the center of each shape to pull the layers apart. Cut out the shapes with the embroidery scissors, being careful to snip only through the top layer, leaving ¼" margin inside the stitched lines.

## what you'll need

- 1½ yards of wool or cotton jersey (for the main body)
- 24" square of contrasting wool or cotton jersey (for the appliqué)
- Approximately 1 yard of fold over elastic
- 1 spool each of coordinating and contrasting thread
- Embroidery thread and needle
- Sharp embroidery scissors
- Flower template (page 309)

There are several fun ways to create layered designs on a reverse-appliqué project, as shown in our examples, including:

- Stitch a shape on top of the cutout reverse-appliqué design.

- Add a second underlayer behind the first. On this skirt, we stitched a piece of cream-colored fabric under the pink, and then cut away the small central circle to reveal it.

- On the big flower with the brown ring, we stitched a cream swatch behind the pink, then hand-stitched the flower's edges and two circles in the middle. Next, we cut away the brown fabric around the outside of the circle, and then we cut through both the brown and the pink layers inside the circle, revealing the cream swatch underneath.

And then, of course, you can always add some embroidery thread accents without cutting anything away, as we've done with the little brown flowers on our skirt.

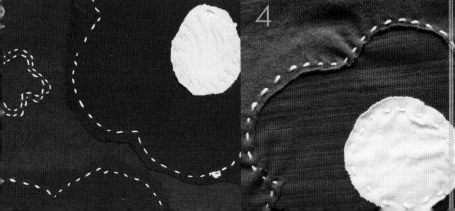

4

pinch fabric inside stitching

cut with opposite hand

# All-Weather Appliqué Mobile

Sometimes even appliqué pieces don't want to be pinned (or sewn) down. This mobile allows them to flutter freely in midair, and will lend a bit of sunny (and cloudy and rainy) color to any bland corner. Buy the canvas in the smallest increment you can purchase at the fabric store (usually ⅛ of a yard), or make it from scraps of any colorful heavy-duty fabric or from wool felt.

## what you'll need

- ⅛ yard each of solid canvas in the following colors: red, orange, yellow, green, light blue, purple, turquoise, gray, white
- Denim sewing machine needle
- 1 spool of black thread
- Embroidery floss and tapestry needle
- Small tree branch or embroidery hoop
- Weather templates (page 306)

## 1. MARK AND CUT THE PIECES

Trace the templates on the right side of the fabrics as follows:

— **outer cloud:** gray

— **interior cloud:** white

— **outer raindrop:** turquoise (cut 4)

— **interior raindrop:** light blue (cut 4)

— **rainbow arcs (in order from smallest to largest):** red, orange, yellow, green, light blue, turquoise, purple

— **entire sun:** yellow

— **sun center:** orange

## 2. STITCH THE PIECES

Install the denim needle in your machine and reduce the thread tension. Determine the best tension setting by test stitching on multiple layers of canvas scraps. Keep in mind that to sew the rainbow, the needle will need to pierce six layers of fabric.

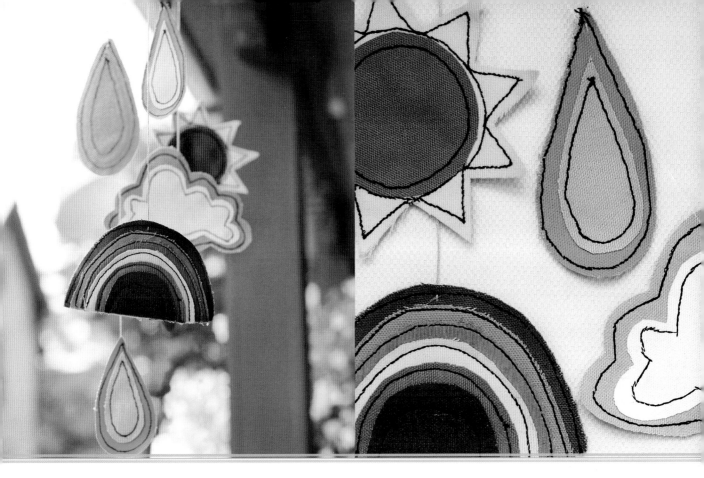

Layer and pin together the various appliqué pieces, as shown. Using the black thread and a straight stretch stitch, sew ⅛" to ¼" from the edge of each appliqué piece.

## 3. ASSEMBLE THE MOBILE

Stitch one end of a 12" length of embroidery floss to the top center of each appliqué. Tie the appliqués onto the branch or hoop by knotting the embroidery floss so the appliqués hang at different heights, then trimming any excess thread. Hang the mobile with more floss.

Design tip:
Want even more rainbow appeal? Spray paint your branch or hoop to match one of the canvas colors or wrap it in coordinating color yarn.

# Modern Stretch Velvet Skirt

**Stretch velvet is a luscious gift** for the one-day sewist. Woven with just enough stretch, it allows for a lovely garment that doesn't require zippers, darts, or anything fussy. Finished at the waist with fold over elastic, with a short or short-ish (just above the knee) hemline, this velvet skirt is a very cool cool-weather look, especially when paired with nice tall boots.

## 1. STITCH A TWO-PANEL SKIRT

With the right sides together, fold the fabric in half so it stretches horizontally (comfortably from hip to hip). Follow the instructions in step 1 to measure, mark, and cut the Two-Panel Skirt (chapter 3, page 46), but make the following adjustments when measuring:

— **Length:** Start from the lower waist and measure just to your knee (or above, for a mini) and add ¾" for a hem

— **Hemline:** draw a line marking the skirt's bottom edge, 10" or 12" wider than the waist (this gives the skirt 5" or 6" of flare on each side)

## 2. ASSEMBLE THE SKIRT

Pin the front and back panels with the right sides together. Using a straight stretch stitch and coordinating thread, sew ½" side seams.

Press the bottom edge ¾" to the wrong side to hem. Using coordinating thread and a zigzag stitch, sew the hem in place.

Sew fold over elastic along the waistband (see page 19).

## 3. EMBELLISH THE SKIRT

Using a straight stretch stitch and contrasting thread, topstitch a few decorative lines at ⅛" intervals just above the hemline.

Trace the flower template onto the remaining fabric and cut along the guidelines. Position as many flowers as you want on the right side of the skirt in the desired locations. Edgestitch them in place with a straight stretch stitch and contrasting thread.

### what you'll need

○ **¾ to 1 yard of stretch cotton velvet (at least 55" wide)**

○ **Fold over elastic (length equal to your waist measurement)**

○ **Spools of coordinating and contrasting thread**

○ **Flower template (page 309)**

# Feast Day Appliqué Tablecloth

**Elegant enough for a fancy dinner,** but still with a distinctly handmade feel, this design looks beautiful in just about any color palette. Choose fabric shades that complement your dining area and dishes, then sit back and soak up the compliments.

- ○ **3 solid color, home-decor weight, woven cotton fabrics as follows\*:**

- ○ **1½ yards of 42"-wide fabric for main panel**

- ○ **1 yard for tree appliqués and side panels**

- ○ **2 yards for short and long borders**

- ○ **Paper-backed fusible web**

- ○ **1 spool of contrasting thread**

- ○ **Tree template (page 303)**

*Fabric yardage is for a tablecloth with the finished dimensions 86" × 50".

## 1. MEASURE, MARK, AND CUT

Press the fabric for the main panel; it doesn't require cutting. Measure, mark, and cut the following pieces from the fabrics you've chosen:

— **side panels\* (cut 2):** 10" × 42"

— **long borders (cut 2):** 6" × 72"

— **short borders (cut 2):** 9" × 52"

*Cut carefully — you need to have enough fabric left over to cut four tree appliqués.

## 2. CUT THE APPLIQUÉS

Press the fusible web to the wrong side of the remaining tree appliqué fabric, following the manufacturer's instructions. Trace the tree template four times onto the paper backing, then cut along the lines.

## 3. FOLD AND CREASE THE MAIN PANEL

Fold and press the main panel fabric in half lengthwise, with the wrong sides together. Open it and fold it in half widthwise, again with the wrong sides together; press. The pressed creases divide the fabric into quadrants to help you position the appliqué pieces.

## 4. POSITION AND FUSE THE APPLIQUÉS

Peel the paper backing from the tree appliqués. Fold the main panel along the widthwise crease, wrong sides together and short edges aligned.

Cutting tip:
The fusible web
makes it easy to
work with the
intricate shape
of the tree.

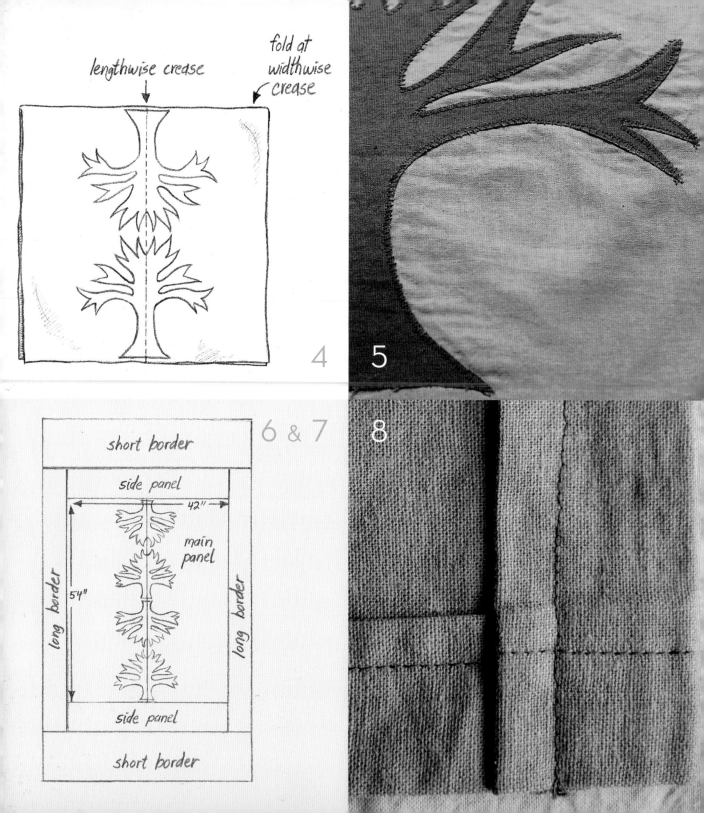

lengthwise crease

fold at widthwise crease

4

5

6 & 7

8

short border

side panel

42"

main panel

long border

54"

long border

side panel

short border

## Feast Day Appliqué Tablecloth

Position two tree appliqués on the tablecloth, centering the trees along the lengthwise crease. Press the pieces in place, following the manufacturer's instructions.

Flip the still folded tablecloth over and repeat on the right side of the other half.

### 5. STITCH THE APPLIQUÉS

With a narrow stitch width setting and full presser-foot pressure, knit stitch around the edges of the tree pieces. It helps to keep the center line on the presser foot lined up with the edge of the appliqué. When negotiating a tight turn, leave the needle in the fabric, lift the presser foot, turn the fabric, put the foot down, and carry on.

### 6. ATTACH THE SIDE PANELS

With the right sides together, pin the side panels to the ends of the main panel. Stitch ½" seams. Trim the seam allowances with pinking shears, and press them open.

### 7. ATTACH THE BORDERS

Pin the long border strips to the longer sides of the tablecloth with the right sides together, and stitch with ½" seams. Trim the seam allowances with pinking shears and press them open.

Pin the short border strips to the side panels with the right sides together and stitch them with ½" seams. Trim the raw edges with pinking shears and press the seam allowance open.

### 8. FINISH THE EDGES

Make a 1" double-fold hem all around (see chapter 1, page 19), folding the corners square as shown. Stitch along the folded edge to hem the tablecloth.

Layout tip: Working on one half of the tablecloth at a time makes this large piece easier to handle.

# Hoodie Scarf

**Here's an awesomely simple and supercozy project** that you can embellish in any way you choose. We added a simple appliqué dressed up with machine sketching. Edgestitching the scarf gives it a pretty frilly look, and we highly recommend splurging on cotton fleece, which is really cuddly.

## what you'll need

- 1½ yards of cotton fleece

- Remnant of felted wool (for appliqué)

- A hooded sweatshirt or other hooded garment (for pattern)

- 1 spool of coordinating thread

- Bird template (page 307)

## 1. TRACE THE HOOD

Fold the fabric in half lengthwise along the straight grain with the right sides and the raw edges together. Fold the hooded garment in half along the center back of the hood. Pin the front edges of the hood together and then to the raw edges of the folded fabric. Loosely trace around the hood ½" from the edges of the hood for seam allowance. End the tracing at the hood/garment seam. Unpin the garment and set it aside.

## 2. MARK AND CUT

Mark a line from the end of the hood tracing to the raw edges of the fabric, as shown. Extend the shaped line from that same point, down to the end of the fabric, gently curving it as shown to create the scarf. Cut along the lines through both thicknesses of fabric.

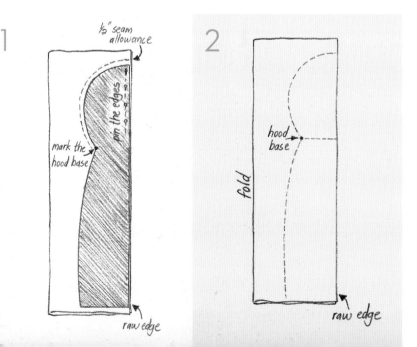

Cutting tip:
The raw edges
of the fabric,
opposite the
folded edge,
will serve as
the front of the
hoodie scarf.

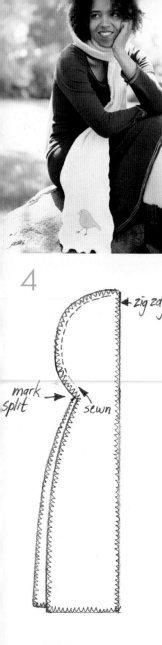

## Hoodie Scarf

### 3. SEW THE CENTRAL SEAM

With the right sides together, straight stitch (our stitch length was 2) the layers together, starting at the top front of the hood and ending at the mark at the base of the hood.

### 4. FINISH THE EDGES

Turn the hood wrong side out. Starting at the front edge of the hood, zigzag along the seam allowances to the base of the hood.

Press the long sides and bottom edges of the scarf extensions ½" to the wrong side and zigzag in place.

Zigzag the raw edges of the hood. Fold the edge ¾" to the wrong side and stitch it in place ½" from the folded edge.

### 5. MAKE AND STITCH THE APPLIQUÉ

Trace the bird template on the felted wool and cut it out. Pin it wherever you want on the scarf.

Straight stitch (ours was set to 2.5) just inside the edges of the appliqué to attach it to the scarf.

Use a vanishing ink pen to draw legs. Using a straight stretch stitch, sew over the marked guidelines. Sew a stitch back and forth to add an eye, if desired.

Stitching tip: When finishing the scarf extensions, use the left edge of the presser foot as a guide, positioning the center of the foot halfway between the seam and the raw edge.

# Custom Ottoman Cover

**Go-anywhere ottomans took the world by storm** a few years back, and they are still popular at many home goods stores. If you have one, treat it to a sweet new outfit. Otherwise, consider acquiring one just so you can deck it out in a cover made to match your room.

## 1. MEASURE, MARK, AND CUT

Fold the canvas or home-decor fabric in half with the right sides together. Measure and mark the following as shown on page 202, then cut through both layers of fabric:

*Cut from the canvas or home-decor fabric:*

— **top panel (cut 1 on the fold):** 8" × 16"

— **side panel (cut 4):** 18" × 16"

*Cut from the contrasting fabric:*

— **appliqué:** 16" square

## 2. PREPARE THE APPLIQUÉ SQUARE WITH CUT OUTS

Following the manufacturer's instructions, fuse the paper-backed fusible web to the wrong side of the appliqué fabric.

Trace the petal template onto the paper backing in the design that appeals to you. We traced 10 petals in a circular pattern. With a craft knife, cut out the petals along the guidelines. Save the square of fabric, not the cut outs.

## 3. ATTACH THE APPLIQUÉ SQUARE

Lay out the top ottoman panel with the right side up. Remove the paper backing from the appliqué square and center it on the top panel. Fuse the appliqué square in place, following the manufacturer's instructions.

Straight stitch ⅛" outside the edge of each cutout on the appliqué square, allowing the raw edges to remain exposed. Baste around the perimeter of the square, ¼" from the raw edge.

### what you'll need

- Cube ottoman (shown is 15" square)

- 1 yard of 60"-wide canvas or home-decor weight fabric

- ½ yard of contrasting woven fabric (for appliqué)

- 1 spool of coordinating thread

- Paper-backed fusible web

- Petal template (page 302)

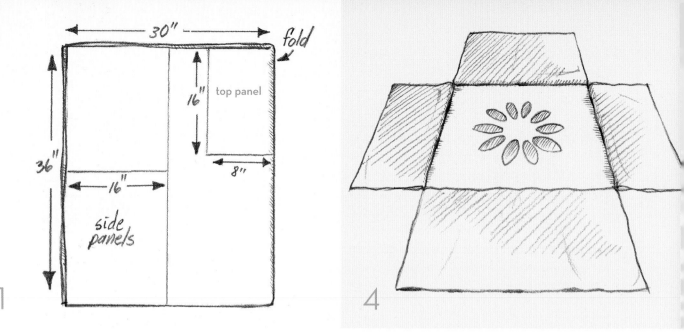

## Custom Ottoman Cover

### 4. ASSEMBLE THE COVER

With the right sides together, pin one side of the top panel to a 16"-long side of one side panel and stitch with a ½" seam. Repeat to attach the remaining side panels to each of the top panel's edges.

With the right sides together, stitch the side panels with ½" seams (start by stitching at the top panel seam). Trim the corners and press the seams open.

Press the bottom edge of all the joined side panels ½" to the wrong side. Then, press another 1" to the wrong side to make a double-fold hem. Straight stitch the hem in place.

Turn the cover right side out and slip it over the ottoman.

# Big-Dot Duvet Cover

**Custom-made linens?** Why not? Take a pair of plain sheets, jazz them up with bold appliqués, stitch them together, and your bespoke bed awaits.

## 1. MAKE THE APPLIQUÉS

Using a compass and pencil to draw, or different size plates and bowls to trace, mark the following circles on the wrong side of the appliqué fabrics and cut them out (mixing the colors as you like):

— **dots (cut 4):** 14"-diameter

— **dots (cut 4):** 8"-diameter

## 2. CREATE GUIDELINES

Fold the sheet that will become the duvet front in thirds lengthwise. Press the creases. Fold each big dot in half and press those creases. These creases will serve as guidelines for centering the appliqués.

## 3. STITCH THE APPLIQUÉS

With right side facing up, pin the larger dots onto the sheet so the crease in each dot aligns with one on the sheet. Pin the small dots on top of the big dots as desired. Straight stitch around the inside edge of one small dot two times. Repeat on the underlying large dot. Complete each pair of dots before moving to the next pair.

## 4. SEW THE SHEETS TOGETHER

Pin the two sheets with the right sides together around three sides, leaving one short edge open. Straight stitch the pinned sides together with a ½" seam.

## 5. FINISH THE DUVET COVER

Measure your duvet. Trim any excess length away from the cover at the open end. On each raw edge, press ½" to the wrong side and then ¾" again. Pin the Velcro strips ¹⁄₁₆" from the pressed edges, extending from seam to seam. Straight stitch the Velcro and then hem in place. Turn the duvet right side out.

## what you'll need

- **2 flat bedsheets (size to fit your bed)**

- **¾ yard each of 2 contrasting cotton fabrics (for dot appliqués)**

- **2 spools of contrasting thread**

- **1½ to 2 yards of sew-on ¾"-wide Velcro**

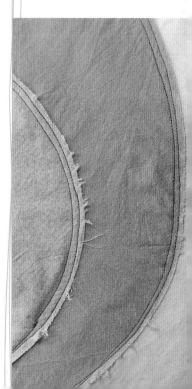

# Blossoming Appliqué Blanket

**Brighten up a tired blanket** by strewing some sweet little flowers across it. Use a blanket from around the house or give a new lease on life to a thrift-store find. If you do the latter, you'll want to give it a good laundering first. We're not big on dry cleaning; instead, we just wash our thrift-store treasures gently in cold water with wool detergent.

## what you'll need

- **Wool blanket**
- **Fabric scraps in 2 colors (we used linen scraps)**
- **1 spool of contrasting thread**
- **Flower template (page 309)**

## 1. MEASURE, MARK, AND CUT

If the binding is tired or torn, cut it off and replace it with new binding (see chapter 1, page 19).

## 2. MAKE THE APPLIQUÉS

Use the template in the size provided, or enlarge it to a variety of different sizes. Trace and cut as many flowers as desired from the fabric scraps. Cut rough circles for the centers. Pin the flowers and centers onto the right side of the blanket in whatever arrangement you like.

## 3. STITCH THE APPLIQUÉS

Set your machine to a straight stitch and presser-foot pressure of 0. Using the Sketching with Thread technique (see page 134), edgestitch around the center circle, then around the flower, backtacking at the beginning and end of the stitching.

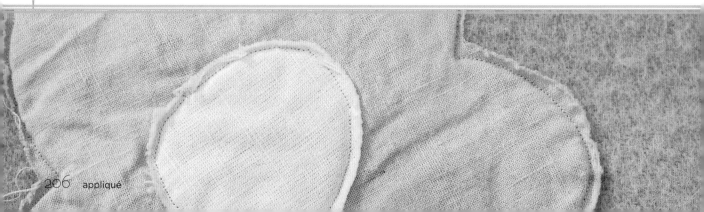

Design tip:
If you like a
rough-edge look,
rub a nailbrush
or toothbrush
along the edges
of the appliqué.
Trim any
long threads.

# 8 stenciling

Freezer paper,
available at the
grocery store,

came on the scene as a printmaking
material a few years ago, and it
has not lost its luster for us — not
one bit. For projects that require
printing, we turn to this paper
(and a handy craft knife) as the
perfect medium for creating quick,
one-time-use stencils. The stuff is
cheap; ask for a piece at the butcher
counter or find it shelved with
the rolls of foil and plastic wrap.

# Making Stencils

**What to know:** Freezer paper has two sides: a shiny, plastic-coated side and a dull paper side. Draw on the paper side. We have provided templates to trace if you want to re-create what we made (we hope so!), but we also encourage you to jump in and design your own stencils.

**How to do it:** Draw or trace a design on the paper side; for extra stability, pin or tape the template onto the freezer paper before tracing it. If you're making your own design, start with a simple silhouette. If you want a more detailed design, trace and cut shapes from the freezer paper that fit within the interior of the main shape. Cut along the traced or drawn guidelines with a craft knife.

# Using Stencils

**What to know:** The plastic side of the freezer paper can be temporarily fused to fabric, using an iron set to the appropriate heat for the project fabric. It's also a good idea to fuse an extra piece of freezer paper, plastic-coated side up, to the back of the fabric being stenciled. This second piece creates a block to minimize bleed-through and further stabilize the fabric, making paint application easier.

**How to do it:** Press the freezer paper stencil in position on the fabric, with the plastic-coated side down. If there are interior elements to the design, press those pieces in place. Apply a thin coat of paint over the entire cutout area (including over any interior elements). Let the paint dry, and if needed, apply a second coat. Once the paint is dry, peel the paper away.

*cut a stencil, add an interior shape. if you like.*

*paint over the whole stencil.*

*remove the paper. nice!*

## A Few Must-Read Notes on Creating Crisp Design Lines

1. When pressing the stencil in place, make sure the edges of the stencil are securely fused with the fabric.

2. Handle the fabric with care when moving it from the ironing board to your work surface; don't rumple it or allow it to pull away from the freezer paper.

3. We prefer foam brushes for stenciling. Stroke your brush in one direction, moving from the paper to the fabric instead of the other way around. This keeps the paint from being pushed under the stencil's edges and blurring the line. Dabbing and gently brushing work best.

4. Apply a thin layer of paint so it isn't wicked under the paper. If you want greater opacity, apply a second coat after the first has dried.

Cutting tip:
Do yourself a favor: when it's time to cut out your shapes, use a craft knife with a new, sharp blade.

# Monogrammed Shaving Pouch

**The perfect traveling companion** for a well-groomed dude, this modern, manly pouch will keep his razor, shaving brush, and extra blades close at hand.

## what you'll need

- ⅓ **yard of natural linen**
- ⅓ **yard of ripstop nylon**
- **1 spool of contrasting thread**
- **Freezer paper**
- **Letter stencil***
- **Craft knife**
- **Fabric paint**
- **Foam brush**
- **18" of ½"-wide twill tape or cotton cord (for drawstring)**
- **Safety pin**

*You can buy a letter stencil, make one from a computer printout in a very large font, or draw one freehand.

## 1. MEASURE, MARK, AND CUT

Press the linen and then measure, mark, and cut the following:

— **linen exterior:** 9" × 12½"

— **nylon interior (it doesn't have a right or wrong side):** 7¼" × 12½"

## 2. STITCH THE CASING

Pin the interior piece to the wrong side of the exterior piece so the bottom and side edges are aligned. Baste the pieces together.

Press the top edge of the exterior piece 1" to the wrong side, over the top edge of the interior piece, and pin it in place.

Starting ½" down from the top edge, sew three or four parallel lines, parallel to the top edge of the outside piece, with a straight stretch stitch. These stitches form a casing for the drawstring and secure the interior piece.

## 3. FINISH THE POUCH

Fold the joined fabrics in half so the short edges meet and the right sides are together. Using a knit or overcast stitch and starting ½" below the top edge (lower edge of the casing), stitch a ¼" seam along the open side and the bottom (your stitches will overcast the edge).

## 4. APPLY THE STENCIL

Turn the pouch right side out. Cut a piece of freezer paper about 1" larger than the design on all sides (our letter measures 4¼" tall). Trace the letter stencil or draw a freehand letter onto the paper side of the freezer paper. Cut along the lines with a craft knife.

Slip another sheet of freezer paper, plastic-coated side up, inside the pouch to prevent bleed-through (it will fuse to the pouch interior piece). Press the stencil with an iron set on the synthetic setting. Paint inside the stencil with fabric paint and a foam brush (see chapter intro for tips). When the paint is dry, peel away the freezer paper.

## 5. INSERT THE DRAWSTRING

Attach one end of the drawstring to the safety pin and slide it through the casing until it comes out the other end. Knot the ends of the drawstring together.

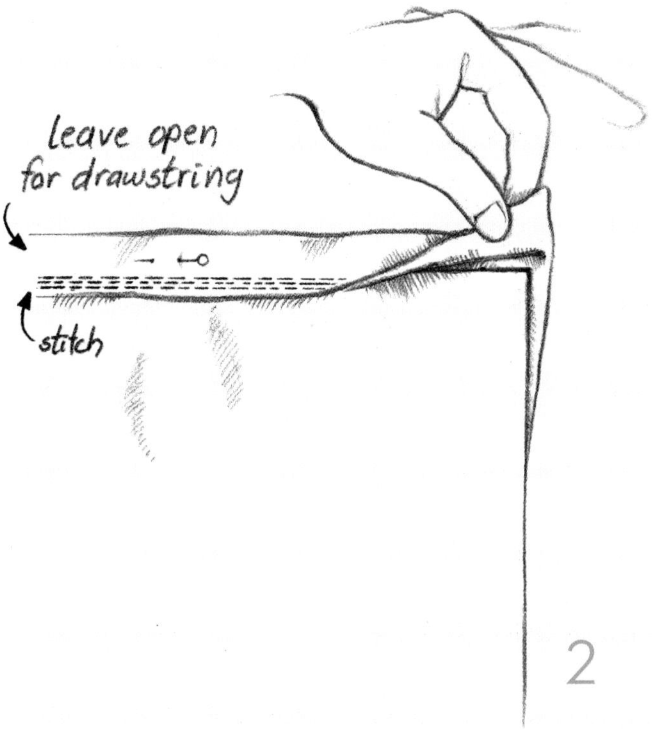

leave open for drawstring

stitch

2

# Pear Produce Bag

**Ditch the plastic and make a bunch of these ecofriendly bags** to bring to market. If you keep the muslin damp, your produce will stay fresh longer, too. We've supplied a suitably fruity template for stenciling, but of course you can draw any shape you can dream up. Or, cut an apple, lemon, or orange in half, brush paint on to the surface, then stamp a design on the bag instead of stenciling.

## what you'll need

- ½ yard of muslin
- 1 spool of contrasting thread
- Freezer paper
- Pear template (page 307)
- Craft knife
- Green and brown fabric paint
- Foam brush
- 58" of cotton cord
- Safety pin

## 1. MEASURE, MARK, AND CUT

Fold the muslin in half, then measure, mark, and cut the following piece through both fabric layers:

— **bag panel (cut 2):** 18" × 12"

## 2. STITCH THE CASING

On each panel, press one short edge 1¼" to the wrong side. Zigzag along the raw edge to create the casing.

## 3. FINISH THE POUCH

With the right sides together, straight stitch a ½" seam along the sides and bottom, starting and finishing the stitching just below the casings. Turn the bag right side out.

## 4. APPLY THE STENCIL

Cut two 8" × 14" pieces of freezer paper. Trace the pear onto the paper side of one of the sheets. Cut along the lines with a craft knife.

Slip the remaining sheet of freezer paper, plastic-coated side up, inside the pouch to prevent bleed-through. Press the stencil with a hot iron onto the front of produce bag, fusing both sheets of paper to the muslin.

Paint inside the stencil with fabric paint and a foam brush (see page 211 for tips). When the paint is dry, peel away the freezer paper.

## 5. INSERT THE DRAWSTRING

Attach the safety pin to one end of the cord and slide it through one panel's casing, then feed it through the remaining casing. Finally, feed it back through the first panel's casing. Trim the cord length as desired, and knot the ends to prevent fraying.

# Sofa Arm Catchall

**Life's too short** to waste time searching for the tv remote or the game controller. Stash it in the small pocket, and stow reading material or a knitting project in the larger pocket of this convenient catchall. The opposite end is anchored under the sofa cushions, so it can securely hold all your couch-time necessities. Don't you feel more relaxed just thinking about it?

## 1. MEASURE, MARK, AND CUT

With the wrong side facing up, measure, mark, and cut the following:

— **body panel (cut 2):** 21" × 36"

— **small pocket:** 7" × 7½"

## 2. SEW THE MAIN PANELS TOGETHER

Align one short edge of the two main panels with the right sides together and stitch a ½" seam, through both thicknesses of fabric. Press the seam open, and zigzag the raw edges of the seam allowances to finish them.

## 3. PREPARE THE SMALL POCKET

On both 7½" sides and one 7" side, press ¼" to the wrong side.

On the remaining 7" side, press ¼" and then another 1" to the wrong side. Straight stitch along the inside fold to form a 1" hemmed edge.

## 4. STENCIL THE SMALL POCKET

Trace all the outlines of the television template onto the paper side of the freezer paper and cut along the outside edges with a craft knife.

Next, cut out the screen along its outer edges, and cut out the switch and knob.

Center the television stencil on the right side of the small pocket with the shiny side of the freezer paper down and a second piece of freezer paper (shiny side up) under the fabric (this will stop paint from bleeding through).

## what you'll need

- 1 **yard of 60"-wide solid canvas (or other fabric that looks good from both sides)**

- 1 **spool of coordinating or contrasting thread**

- **Freezer paper**

- **Craft knife**

- **Fabric paint**

- **Foam brush**

- **Television template (page 307)**

4

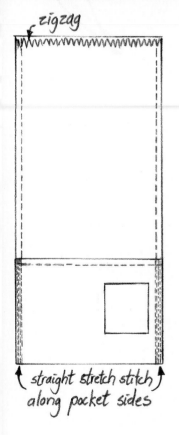

zigzag

straight stretch stitch
along pocket sides

7 & 8

## Sofa Arm Catchall

Position the screen, switch, and knob within the stencil, referring to the photograph at left for placement, and press them in place.

With the foam brush, dab brown paint over the stencil. Once the brown paint has dried, remove the stencils. Cut out the inside rectangle from the screen border rectangle and fuse the screen border back in place. Dab blue paint within the stencil. Let the paint dry and remove the paper.

### 5. HEM THE LARGE POCKET

Press one short edge of the main panel ½" and then another 1" to the wrong side to make a double-fold hem. Topstitch the hem in place 1" from the folded edge.

### 6. ATTACH THE SMALL POCKET

Pin the small pocket to the main panel so the hemmed edge of the pocket is 2½" from the hemmed edge of the panel and 3" from the right side. Edgestitch the pocket in place, leaving the top, hemmed edge unstitched.

### 7. ASSEMBLE THE CATCHALL

Fold the hemmed edge of the main panel, with the stenciled pocket facing out, up 10" to create the large pocket. Press the crease and pin the sides together.

Press the long edges (including the pocket edges) ¼" to the wrong side and then ¾" again to make a double-fold hem.

Straight stitch ¼" from each long edge to secure the hem and the pocket. Use a smaller stitch when stitching the pocket, and switch to a longer stitch length (ours was 3) for the remainder of the panel (a reinforced stitch isn't necessary beyond the pocket).

For extra reinforcement, stitch three parallel rows of straight stretch stitches along the pocket sides at ⅛", ¼", and ½" in from the edge.

### 8. FINISH THE HIDDEN EDGE

Zigzag along the remaining raw edge to prevent fraying. (No need to make it too beautiful; it will be under the sofa cushions.)

# Mod Flower Skirt

While making this skirt, we had a *Sound of Music* moment. Remember how Maria was outraged that the von Trapp children didn't have any play clothes? To rectify this situation, she sewed the kids some outfits from her bedroom's brocade curtains. We prefer a nice soft jersey, either from yardage or upcycled adult t-shirts, which we then double-stencil for fun. The results are comfy, stretchy, and one of our "favorite things"— well suited for marching and singing, eating schnitzel, or putting on a marionette show.

## 1. MEASURE, MARK, AND CUT A TWO-PANEL SKIRT

Follow the instructions for step 1 of the Two-Panel Skirt (see chapter 3, page 46).

## 2. CUT THE STENCIL

Place a large piece of freezer paper with the paper side up on the right side of the front skirt panel to plan the stencil layout. Using the template, trace the dots onto the paper at the desired locations. Take the paper off the skirt and cut out the dots with the craft knife.

Trace the cutout dots onto another large sheet of freezer paper. Trace the flower template over the dots. They don't need to be centered; make them a little wonky and playful. Cut out just the flower shapes.

## 3. FUSE AND PAINT

Place a piece of freezer paper plastic-coated side up on your work surface, and then place the skirt front panel on top of it with the right side facing up (the paper should extend beyond the skirt panel edges). Position the dot stencils on the panel and press them in place with a hot iron.

Using the foam brush, dab paint over the stencil. Let the paint dry, then peel off the paper.

Position the flower template sheet on top of the stenciled dots, fuse it in place with a hot iron, and apply paint. Let the paint dry, then peel off the paper.

- 1 yard of 60"-wide jersey fabric
- 1 spool of coordinating thread
- Fold over elastic
- Freezer paper
- Craft knife
- Fabric paint
- Sponge brush
- Templates (page 308)

## Mod Flower Skirt

### 4. ASSEMBLE THE SKIRT

When the paint is completely dry, align the panels with the right sides together. Sew ½" side seams with a straight stretch stitch. Attach fold over elastic along the waistband (see chapter 1, page 19).

# Rainy Day Wrap Skirt

Our wrap skirt design is made from a bouncy bamboo jersey and contrasting homemade binding. The crowning touch is a stenciled umbrella. Don't feel as if you have to save this one for a rainy day, though — it's a great look no matter what the weather promises.

## 1. SEW A THREE-PANEL WRAP SKIRT

Follow the instructions through step 2 for the Three-Panel Wrap Skirt (see chapter 3, page 49). Finish the bottom edge and both side edges of the skirt with a knit stitch in contrasting thread.

## 2. ATTACH THE BINDING

On the fabric cross grain, cut a strip of jersey fabric that is 2" wide by the skirt waist measurement (all three panels) to use to make binding. Follow the instructions for making binding (chapter 1, page 19), folding and attaching it to enclose the skirt's raw top edge. Gently stretch the binding as you sew, but avoid stretching the skirt material. Cut any excess binding flush with the skirt ends.

## 3. ADD THE BUTTONHOLES AND BUTTONS

Following the directions for your sewing machine, sew two vertical button-holes (sized to accommodate your buttons) on the waistband, one at the seam joining the middle and front panels, and the other at the end of the

what you'll need

- 2 yards of bamboo jersey
- Jersey fabric for binding strip
- 1 spool of contrasting thread
- Freezer paper
- Craft knife
- Fabric paint
- Foam brush
- Umbrella template (page 306)
- 2 coordinating buttons

waistband on the front panel. Slit the buttonholes with a seam ripper or craft knife, being careful not to cut any stitches.

Try the skirt on and mark the proper button placement, then hand-sew the buttons on at the marks.

## 4. STENCIL YOUR DESIGN

Trace the template onto the paper side of a sheet of freezer paper. Cut along the lines with a craft knife, including the four interior umbrella shapes. Position the iron template on the skirt front panel as desired, with a second sheet of freezer paper beneath the stencil area to stabilize and protect the back of the skirt from seeping paint. Press with a hot iron, fusing both sheets with the fabric (see page 210 for illustrations).

Using the foam brush, dab paint over the stencil. When the paint is dry, peel away the paper.

Cut and use the raindrop stencil included with the umbrella or paint raindrops freehand as desired.

Design tip:
Feel free to add some hand-stitched raindrops for extra rainy day fun.

# Ollie and Opal's Big Dog Bed

**We both share our homes with a big dog,** and we have both found that big dog beds are either incredibly ugly or outrageously pricey. Finally, we came up with this simple solution, which can be color matched to complement any room and personalized with any motif; we chose a bouncy tennis ball for our inexhaustibly enthusiastic canines.

## what you'll need

- **1¼ yards of 60"-wide canvas***

- **23" of 1"-wide sew-on Velcro**

- **1 spool of coordinating thread**

- **Freezer paper**

- **Craft knife**

- **Tennis ball template (page 308)**

- **Fabric paint**

- **Foam brush**

- **3" × 24" × 32" piece of high-density foam***

  *For a dog bed with finished dimensions of 24" × 33"

## 1. CUT AND HEM THE FABRIC

Cut the canvas to measure 38½" x 54½". Press one long edge 1¼" to the wrong side. Zigzag the hem in place.

## 2. STENCIL THE DESIGN

Stack together three of four squares of freezer paper, larger all around than the tennis ball template. Trace the template, including the U-shaped center marking on the top sheet, then cut along the outline through all the layers. Cut the U-shaped motif out of each tennis ball shape and save them. Repeat until you have the desired number of stencils.

Position the tennis ball stencils as desired on the right side of the fabric. Be sure to include a U-shaped motif inside each stencil. Press them in place with a hot iron. Brush the stencils with paint (see page 211 for tips). When the paint is dry, peel away the freezer paper.

## 3. ATTACH VELCRO

With the hemmed edge along the top, fold the fabric in half with the right sides together and the short edges aligned. Press the crease. With the fabric

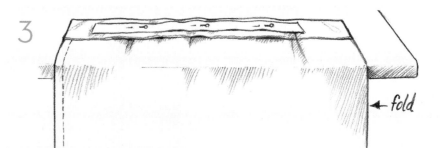

3

← *fold*

Stitching tip:
Sewing Velcro
onto large pieces
of fabric can
make sewing in
a straight line
trickier than
normal. Take
extra care and
sew slowly.

still folded, center and pin the hook side of the Velcro ⅛" from the hemmed edge on one side of the cover. Starting and ending with a box stitch, stitch the Velcro in place along the edges. Flip the cover so the opposite half is facing up, and repeat with the loop side of the Velcro.

## 4. STITCH THE SEAMS

Starting at the hemmed edge and using a straight stitch, stitch a ½" seam along the open side and the bottom edge. Be sure to backtack at both ends. Turn the cover right-side out and insert the foam or other cushioning.

beyond fabric

You know that you've really become a free-thinking sewist when you start musing about the inherent stitch-worthiness of a FedEx envelope or a cork coaster. Once you view the world this way, you'll find many different materials that can flow beneath your machine's needle, and you'll discover just how much you can make and repair. We've even tried sewing on wood (we used thin balsa sheets, and it was a bit tricky to manage the stitching without splitting the wood, but we're going to keep experimenting). With imagination and the right sewing machine needles and settings, there's a whole world beyond everyday fabrics just waiting to be stitched in all sorts of playful, beautiful, and useful ways.

# Sewing on Paper or Cardboard

**What to know:** Stitching on paper or cardboard is simple and lets you get wildly creative, but keep in mind that each time the needle perforates the material, it compromises the surface. If too many stitches are made in one small space, paper can tear. For this reason, it's easiest to use thick, high-quality paper or cardstock. Cardboard should be single-ply (steer clear of the corrugated stuff).

**How to do it:** After experimenting to find the proper settings, sew decorative lines using the Sketching with Thread technique (page 134). Keep your material moving, never letting the needle stay in one spot for more than a stitch or two.

## A Few Notes on Going Beyond Fabric

1. **You don't need an industrial machine to stitch through unconventional materials like plastic, paper, and cork. A basic home machine can easily handle these and many others, as long as the material fits under the presser foot and the needle can pierce it.**

2. **Universal needles work for all of the projects in this chapter. Before beginning, experiment with your machine's settings, working on scraps of your project material to find the right stitch length and width, thread tension, and foot pressure. If you are running into trouble, you may want to use a specialty needle. To determine the right needle type and size, refer to your machine's manual and talk to a knowledgeable sewing machine salesperson.**

Stitching tip:

To stitch on cork, use basting stitches (stitch length at 4) or straight stretch stitches (also at a long stitch length) for greatest ease and visibility. The thread tension will probably need to be lowered as well (ours was set at 2).

# Cork Trivet

**Personalize a set of trivets or coasters** with graphic stripes. Sewing on cork is easy if you stick to straight lines, such as the design shown here.

## 1. STITCH THE LINES

Simply sew a mix of colorful lines across the trivet as desired. To create our design, stitch as follows:

— Starting ½" from one edge, stitch three lines of basting stitch at ⅛" intervals.

— Leave ¼" of blank space, and then stitch two lines of straight stretch stitch ⅛" apart.

Change thread color and stitch additional lines between the ones you just stitched.

### what you'll need

- **6" square of ⅛"-thick cork**

- **2 spools of contrasting thread**

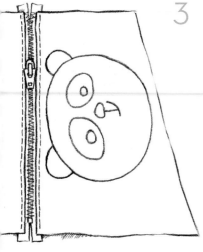

3

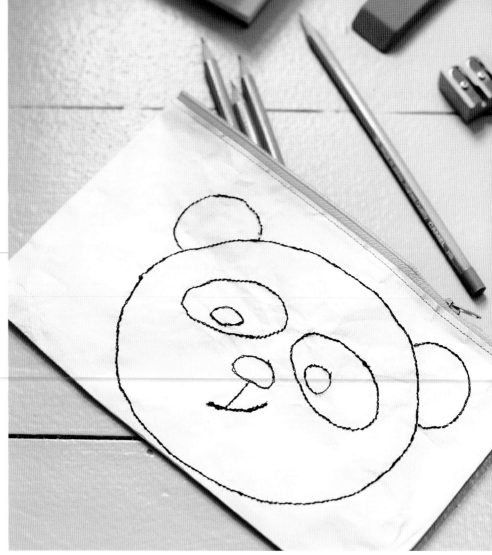

# Tyvek Pencil Pouch

**Tyvek is an almost indestructible material** used in building and, of course, in those express mailing envelopes that are available for free if you know where to look. They are a great canvas for decorative stitching. This little pouch can hold anything from pencils and lunch money to makeup and medicine.

# 1. MEASURE, MARK, AND CUT

Lay the Tyvek flat. Measure, mark, and cut the following pieces:

— **pouch panel (cut 2):** 6" × 10"

# 2. SKETCH AND STITCH YOUR DESIGN

On the right side of one panel, use a pencil to trace the template provided or to make your own line drawing.

With a straight stitch (our stitch length was 2; presser foot pressure was 1), use the Sketching with Thread technique (see page 134) over the sketched guidelines.

Working on the facial features, shorten the stitch length to 1 and stitch quite slowly. The smaller stitch makes the lines sharper and easier to curve when turning sharply.

# 3. ATTACH THE ZIPPER

Pin the top edge of the embellished panel on the zipper tape, about ⅛" from the zipper coil. Install the zipper foot and stitch along the top edge of the Tyvek, ⅛" from the edge. Turn the panel and zipper over and repeat this process on the other side of the zipper with the remaining Tyvek panel.

# 4. ASSEMBLE THE POUCH

Unzip the zipper halfway and fold the pouch at the zipper with the right sides together and panel edges aligned. Pin along the edges (not in the center of the pouch because pin holes don't go away in Tyvek).

With the regular presser foot and a straight stitch, sew a ½" seam around the side and bottom edges, starting at one end of the zipper tape and finishing at the opposite end. Trim the corners and any excess zipper tape.

Turn the pouch right side out.

## what you'll need

- Tyvek mailing envelope or piece from a builder's roll
- 10" all-purpose zipper
- 1 spool of contrasting thread
- Zipper presser foot
- Panda template (page 308)

# Sewn Cardboard Gift Tags

**When you're really in love with a fabric**, even the tiniest scraps are precious. Here's a great way to make use of them. We appreciate the contrast of the lavishly colorful appliqués and the homespun cardboard — and your gift recipient will too.

## what you'll need

- **Shirt cardboard (cereal boxes also work well)**
- **Colorful fabric scraps**
- **Spools of contrasting thread**
- **Hole punch**
- **Embroidery floss or yarn**
- **Permanent pen**

## 1. MEASURE, MARK, AND CUT

Draw the flower center and petals freehand; the more imperfect they are, the cuter the finished product looks. Measure, mark, and cut the following pieces for each tag:

*Cut from the cardstock or cardboard:*

— **tag front:** 3" square

*Cut from the fabric:*

— **flower petals (cut 5 or 6):** about 1" from tip to tip

— **flower center:** about 1"-diameter circle

## 2. APPLIQUÉ THE DETAILS

Stitch the petals and centers to the front of each tag by sewing just inside the shapes' edges or decoratively in the center of them (see page 172 for tips on appliqué). Straight stitch a border (our foot-presser pressure was 0 and stitch length was 2), just inside the tag's edges. Be sure to leave a bit of space on the cardboard for writing.

## 3. FINISH THE TAG

Handwrite your message with permanent pen. Punch a hole and thread it onto the ribbon on the package, or add with a loop of embroidery floss or yarn.

Design variations tip: These simple cards can be made in any shape. Instead of appliqué pieces, decorate the tags by stitching on photos or little drawings. Or add sparkle to your stitched-on scraps with hand-sewn sequins or a few lines of glitter glue.

# Wind Spinner

**We like these spinners best** when they're made in multiples, strung up along the porch eaves to catch the breeze. They also make terrific party trimmings, since you can match them to any color scheme or holiday theme. They're possibly the easiest, cheapest, and twirliest decoration ever.

## what you'll need

- Cardstock in bright colors
- Craft knife
- Ruler
- 1 spool of white thread

## 1. CUT THE STRIPS

Use a craft knife and ruler to cut 24 spinner strips, each ½" × 5", to make a spinner approximately 15" long.

## 2. STITCH THE SPINNER

With your machine set for a straight stitch (our stitch length was 2), feed the center of the strips under the presser foot, leaving about ⅛" to ¼" between each strip. At the end, leave a long tail for hanging the spinner.

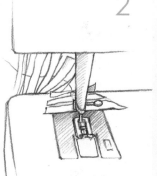

2

## design variations

— Instead of a dangling spinner, add more strips and make a garland using the same technique, leaving long tails at the start and the end for hanging.

— Use a mix of decorative papers for a patchwork-quilt look. Shrink down the strip size; try ½" × 2" to make a mini-garland to string in your Christmas tree.

— Change the shapes of the strips: try circles, squares, ovals, triangles, or hearts.

Design tip:
Any printing on the
bag should face the
interior or at least be
turned so the iron
can't touch it because
the ink could bleed.

3

# Fused Plastic Wallet

**Plastic bags can be gently ironed into an amazingly tough fabric.** Find a bag with an attractive color or pattern, and you can whip up a holder to stash coupons or loose change. Be sure to do the ironing in a well-ventilated spot.

## 1. CUT AND FOLD

Trim off the bag's handles. Cut the bottom seams open and flatten the bag with the front and back panels aligned. Fold it in half, being sure to fold the printed sides in. Sandwich the plastic between layers of parchment or white tissue paper.

## 2. FUSE THE LAYERS

With the iron set on the synthetic setting, press the layers, keeping the iron moving across the paper. After a few passes, check to see if the plastic layers have fused together. Press more, if needed. When the plastic layers are fused, peel off the parchment or tissue paper.

## 3. MAKE THE POUCH

Cut a piece of the fused material measuring 5" × 8½".

With a straight stitch, sew the hooked side of the Velcro along one short edge of the fused plastic, stitching all around the perimeter of the Velcro.

Fold the remaining short edge of the plastic up 3½" toward the top, so it forms the wallet shape. Pin the loop side of the Velcro strip along the top of this edge, making sure it aligns with its mate.

Open the fold. Stitch the Velcro in place as pinned. If you like, use a straight stretch stitch to embellish the wallet's exterior.

Refold the wallet. With a decorative stitch (we used the feather stitch) sew along the sides and the flap edge.

## what you'll need

- Plastic shopping bag
- Parchment or white tissue paper
- 4½" of 1"-wide Velcro
- 1 spool of contrasting thread

# Mail Organizer

Stash the bills as they arrive in these pretty pockets, and maybe they won't seem so onerous. The tear-away paper technique used here is truly nifty.

## what you'll need

- ⅓ yard of heavyweight canvas

- ¼ yard of vinyl (with its protective tissue layer)

- Decorative paper (with closed-edge designs)

- Spools of coordinating and contrasting thread

- 23"-long dowel, ¼" in diameter

- 18" length of cord or ribbon

- Mod Podge or white glue

## 1. MEASURE, MARK, AND CUT

With the wrong sides of the fabrics facing up and the protective tissue still on the vinyl, measure, mark, and cut the following:

*Cut from the fabric:*
— **main panel:** 22½" × 12"

*Cut from the vinyl:*
— **pocket (cut 2):** 7" × 10" wide

## 2. HEM THE MAIN BODY

Straight stitch a ½" double-fold hem on both long sides and the bottom edge of the main panel (see page 19) with coordinating thread.

To make the casing at the top edge for the dowel, press a 1" hem to the wrong side and then zigzag with coordinating thread close to the raw edge, leaving the ends open.

## 3. MAKE THE POCKETS

Working with one pocket piece at a time, place the vinyl over the decorative paper, with the right sides of both facing up. With a straight stitch (our stitch length was 2) and using the free-motion drawing technique (see page 134), sew over and around the design printed on the paper, which is visible through the vinyl. The more stitching there is in your design, the more secure the paper will be.

Carefully tear away the paper around the perimeter of the stitching that outlines the shapes, leaving only the filled interior of each shape.

Brush a coat of Mod Podge or white glue over the backs of the stitched shapes and let it dry.

Design tip:
The paper shapes
need to have
closed edges.
We chose a floral
paper and simply
sewed around
the outlines
and through the
interiors of some
of the flowers.

Stitching tip:
Vinyl is a little
sticky, so layering
it with tear-away
tissue makes it
easier to move
during stitching.

Position the pockets on the main panel with the right sides facing up. Straight stitch the pockets in place ¼" from the side and bottom edges of the vinyl, leaving the top edges open.

## 4. HANG THE ORGANIZER

Slide the dowel into the casing. Knot the cord onto it at both ends and hang it in a place of honor.

**Design tip:** Add texture and color by stitching on some paper appliqué.

**Stitching tip:** Be sure to check out the tips for sewing decorative lines on page 106 and for free-motion drawing on page 134.

# Custom-Stitched Card and Envelope

**Once you've embellished paper with thread,** you may never go back to pen and pencil! And one great plus: with paper, the stakes are delightfully low, so you can play around with different techniques and stitches until you get a feel for them. This project makes a beautiful keepsake for birthdays, holidays, or any time at all.

## 1. MEASURE, MARK, AND CUT

From the cardstock, measure, mark, and cut the following pieces:

— **card:** 5½" × 11"

— **envelope:** 6½" × 11"

— **flap:** 6½" × 2"

## 2. MAKE THE CARD

Fold the card in half so the short edges align.

With a sharp pencil, lightly draw a simple design and lettering on the front of the card.

With a straight stitch (our stitch length was 2.5), sew over your guidelines using the Sketching with Thread technique (see page 134). Sew straight lines with full presser-foot pressure, and sew curved ones with decreased pressure.

## 3. MAKE THE ENVELOPE

Align the 6½" edges of the flap and envelope so that the flap overlaps the envelope by ¼". Zigzag the overlapped edges (our stitch length was 2); backstitch at both ends to secure.

Fold the opposite edge of the envelope up to meet the seam.

With a straight stitch, sew the envelope sides closed with a scant ¼" seam, backstitching at both ends.

## what you'll need

- **Cardstock**

- **1 or more spools of contrasting thread**

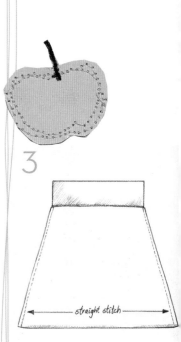

3

*straight stitch*

upcycling

# Gosh, there's a lot of fabric in this world.

Our drawers and closets are stuffed, our thrift stores are brimming with castoffs. We love gorgeous new fabrics as much as anybody, but we feel a responsibility and desire to make good use of what's already out there. Throughout this book, we've created projects that repurpose t-shirts, blankets, sweaters, and other goodies, and in this chapter we've fashioned a few more favorites. We hope they'll inspire you to cast a fresh eye on preworn and preloved items. Here's our quick summary of what to look for to ensure the best upcycling results.

# T-Shirts

We highly recommend buying 100% cotton tees, though if you have a project in mind that calls for something slinky, then go for a silk, rayon, or polyester one. Always check for stains. You may be able to appliqué or cut around a stain, but if it's in a tricky spot, keep looking for a different t-shirt; there are so many to choose from. Pockets can be clever additions to the design of a skirt or dress, but if you don't want to keep the pocket, skip the garment, since removing it will leave holes. We generally work with solids, but sometimes we come across a graphic that is beautiful and interesting, and it's fun to incorporate that into a project (see the Reversible Graphic Belt, page 248, for a good example).

# Tablecloths, Curtains, and Sheets

Once you've caught the upcycling fever, you'll find yourself prowling the racks and yard sales where the used home-decor items hang. These large pieces can be repurposed in so many ways. Dye them. Cut them up. If there are stains on a tablecloth, appliqué over them. Vintage pillowcases can be turned into all kinds of small projects. Even a vinyl cloth can be used to make bags and pouches. Treat these items like yardage; they'll pay you back big time.

# Vintage Wool Blankets

Don't miss our favorite idea for dressing up an old blanket (see page 206): appliquéing it with fabric or felted wool. Blankets are also great as batting for quilts, pot holders, rugs, or anything that needs insulating qualities or heft. We buy them, stick them right in the washing machine, and then air-dry them. Dry cleaning works well too. However, if a garment or store smells like mothballs, run the other way!

# Sweaters

Felting old sweaters in the washing machine is a simple form of upcycling, but you need to start with the right wool. Read the label carefully, and skip sweaters that don't have a label.

## Felting Sweaters

**What to know:** Sweaters made of 100% wool or cashmere felt the best. Merino wool shrinks up nicely, while lambswool might be a little stubborn or it might felt right away. Sweaters with a small percentage of synthetic fibers may felt, or they may not; the stakes are low if you want to try it. Pick colors you love and don't shy away from really ugly-shaped sweaters since you will be disassembling them anyway. Very thick sweaters, like Irish fisherman's sweaters and other items knit from superbulky yarns, will result in a very thick piece of felted wool, often too thick to get under your presser foot. Steer away from those.

**How to do it:** To felt a sweater, wash it in the washing machine on the hot wash/cold rinse setting with regular laundry detergent. Dry it in the dryer on high heat. Repeat the process as often as necessary until the ribbing or knit stitches become very tight and you can snip and cut away the edges without any raveling.

# Vintage Pot Holder

**Salvage the pretty parts of a timeworn vintage tablecloth** by turning them into a set of pot holders, embellished with outline stitching for a modern dimension. It's easy to move the multiple layers through the sewing machine, making this project a good one for honing your thread-drawing skills.

## 1. MEASURE, MARK, AND CUT

With the right side of the fabric facing up, measure, mark, and cut two 8" squares.

## 2. ASSEMBLE THE POT HOLDER

With the right sides together, straight stitch around three sides of the cotton squares with a ½" seam.

Turn the pot holder right side out and insert the felted wool square or batting squares into the pocket. Press the open raw edges to the wrong side, with one of the raw edges encasing the exposed edge of the wool or batting.

Fold the twill tape in half and tuck the ends in one side of the opening to make a hanging loop.

Straight stitch ⅛" from the edge around the entire perimeter of the pot holder, starting at the corner with the loop.

## 3. STITCH OVER THE PRINT

Straight stitch over some of the outlines of the fabric print using the free-motion drawing technique (see page 134). Stitch on one side or both, as desired.

### what you'll need

- Vintage or other printed cotton fabric (at least 8" × 16")

- 7" square of felted wool or three 7" squares of cotton batting

- 1 spool of contrasting thread

- 4" of ½"-wide cotton twill tape

Stitching tip: Your stitched lines will appear on the flip side of the pot holder, creating lovely layered patterns.

# Blanket-Stitched Armies

**Arm warmers have a practical Dickensian chic.** We love to wear them when we're sewing or typing on a cold winter's day. You can make these in a flash out of any felted sweater, but we highly recommend using cashmere if you can swing it.

## what you'll need

- Sleeves from a felted sweater (see page 244)

- 1 spool of coordinating thread

- Embroidery thread and needle

## 1. FIND THE FIT

Cut off the sleeves from a felted sweater, near the armhole seam. Turn the sleeves inside out and slide them onto the wearer's arms. Pin the sleeves along the seam for a snug fit at the wrist and up the arm. Pin mark the desired length (ours reach about 2" above the elbow). Take the sleeves off.

## 2. TRIM AND STITCH

Lay the sleeves flat with the wrong side out and trim them at the marked length. Using a straight stretch stitch, stitch a new seam along the pin markings up each arm. Cut off the extra fabric along the new seam. Turn the sleeves right side out.

## 3. FINISH THE ARM WARMERS

On each arm warmer, measure 2" up from the finger opening (wrist) along the seam and snip a thumb hole opening about 1½" long.

With the embroidery thread and needle, hand-sew a blanket stitch along the thumb holes and finger openings. Leave a 2" tail of thread at the beginning and end of the stitching. When the stitching is complete, knot the thread tails together securely and then trim them.

Stitching tip: For easier hand sewing, slip each armie on your nondominant arm (we find it easier anyway).

# Reversible Graphic Belt

**Rescue that loved-to-pieces tee from the rag bag** by turning it into cool accessory. The leather backing is more than just good-looking; it also gives the belt structure and keeps the jersey from stretching. If you don't have upcycled leather on hand, you could also use canvas or any other sturdy fabric.

## 1. MEASURE, MARK, AND CUT

Measure the wearer's waist (or hips, depending on how the wearer wears belts) and add 5" to 6".

Determine which part of the t-shirt graphics you want to use and be sure to mark and cut there. It's hard to get a long enough strip of fabric for a belt from a t-shirt, so you'll cut two pieces and sew them together.

With the right side facing up, measure, mark, and cut two pieces each from the jersey and the backing fabrics as follows:

— 1¾" × half the desired finished belt length

## 2. JOIN THE STRIPS

Align the jersey strips with the right sides together along one short edge. Straight stitch a ¼" seam to join the strips. Press the seam allowances open.

Lay the leather strips end to end, overlapping the ends by ½". Straight stitch along the overlap to join the strips.

## 3. ASSEMBLE THE BELT

Align the jersey and leather strips with the wrong sides together.

Straight stitch (our stitch length was 2) around the perimeter of the strips, as close as possible to the edges.

Use a straight stretch stitch to secure the strips together (especially if your leather strips include seaming from the original garment or bag) and embellish it with Xs and straight lines of stitches, as shown.

Overcast the short edge with stretch zigzag stitches for reinforcement.

## 4. ATTACH THE BUCKLE

Thread one end of the belt through the buckle, loop it back, and straight stitch it in place to secure the buckle.

## what you'll need

- 1 cotton jersey t-shirt with graphics

- Upcycled leather (from a bag or garment) or a sturdy fabric for backing

- 1 spool of contrasting thread

- 2"-wide slide-on belt buckle

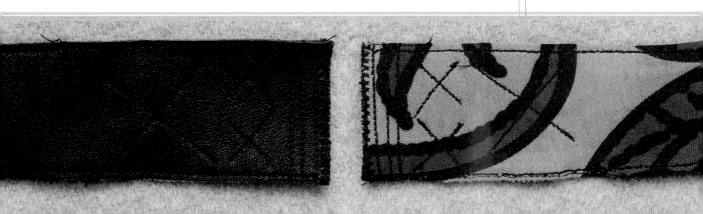

# Wool Jumper

A sweater with a color or pattern that's a bit too raucous for the grown-ups in the house can be perfectly adorable on a child. This two-panel dress is supersweet over a tee and tights, and can be embellished with a simple circle blossom, as shown here, or thread-sketched with any design that might tickle its wearer's fancy.

## what you'll need

- Adult (size large) wool sweater, felted (see page 244)

- Two-panel dress pattern, sized to fit wearer (see page 34)

- Button

- 1 spool of coordinating thread

- Embroidery thread and needle for attaching the button

- Hand needle

## 1. SEW A TWO-PANEL DRESS

Cut apart the sweater along the seams so you can use the front of the sweater to cut the front of the dress and the sweater back for the dress back.

Follow the instructions for the Two-Panel Garment, (see chapter 3, page 34) through step 2, making the following adjustments:

— Fold each sweater panel in half lengthwise, and pin the pattern with its marked "center" aligned on the fold.

— To add flare at the hem, mark the bottom edge 3½" wider than the pattern piece, for a total of 7". Trace around the pattern, drawing the side seams to add the flare.

## 2. STITCH THE SHOULDERS AND SIDE SEAMS

Pin the front and back panels with the wrong sides together.

Straight stretch stitch ¼" seams at the shoulders and sides, taking care to keep the stitches straight since they will be exposed.

Zigzag through the center of the seam allowances to hold them flat and give them a nice finish.

## 3. ADD THE FLOWER

From the sweater scraps, cut a 2½"-diameter circle and a 2"-diameter circle. Stack them with the smaller circle on top.

Attach the flower to the dress shoulder with a button, stitching it in place with embroidery thread.

Design tip:
Zigzag edgestitching creates a lettuce-edge effect for your bloomers.

# Girl's Bloomers

**Whether you call them pantaloons,** baggies, or bloomers, these sweet bottoms are designed to wear under a skirt, dress, or tunic for maximum style and playground practicality (hang from the monkey bars without fear of undie exposure!). You can make them from jersey yardage, but we think it's more fun to upcycle fabric from a roomy men's t-shirt, plucked out of Dad's cast-off pile or thrifted from a secondhand store.

## 1. MEASURE, MARK, AND CUT YOUR FABRIC

Cut the sleeves off the shirt and lay out the torso piece with the front side facing up.

Fold the pants in half at the crotch seam with the legs aligned, and place them on the fabric as shown, aligning the side seam of the pants close to one of the shirt side seams. Trace around the pants, leaving an extra ½" for seam allowance as shown, widening the marked (inseam) line so it is more or less vertical. This makes the pattern piece for one pant leg.

Flip the pants over and align the side seam with the other side of the shirt to make the pattern for the other leg. Repeat the tracing as above.

Cut along the lines through both thicknesses of fabric.

1

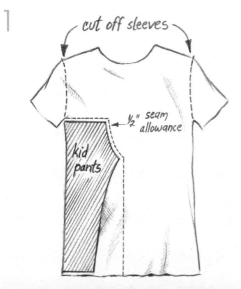

*cut off sleeves*

½" seam allowance

kid pants

2

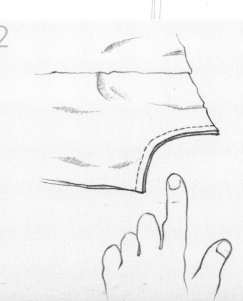

## 2. ASSEMBLE THE BLOOMERS

Unfold both pieces and align them with the right sides together.

Straight stretch stitch a ½" seam from the waist down to the crotch point (as shown in illustration on page 253). Repeat on the opposite side.

Pin the pants with the right sides together so the crotch seams are aligned. Starting at the bottom edge of one leg, straight stretch stitch up the inside leg seam, across the crotch seam, and then back down the other leg inseam.

Then, working again from bottom edge to waist, sew up the outer side seams on each leg.

## 3. ADD THE WAISTBAND

Turn the bloomers right side out. Finish the waistline with fold over elastic. (See chapter 1, page 19).

## 4. FINISH THE LEG BOTTOMS

Zigzag around the raw edges of each leg opening.

Working on one leg at a time, mark a line all the way around the leg about 1½" above the opening.

Measure the circumference of the wearer's leg at the point where the bloomers will end. Cut a piece of fold over elastic two times the leg measurement. Cut the elastic in half so you have a piece for each leg.

Align the bottom edge of the elastic along the marked line. Edgestitch the elastic in place along the top and bottom edges with a small zigzag stitch, pulling the elastic taut as you stitch. Overlap the ends by ½" and backtack.

Trim the excess elastic close to your stitching (but don't cut the stitches).

4

# Clever Leather Shoulder Bag

**Out-of-fashion leather coats,** jackets, bags, and even belts can be miraculously transformed into this hip and handy tote with a little snipping and stitching. We cut our own shoulder strap, but if you're lucky enough to thrift a belted coat, you're a step ahead of the game.

## Clever Leather Shoulder Bag

### what you'll need

- Leather jacket (for the main body)
- Contrasting leather (for appliqué pieces)
- ½ yard of lining fabric
- ⅛ yard of fabric for pocket
- Leather sewing machine needle
- 1 spool of contrasting thread
- Side panel and flower appliqué templates (pages 309 and 311)

## 1. DISASSEMBLE THE LEATHER JACKET

Use sharp scissors to cut off the jacket sleeves and open the side seams, doing your best to preserve large swaths of the leather. Remove any lining or interfacing from the jacket interior. Repeat, if necessary, with another jacket, to obtain leather for the appliqué pieces.

## 2. MEASURE, MARK, AND CUT

With the wrong side of the fabrics and leather facing up, measure, mark, and cut the following pieces:

*Cut from the main-body leather:*

— **exterior bottom panel:** 2½" × 15½"

— **exterior side panel (cut 2):** Trace the side panel template*

— **shoulder strap:** 2" × 35" (if necessary, piece several shorter lengths end to end)

*Cut from the lining fabric:*

— **interior bottom panel:** 2½" × 15½"

— **interior side panel (cut 2):** Trace the side panel template

*Cut from the pocket fabric:*

— **pocket (cut 2):** 4½" × 6½"

*Cut from the contrasting leather*

— **appliqué:** see step 5

— **binding:** 1" × 25" (or cut 2 pieces 1" × 13" to allow for a seam)

— **strap lining:** 1¾" × 33"

*If you don't have a large enough piece of leather to cut the side panels on the fold, cut two pieces and stitch them together, allowing enough for seam allowance at what would have been the fold.

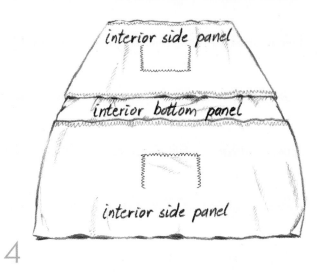

### 3. ATTACH THE POCKETS

Hem the top of each pocket by pressing the top raw edges ½" to the wrong side; zigzag them in place.

Center each pocket on an interior side panel piece, 1" below the top edge; pin them in place.

Zigzag (our stitch width was 2) along the sides and bottom of the pockets to attach them to the lining.

### 4. ASSEMBLE THE LINING

Pin an interior side panel to each long edge of the interior bottom panel with the right sides together; straight stitch with ¼" seams.

Fold the two interior side panels so they are aligned with the right sides together, tucking the bottom panel within the fold (between the side panels). Straight stitch the panels together along the sides with ¼" seams. Turn the lining right side out and set it aside.

Detail of finished lining

5

6

**Design tip:**
Invent your own stitched design for the strap ends — anything will look great as long as there's plenty of stitching to attach the strap securely — and the stitching adds a little whimsy in the process.

## 5. CREATE THE APPLIQUÉS

Trace the flower template as many times as desired on the wrong side of the contrasting leather and cut the flowers out with sharp scissors.

Pin the appliqués on the exterior side panels. Trim any that extend beyond the panel edges.

Install the leather needle (you'll use it for the rest of the project) and straight stitch the appliqués in place several times around and just inside the edges.

## 6. ASSEMBLE THE EXTERIOR

As for the lining in step 4, pin an exterior side panel to each long edge of the exterior bottom panel with the right sides together; straight stitch with ¼" seams.

Fold the two side panels so they are aligned with right sides together, tucking the bottom panel within the fold (between the side panels). Using a straight stretch stitch, sew both sides with ¼" seams.

# 7. JOIN THE EXTERIOR AND INTERIOR

Slip the lining inside the exterior so the wrong sides are together and the top edges are aligned. Baste or pin the top edges together.

Piece the binding strips if necessary to make one strip 25" long. Fold it in half lengthwise and position it over the top of the bag, encasing the top edges of the lining and exterior in the fold.

Starting at one side seam, zigzag the binding in place, around the entire top edge of the bag. Overlap the narrow ends slightly.

# 8. MAKE AND ATTACH THE STRAP

If necessary, piece the strap pieces to obtain the desired length.

Trim the leather strap ends as desired; ours has a scalloped edge. Add decorative stitched lines across the strap to embellish and strengthen the leather.

If you like, trim the ends of the strap lining to complement the leather strap ends. Pin the lining to the strap with the wrong sides together; the lining straps are shorter. Straight stitch the lining and leather pieces together close to the edge.

Position one side seam of the bag under the sewing machine needle. It might help to convert to the machine's sleeve arm for easier maneuvering. Center one strap end over a side seam so it extends about 2" below the top edge. Using a straight stretch stitch, edgestitch all around the strap end. Then stitch a U shape inside the stitches and fill in the U shape with straight lines of stitching. Repeat for the opposite strap end and side seam.

8

# Vintage Tablecloth Floor Cushion

**The envelope closure on this cushy item** makes construction a breeze. Of course, Nicole's husband looked more than skeptical as he saw her making this lovely *white* cushion. But it is crazy beautiful, and soft as can be. In her fantasies, Nicole's home is filled with white cushions made from fabulous fabric like this!

## what you'll need

- **32" square cushion form (we used one stuffed with feather and down)**
- **A vintage tablecloth, at least 66" long**
- **1 spool of coordinating thread**
- **30" length of sew-on Velcro**

## 1. MARK, MEASURE, AND CUT

Spread the tablecloth out and determine which section you'd like to highlight. With this section as centered as possible, measure, mark, and cut the following:

— **cushion cover:** 34" × 66"

## 2. HEM THE EDGES

Straight stitch a ½" double-fold hem (see page 19) along both short sides.

## 3. STITCH THE SIDES

Fold both short ends toward the middle with the right sides together, so the length from folded edge to folded edge is 32". The hemmed edges will overlap slightly to form the cushion cover opening. Pin the overlap closed.

Using a knit stitch, stitch a ½" seam along each side, sealing the raw edges as you stitch.

## 4. FINISH THE CUSHION

Unpin the overlap and position the Velcro strips on the hemmed edges, at least ⅛" in. Straight stitch just inside the edges of the Velcro strips to secure them. Turn the cushion cover right side out and stuff the cushion inside.

4

# Two-Tee Dress

**Your favorite little girl will love this comfy dress** styled from Mom or Dad's tees or from sweet thrifted finds. We finished our version with short sleeves, but it's also delightfully cool as a tank dress. P.S. You could make one of these as a woman's tunic, too.

## 1. PREPARE FOR CUTTING

Determine the desired dress length and make the torso and sleeve patterns (see chapter 2, pages 29–30). Decide which shirt will supply which panels (we used a brown t-shirt for one front and two back panels, and a printed shirt for the remaining front panel). Place the pressed shirts right side facing up.

## 2. MEASURE, MARK, AND CUT

Follow the instructions for the Four-Panel Garment (see chapter 3, page 38) through step 3, positioning the torso pattern piece on each t-shirt to trace it, as shown on page 263. When cutting the panels, cut through both the front and back of the shirts.

## 3. MAKE THE SLEEVES

For a dress with sleeves, follow the instructions for Sleeves Made Simple (see chapter 3, page 42), using the leftover t-shirt fabric, or (as we did here), cutting off and repurposing the sleeves from one of the shirts. If the sleeves are too large, cut them apart at the underarm seams, fold them in half with seam edges aligned, and trace the sleeve pattern onto each one.

## 4. COMPLETE THE DRESS

Join the panels and sleeve pieces and finish the bottom edge as directed in the Four-Panel Garment instructions (see chapter 3, page 38). Trim the sleeves to the desired length. With a tricot stitch and contrasting thread, topstitch over the front and back center seams.

## what you'll need

- 2 adult t-shirts, plain or printed, both the same size*

- Torso and sleeve pattern pieces, sized to fit for wearer (see chapter 2, pages 29–30)

- Spools of coordinating and contrasting thread

*The length of the shirts will determine how long the dress can be. Adult small t-shirts will most likely work for a toddler's garment; however, an older (and taller) child might need large or extra-large shirts as starting points.

Cutting tip:
You will probably
end up cutting
extra panels, but
they can be used
as sleeve fabric.
You could also
make ruffles from
them (see page
60) to sew at
the neckline or
bottom edge.

2

↖ ½" seam allowance

Cutting torso piece

Stitching tip: Make sure to stitch plenty of lines so that the layers of fabric won't shift when the mat is used.

# Reversible Loopy Bath Mat

**Towels with frayed edges are the perfect candidates** for this makeover.
Find a complementary fabric that makes you happy, stitch it to the towels
with some free-flowing thread doodles, add bias tape, and you've just
upgraded your bathroom decor.

## 1. MEASURE, MARK, AND CUT

Measure, mark, and cut both towels and the cotton fabric (grain can run
either direction) so there are three pieces, all 20"x 32".

## 2. JOIN THE PIECES

Layer the cut pieces as follows: the top piece with the wrong side facing up,
then the toweling pieces over it, with the right side of the better looking
towel on top. The middle toweling piece simply serves as an interfacing, giving
the mat more heft, so choose the more tired-looking towel for the center.
Pin the layers together and straight stitch around all the edges with a ¼" seam.

## 3. SKETCH THE DESIGN

Straight stitch, using the Doodling with Thread technique (see page 134),
squiggly lines approximately 2" to 3" apart on the toweling side, adding a loop
to the lines every so often.

## 4. FINISH THE EDGES

Pin bias tape along the short sides, enclosing the raw edges. Edgestitch it in
place with a straight stitch. Repeat on the long edges, mitering the tape at
the corners (see page 21). To finish, stitch a few free-motion doodled circles
in each corner of the mat.

### what you'll need

- 2 bath towels (one
  will be hidden as
  an interfacing
  layer, so the towels
  needn't match)*

- ¾ yard of cotton
  fabric for the top

- 1 spool of
  contrasting thread

- 1 or 2 packages of
  wide double-fold
  bias tape

  *For a finished size of
  21" × 33".

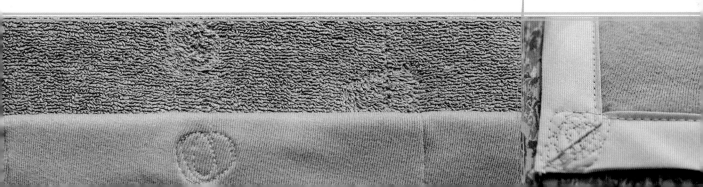

# Dress Shirt Wrap Skirt

To make this cool cotton wrap skirt, head to the thrift store and pick out three generously sized men's dress shirts. The shirts can be as alike or different as you desire; the skirt will be extremely cute either way.

what you'll need

- 3 extra-large men's cotton dress shirts
- 3 yards of double-fold ½"-wide cotton bias tape
- Spools of coordinating and contrasting thread

## 1. DISASSEMBLE THE SHIRTS

Wash and press the shirts. Cut off the sleeves and shoulder yokes at the seams; then cut the side and shoulder seams to remove the front. You will use only the back panels.

## 2. STITCH A THREE-PANEL WRAP SKIRT

Follow the instructions through step 2 for the Three-Panel Wrap Skirt (see chapter 3, page 49), cutting one panel from each piece of shirt fabric and making the following changes when measuring and marking:

— **length:** add ¾" for the hem

— **hem flare:** mark the panel's bottom edge 3" wider than the waist on each side

Instead of pinking the raw edges of the side seams, zigzag with contrasting thread as in step 2 (see chapter 3, page 50).

## 3. FINISH THE BOTTOM AND SIDE EDGES

Stitch ¼" double-fold hems along the outside edges of the skirt (see chapter 1, page 19) with coordinating thread.

Press a ¾" hem to the wrong side along the bottom edge of the skirt and zigzag it in place with contrasting thread.

## 4. ADD THE WAIST TIES AND WAIST-TIE OPENING

To finish the waist, follow steps 4 and 5 for the Three-Panel Wrap Skirt (see chapter 3, page 49), attaching the bias tape with coordinating thread.

**Design tip:**
If you're feeling
really inspired,
add pockets from
the original shirts
or snip off some
of the buttons
and stitch them
to the skirt as
fun trimming.

# Lettuce-Edge Neck Warmer

**We love a lot about this little item.** First, it's a fantastic use for upcycled fabric, giving a whole new life to swatches from an old sweater and an old tee. Second, the clever layering of fabric means no itching, with soft jersey wrapping your neck, and warm wool on the outside. Third, the lettuce-edge frames the wearer's face in an adorable way, and the little felted flower is like a cherry on top.

## what you'll need

- 5" × 16" length of felted wool (see page 244)
- 5" × 16" piece of cotton jersey
- 1 button
- 1 spool of contrasting thread
- Needle and embroidery thread
- 1 sew-on snap
- Pinking shears

## 1. MAKE THE NECK WARMER

Pin the wool and the jersey with the wrong sides together. Using a knit or zigzag stitch, edgestitch around all four sides.

## 2. MAKE THE BUTTON FLOWER

With pinking shears, cut three circles from the remaining wool, each a little smaller than the last (ours measured 2½", 2", and 1½" in diameter.)

Stack the circles with the smallest circle on top and a button centered over the circles. Hand-sew the circles and button together and onto the end of the neck warmer, centered about 1" from the edge.

## 3. ADD A CLOSURE

Hand-sew a snap, with one side beneath the flower and the other at a corresponding spot on the opposite end of the neck warmer.

Cutting tip: We used pinking shears for a decorative edge, but they could be cut with straight scissors.

**Stitching tip:** Edgestitching on these fabrics accomplishes two tasks at once; it creates a flouncy lettuce edge while joining the inner and outer layers.

**Finishing tip:** We like sew-in snaps for their utter lack of fussiness. With a needle, thread, and a few quick stitches, you have a secure closure for your garment, which sometimes is a much better option than sewing buttonholes.

# Four-Panel Hat

**This cold-weather essential** is twice as cozy when it's sewn from a favorite old sweater, and it gets extracool with the addition of a striking graphic appliqué, cut from a t-shirt or fabric. If your fabric has good stretch, this hat should fit just about anybody.

## 1. TRACE AND CUT

Fold the fabric in half and position the template on top of it. Trace the template twice, then cut through both thicknesses of fabric for a total of four panels.

## 2. JOIN THE PANELS

With the right sides together, straight stretch stitch two panels together from the top point down to the bottom edge with a ½" seam. Press the seam open. Repeat with the remaining two panels. Then, stitch the two joined panels with the right sides together in the same way, so all four panels are joined together.

## 3. HEM THE BOTTOM EDGE

Roll the bottom edge ½" to the wrong side and then another 1½" and pin. Turn the hat right side out. Straight stretch stitch the hem in place 1" from the fold.

## 4. STITCH THE APPLIQUÉ

Cut out a small graphic from print yardage or an old t-shirt. Stitch the graphic appliqué to the hat where desired, straight stitching just inside the edges. Leave the edges rough.

### what you'll need

- ⅓ yard of felted wool or stretch fabric (stretch terry or wool or cotton jersey)

- Graphic cut from a t-shirt or print fabric

- Hat template (page 310)

- 1 spool of coordinating thread

one size fits all!

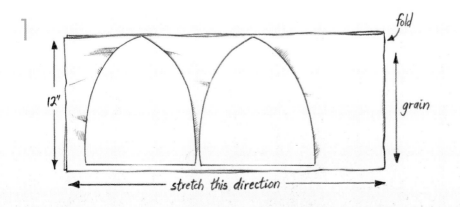

1

12"

fold

grain

stretch this direction

# Ugly Sweater Turned Pretty Cardigan

**Most of us have an unloved old sweater** lurking in the bottom of a drawer or the back of a closet. Make a trip to the notions store, pick up whatever trimmings strike your fancy, and get that woeful woolly garment back into circulation fast.

## what you'll need

- **Large wool sweater, washed and felted (see page 244)**
- **Velvet ribbon and other trimmings as desired**
- **1 spool of coordinating thread (matched to ribbon)**
- **Embroidery thread and needle**
- **Hook and eye closure**

## 1. CUT THE SWEATER

Cut off any unwanted sweater parts such as cuffs and turtlenecks. Fold the front panel in half from the neck to the bottom edge, aligning the side and shoulder seams. Cut along the fold to open the sweater front (see illustration on page 109).

## 2. ADD THE RIBBON TRIM

Trim one end of the ribbon into a point. Fold the pointed end over ½".

With a tiny zigzag (our stitch width was 1.5; stitch length 2), edgestitch the ribbon in place along the edges of the sweater's front opening, allowing the stitch to overcast the ribbon a bit. At the bottom edge of the sweater, trim away the excess ribbon. Repeat to sew more ribbon around the sleeve openings.

## 3. EMBELLISH AND ADD THE CLOSURE

Add more trim as desired, by machine or by hand, as appropriate. We stitched lengths of velvet rickrack over the ribbon along the front openings, hand-embroidered cross-stitches at the neckline and running stitches around the sleeves, and added two velvet flowers (cut from a ribbon) at the neck closure.

Hand-sew the hook and eye closure on the wrong side at the top of the center opening.

# 11 instant gifts,
## instant gratification

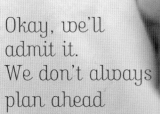

## Okay, we'll admit it. We don't always plan ahead

when it comes to gifts. Even when we have time to run out to the mall, we usually decide to take the cheaper, faster, and more meaningful route by making something at home. In the 20 or 30 minutes it takes to stop off and pick up flowers or a fancy bath potion on the way to your friend's birthday dinner, you could stitch up one of the projects in this chapter (there's quite a few superfast projects in the previous chapters too). Plus, don't you just adore thwarting consumerism from time to time? And isn't it nice to know that the one-of-a-kind, love-infused doodad we sewed in minutes will be treasured forever, long after the last of that bath potion would have swirled down the drain?

P.S. This chapter title includes the phrase "Instant Gratification." That's because it's perfectly fine to sit right down and stitch up a quick gift just to gratify yourself!

## A Few Notes on Stockpiling Instant-Gift Stash Supplies

**You'll always be ready to make a quick homemade present if you keep some basic supplies on hand.**

- Cut fabric carefully when you make projects, and you'll soon have a stash of lovely scraps. In addition, build up a stock of neutral fabrics like natural canvas, linen, and muslin, and be on the lookout for outgrown or no-longer-loved items with great prints, textures, or graphics.

- Buy fine ribbon when it goes on sale. You will use it sooner or later, whether for embellishing or wrapping.

- Stock up on notions that will dress up a last-minute gift — brightly colored thread, eye-catching buttons, snap closures, different types of elastic, Velcro, and silk cord.

- Buy some good notepaper and save shirt or cereal-box cardboard so you can always add a sewn card or gift tag (you'll find those projects in the previous chapter).

# Simple Jersey Shawl

**You love your sleeveless dresses,** but weather and air-conditioning often call for a cover-up. Pick up some pretty yardage to match your favorite frock and stitch one up in no time. Just wrap it around you or add a snazzy brooch to pin it gracefully across your chest.

## 1. ATTACH VELVET RIBBON

Cut the ribbon into two 18" lengths. Pin each length of ribbon on the right side of the fabric, ¾" in from the short (selvage) edges. Stitch around all the edges of the ribbon with a narrow zigzag.

## 2. EMBROIDER LINES

With the embroidery thread, hand-sew a line of running stitches parallel to each short end, between the ribbon and the edge.

## what you'll need

- ½ yard of 66"-wide rayon or bamboo jersey*
- 1 spool of thread to match ribbon
- 1 yard of velvet ribbon
- Embroidery floss and embroidery needle

  *Yardage is for a shawl that measures 18" × 66".

## design variations

Roll the edge and secure it with a narrow zigzag in coordinating thread. //// Use one of our flower or leaf templates (pages 302–311) to add appliqués from the same jersey for a tone-on-tone look. //// Stitch on color-matched seed beads for subtle sparkle.

# Vintage Hankie Tissue Case

**Debra inherited a box of fine vintage handkerchiefs** from her grandmother.
They were made of Madeira and Irish linen, embroidered with monograms
(a curly S for Sylvia) and featuring all kinds of gorgeously stitched edges.
If you have a similar treasure trove (or spot one in a flea market), here's one
way to put old hankies to a new use: holding packets of the paper version
that ultimately supplanted them.

## 1. MEASURE, MARK, AND CUT
Choose the prettiest part of the hankie and cut out a piece that measures
6" × 10".

## 2. FOLD AND STITCH
Press each short edge 1½" to the wrong side. Turn the fabric right side up.
Fold the short edges so they overlap at the center by ¼" (this will be the top
opening).

Press the side edges ½" toward the back (the side opposite the overlapped
flaps). Straight stitch the side folds in place with a ¼" seam. Leave the opening
unstitched for inserting the tissue pack and removing tissues.

**what you'll need**

- **Vintage
  handkerchief**

- **1 spool of
  coordinating or
  contrasting
  thread**

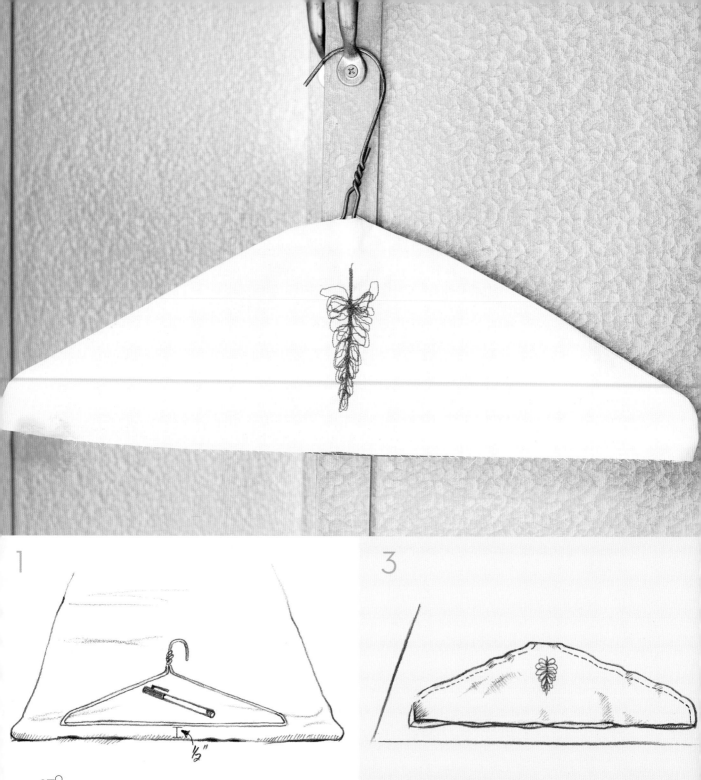

1

½"

3

# Guest-Worthy Hanger

Once you learn to draw with your sewing machine, your desire to pretty up everything can become a bit overwhelming. Take the wire hanger. If we had a guest room, a dozen of these would hang in each closet to greet our guests.

## 1. MEASURE, MARK, AND CUT

Press the muslin, and fold it. Position the bottom edge of the hanger ½" from the fold. Draw a line all around the hanger (skipping over the hook portion), allowing for ½" seam allowance on all sides. Cut along the marked lines and along the fold to make two separate panels. Then, in order for the panels to be identical on each side of the hanging hook, fold them in half, bringing the points together and trimming them if necessary to even out the markings (wire hangers can be less than symmetrical).

## 2. SKETCH YOUR DESIGN

Use a vanishing ink marker to draw a design at least 2" from the top. We freehand sketched a pinecone, but you could also embellish with lines, abstract shapes, or add a simple appliqué. Using a straight stitch and the Drawing with Thread or Doodling with Thread technique (see page 134), stitch over the guidelines.

## 3. JOIN THE PANELS

With the right sides together, straight stitch a ½" seam on both sides from the neck to the bottom edge. Turn it right side out and insert the hanger.

### what you'll need

- Wire coat hanger
- ½ yard of muslin fabric
- 1 spool of contrasting thread

# Modern Onesie

**Four lines and a circle are all it takes** to whip up this look for your favorite cool baby. This project is almost embarrassingly easy, but the tiny tot won't know that! Birds, trucks, monograms, or just about any other shape, topstitched with contrasting lines, can be substituted for our simple circle.

## what you'll need

- **Onesie**
- **Scrap jersey**
- **1 spool of contrasting thread**

## 1. CUT THE APPLIQUÉ

On the scrap jersey, draw a circle or any desired shape and cut it out with sharp scissors.

## 2. STITCH THE LINES

Pin the appliqué on the onesie in the desired location. Taking care to only stitch through the front layer of the onesie, and starting and finishing about ½" outside the appliqué, straight stretch stitch a line across the appliqué. Repeat, stitching three more lines to create a starburst pattern.

Stitching tip: When the stitching reaches the edges of the appliqué, use your fingers to gently apply tension to the jersey on either side of the needle to keep the fabric flowing smoothly.

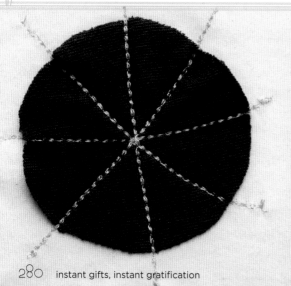

Cutting tip:
To cut a nice
even circle, fold a
square of fabric in
quarters, and then
cut a quarter-circle.
Unfold and trim the
curves as needed.

# Ponytail Flower

**Whip up a few of these charming hair accessories** to please a flower child of any age. We used solid fabric scraps, but you can experiment with a mix of prints for a cute twist.

## 1. MARK AND CUT

Trace the flower templates onto the wrong side of different color fabrics and cut them out. Layer the flower shapes right side up with the smallest on top.

## 2. SKETCH THE DESIGN

Use the free-motion drawing technique (see page 134) to straight stitch a circular flower center in the middle of the stacked fabrics. Then stitch narrow petal shapes. Move at your own pace and leave the needle in the fabric when you readjust your hands so the fabric doesn't shift (our foot pressure was 0 and stitch length was 1).

## 3. STITCH THE EDGES

Zigzag with increased presser-foot pressure (our pressure was 2, stitch width was 3, and stitch length was 1) around the perimeter of the larger flower, turning the fabric as you stitch.

## 4. ATTACH THE ELASTIC

With the tapestry needle and embroidery thread, make a stitch through the center of the flower, beginning and ending on the wrong side. Knot the thread around the elastic. Take one or two additional stitches, turning the flower to create an X or starburst on the right side, and firmly securing the elastic by stitching over it with each stitch. Triple knot the thread and trim.

## what you'll need

- Colorful fabric scraps (we used canvas, but any home-decor or quilting-weight fabric will do)

- Spools of contrasting thread

- Hair elastic

- Embroidery thread

- Tapestry needle

- Large and small flower templates (page 309)

# Canvas Loose-Leaf Paper

**Stitch a love note** on one of these sheets, and it will be saved for posterity. Or make a set for a gift; it's the perfect stationery for anyone who enjoys playing with needles and thread. One young friend used them for secret notes with a vanishing-ink fabric pen, so she could reuse the sheets again and again. Clever!

## 1. MEASURE, MARK, AND CUT

Fold the fabric in half with the short edges aligned so you'll be cutting two sheets at one time. Measure and mark the following measurements as many times as desired:

— **sheet:** 7" × 5"

## 2. STITCH THE LINES

On each fabric sheet, mark the following guidelines: a (horizontal) top line 1½" down from the top edge and a (vertical) margin line 1" in from the left edge.

With the blue thread and a straight stretch stitch, sew the top line. Align the right edge of the presser foot with the sewn top line and stitch the next line beneath it. Repeat, aligning the right edge of the foot with each preceding line as you continue to stitch the horizontal lines all the way down the fabric.

With red thread and a straight stretch stitch, sew the margin line.

If you like, stitch black-thread letters with your machine (see tips for writing with thread, page 135), or hand-sew a message with embroidery thread.

2

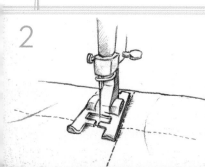

# Leather Bookmark

**Present this little item tucked into a book** chosen especially for the recipient, and you've got a truly meaningful gift. It's a thrifty way to use up scraps left over from other leather projects, but you can also purchase inexpensive leather sheets at a craft store.

## 1. MARK, MEASURE, AND CUT

Measure and mark the following pieces on the wrong side of the leather, then cut them out:

— **bookmark:** 8" × 2"

— **tassel:** 8" × ¼"

## 2. MARK AND STITCH YOUR DESIGN

If necessary, mark the location of the square designs as desired with a fine pencil line on the leather. Using one color at a time and a straight stitch, stitch the square outlines (our stitch length was 4). When you're happy with the number of square outlines in one thread color, change the thread color and continue stitching the square outlines. Vary the sizes and allow the square outlines to overlap.

## 3. MAKE A TASSEL

Cut a small slit at the top of the bookmark, about ¼" from the edge. Thread the tassel piece through the slit and make a slip-knot.

## what you'll need

- Leather scrap, at least 8" × 2¼"
- 2 to 4 spools of contrasting thread

Design tip:
Add a name or monogram to personalize this little gift even more.

# Beaded Cuff

**Here's a lovely way to use up scraps** of just about any fabric you like. We chose a pretty strip of jersey that we upcycled from a screen-printed shirt. With some seed beads sewn on, it looks really special.

## 1. HEM THE FABRIC

Press the edges of both long sides ½" to the wrong side.

Fold roughly in thirds, so that the finished width of the cuff will be about 1½".

From the right side, zigzag all around perimeter of the bracelet, very close to the edge.

## 2. ADD SNAPS

Following the manufacturer's instructions, attach two snaps at the opening of the cuff as shown.

## 3. EMBELLISH WITH BEADS

With a beading needle, thread, and seed beads, stitch beads to the right side of the cuff as desired.

## design variations

Use beads to outline elements of the fabric print or the graphic pattern from a repurposed t-shirt. //// Use free-motion sketching (see page 134) to add a design to a solid-color fabric, then stitch beads to add dimension to the design. You might want to fold the cuff first as in step 1 and then unfold it to stitch the design in the correct spot. //// Make an elegant cuff by using dark velvet fabric with matching velvet ribbon, sprinkled with coordinating seed or bugle beads.

(see page 134)

### what you'll need

- 5" × 8" piece of fabric (we used a swatch from a t-shirt, but just about any fabric will do)

- 2 sets of ⁷⁄₁₆" pearl snaps

- 1 spool of coordinating or contrasting thread

- Seed beads

- Beading needle and thread

# Modern Guest Towels

These updated versions of the lacy numbers your mom got as a wedding present make even the most modest bathroom seem chic. The best part is that they'll give you an excuse to buy a tiny amount of that out-of-your-price range fabric you've been dreaming about. They make a really classy hostess gift too.

## what you'll need

- **1 yard of white linen or Birdseye cotton (44" wide)***

- **¼ yard of cotton print fabric**

- **1 spool of coordinating thread**

*Makes four towels. You can also purchase plain guest towels and decorate them.

## 1. MEASURE, MARK, AND CUT

Fold the white fabric with the right sides together and the selvages aligned. Measure, mark, and cut the following:

*Cut from the white fabric:*

— **main body (cut 4):** 22" × 14" (cut across the fabric then parallel to the fold, include selvages)

*Cut from the printed fabric:*

— **top trim (cut 4):** 3½" × 13"

— **bottom edge trim (cut 4):** 2" × 13"

## 2. STITCH THE ROLLED SIDES

Make a ¼" double-fold hem on both long sides (chapter 1, page 19) of each towel. Stitch the hems with a narrow zigzag.

## 3. ATTACH THE TOP TRIM

Press ¼" to the wrong side around all four edges of each of the top trim pieces. Trim the corners at a 45-degree angle to make them easier to hem.

For each towel, pin the top piece so it folds over and encloses the panel's top raw edge.

Pin the rest of the trim in place on the front side of the panel (no other edge wraps around to the back side). Narrow zigzag (our stitch width was 2) the folded-over edge of the trim ⅛" from the top edge of the towel. Edgestitch the remaining three sides with the same narrow zigzag.

Repeat to sew the top trim to all the main body panels.

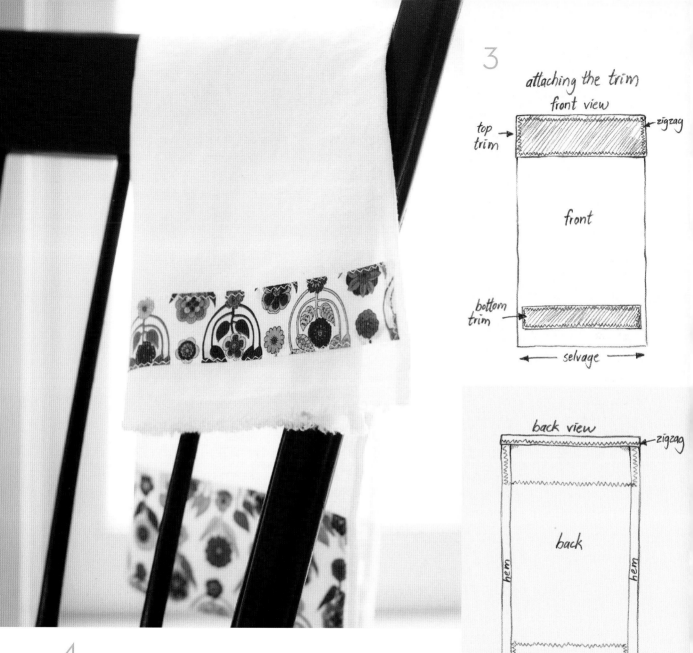

attaching the trim
front view

top trim →

zigzag

front

bottom trim →

← selvage →

back view

zigzag →

back

hem    hem

← selvage →

## 4. ATTACH THE BOTTOM TRIM

Press ¼" to the wrong side around all four edges of each of the bottom trim pieces. Pin the trim on the main body panel, 1" from the bottom edge. Edgestitch the trim in place with the same narrow zigzag. Trim the edges and, if desired, leave raw.

# Linen Votive

For a quick excursion into the fabulous realm of thread sketching, this fast and pretty votive is ideal. Begin by stitching a field of straight lines, then cut loose by layering free-motion circles over the lines. The final result will give your home a warm glow. This also makes the perfect holder for a small posy.

## what you'll need

- **Half-pint mason jar***
- **¼ yard of linen**
- **2 spools of contrasting thread**
- **Pinking shears**

*Any straight-sided glass jar in your recycling bin will work for this project.

## 1. MEASURE, MARK, AND CUT

For a half-pint mason jar, measure, mark, and cut out the following piece:

— **votive cover:** 3" × 8½"

To use a jar other than a half-pint mason jar, just measure the height of the jar from the bottom to just beneath the lid threads. Next, measure the circumference and add ½" for seam allowance. Mark and cut the fabric accordingly.

## 2. STITCH THE LINES

Straight stretch stitch straight lines across the width of the fabric at ¼" intervals. Leave the edges raw.

## 3. SKETCH YOUR DESIGN

Practice the Sketching with Thread technique (page 134) on a scrap of the project fabric. With the contrasting thread and using a straight stretch stitch (set the presser-foot pressure on 1), sketch circles over the lines. Turn the fabric slowly as you stitch.

## 4. FINISH THE COVER

Pin the short edges with the wrong sides together. Straight stitch two seams, ¼" and ⅛" from the edge. Pink the raw edges. Slip the cover over the jar.

# Log Lugger

Indoor/outdoor fabric comes in fantastic colors these days, and you only need a yard to make this practical gift. The ruggedly attractive jute strapping can be found at the hardware or fabric store.

## what you'll need

- 1 yard of 60"-wide canvas (the outdoor kind is best for this project)
- 102" (2 yards + 30") of 3½" jute strapping
- 1 spool of contrasting upholstery thread
- Denim needle
- Large pins (safety pins may work best)

## 1. HEM THE EDGES

With the iron set on low, press both short edges of the canvas 1" to the wrong side. Zigzag the edges in place. Repeat to hem the long edges, letting the hems overlap at the corners.

## 2. PLACE THE STRAPS

Fold the fabric in half so the short edges align, and lightly press the crease. Unfold and lay out the fabric in a single layer with the right side facing up. Measure and mark a dot on the pressed crease 5" in from each edge.

Start pinning the strapping to the fabric with one end at the pressed crease and the outer edge aligned at the dot, as shown. Pin every 2", extending the strapping toward the top edge. At the top edge, curve the strapping in a U shape to create the handle (each handle measures 18"). Continue pinning the strapping straight back down to the pressed crease so the outer edge of the strapping aligns with the other dot.

Continue pinning the strapping across the pressed crease onto the opposite side of the fabric in the same way (forming a U-shaped handle on the bottom edge).

The two ends of the strapping should meet at the fold.

## 3. ATTACH THE STRAPS

Attach the strapping to the fabric by zigzagging along both long edges. Add extra stitched lines for reinforcement across the straps near the top and bottom edges of the canvas panel and at the point where the strap ends meet.

For carrying ease, fold under the edges along the center of the handles and stitch them in place with a straight stretch stitch.

2

overlap and
stitch here

start
here

crease

5"

5"

pins

# Wild Thing Newborn Bonnet

**Here's a sweet slip-on hat for a newly arrived beastie** boy or girl. Choose the softest wool jersey or a fine cotton fleece (cotton jersey will work well for a summer baby). Make the matching sweater on page 296, and you've got an outfit.

## 1. MEASURE, MARK, AND CUT

With the wrong side of the fabric up, measure, mark, and cut the following piece:

— **hat:** 9" × 14" (cut longer dimension on straight grain)

## 2. STITCH THE HAT

Topstich ⅛" from the short edges of the hat piece with a decorative utility stitch.

With the right side facing up, fold the short edges so they overlap by ¾" in the center; pin them together.

Straight stitch a scant ¼" seam along the top edge to sew the hat closed.

Starting at the bottom edge, zigzag the overlapping edges together for 1". Take care to only stitch the overlapping edges and not through to the other side of the hat.

Starting at the top edge, hand-stitch the overlapping edges together for 1", as for the bottom edge.

Turn the hat right side out.

2

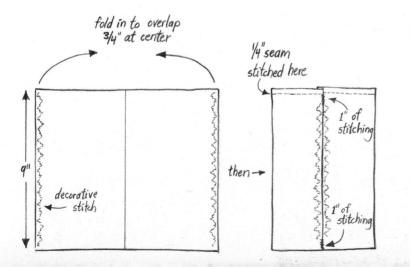

## what you'll need

- ¼ **yard of wool jersey or cotton fleece**
- **1 spool of contrasting thread**
- **Hand-sewing needle**

# Sweet Thing
# Newborn Cardigan

**Get ready for total adorableness** when you slip this little number on your favorite new babe. Add a matching Wild Thing Newborn Bonnet (page 294) to up the cute quotient even higher. By the way, adjust the measurements as needed, and this also works as a quick new outfit for a beloved doll or teddy bear.

(page 294)

## what you'll need

- ½ yard of wool jersey or fine cotton fleece (a sturdy cotton jersey also works for a summer baby)

- Contrasting fabric scrap (we used felted wool)

- 1 spool of contrasting thread

- 4"-diameter paper circle

- Sew-on snap

- Embroidery thread and needle

## 1. MEASURE, MARK, AND CUT

With the right side of the fabric facing up, measure, mark, and cut the following piece:

— **sweater:** 15" × 20"

## 2. MAKE THE NECK OPENING

Fold the fabric in half with the short edges aligned and the right sides together; fold it in half again so the short edges align once more. The fabric should now measure 7½" × 10".

Fold the paper circle into quarters. Lay the folded circle over the inner corner of the folded fabric (the corner with no open edges) and trace around it. Cut along the traced line through all the thicknesses of fabric.

2

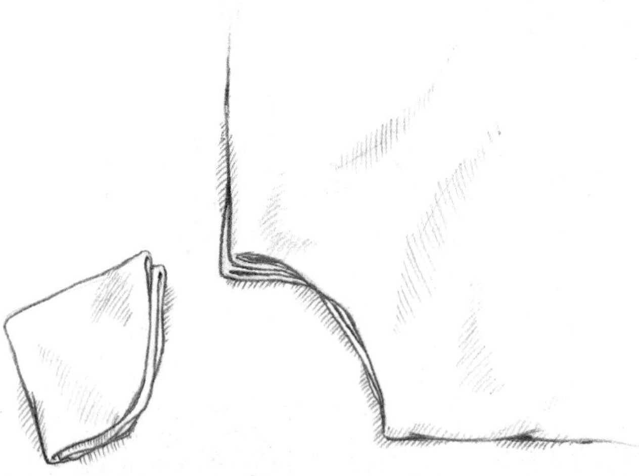

### 3. DRAW AND CUT THE SWEATER SHAPE

Lay out the still folded fabric with the neck opening at the top left. Mark the sleeve depth and hem width measurements as shown, and then freehand draw a swooping curve to connect the sleeve with the bottom edge. Cut along the marked line through all the fabric layers.

### 4. SEW THE SIDE SEAMS

Unfold the fabric so the front and back panels are aligned, with the right sides together. Use a knit or stretch stitch to sew the sides and sleeves with ½" seams.

### 5. MAKE A CARDIGAN AND ADD THE SNAP AND APPLIQUÉ

Mark the center line of the front panel, and cut along the line.

With the embroidery thread and needle, hand-stitch the snap closure in place at the top corner of the neck opening, making sure to sew the pieces very securely so they don't fall off and become a choking hazard.

Trace or draw a 1½" × 1" heart on the contrasting scrap and cut it out. Pin it to the sweater to cover the exposed snap stitching near the neckline. Attach it to the sweater with hand-sewn running stitches around the inside edges.

# Stitched Silk Bracelet

**This tie-on wrist adornment is a last-minute gift** any girlfriend would be thrilled to receive. Choose a motif to suit that gal (though if you're drawing a blank, flowers are always a good bet). We used a scrap of stretch silk, but a lightweight, silky jersey in wool, rayon, or cotton would be nice too. Remember, the design needn't be perfect; its wabi-sabi is what makes it special.

## 1. MARK AND CUT

Fold the fabric with right sides together and short edges aligned. Trace the template and cut along the marked lines.

## 2. STITCH THE EDGES

Zigzag all the edges around the bracelet.

## 3. SKETCH YOUR DESIGN

If desired, draw a design on the right side of the fabric (or just freestyle stitch). Turn the bracelet lengthwise to sew, so you have ample fabric to grab. Using the Doodling with Thread or Sketching with Thread technique (see page 134) (our presser-foot pressure was 0), stitch your design.

### what you'll need

- Scrap of solid color stretch silk, 2" × 14" (a longer piece if cut on the crossgrain)

- 1 spool of contrasting thread

- Bracelet template (page 304)

**Stitching tip:** The center of the presser foot should align with the fabric edge, so the stitches truly lie right on the edges.

# Pretty Pendant Necklace

**A showcase for bits of gorgeous fabric,** this necklace is fast to make and easy to wear. Whether you make it with one stunning pendant, or string a few on the cord, you end up with an eye-catching, conversation-starting accessory.

## 1. FUSE THE FABRICS

Press the fusible web to the wrong side of the canvas as directed by the manufacturer. Peel off the paper backing and place the canvas on top of the print fabric, wrong sides together. Press the pieces to fuse them.

## 2. CUT THE FABRIC SHAPES

Carefully cut out motifs from the fabric, or trace a jar lid, cookie cutter, or other simple shape onto the fabric and cut out.

## 3. STITCH THE EDGE AND CORD HOLES

Use a small zigzag (our stitch width was 3, stitch length was 1, and presser-foot pressure was 2) to edgestitch around the perimeter of each shape.

To create reinforced holes for the neck cord, mark a dot on both sides of the center of the pendant, just inside the stitched edge. Using the Doodling with Thread technique (see page 134) and a straight stitch (our stitch length was 1; presser-foot pressure was 0), sew at least five circular orbits around the dot, leaving an open center through which the tapestry needle and cord will pass.

## 4. FINISH THE NECKLACE

Thread the tapestry needle with the cord and thread the pendants on the cord, running the needle through the center of the circular stitching. Make a knot behind each pendant hole if you don't want the pieces to slide along the cord. Tie the cord with a bow around the wearer's neck.

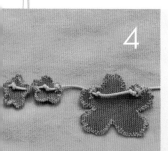

**design variations** Use this idea to show off a thread drawing done on a solid fabric. //// Add a few strategic hand-sewn beads. //// String a fabric pendant on a delicate gold or silver chain for striking contrast.

# Templates

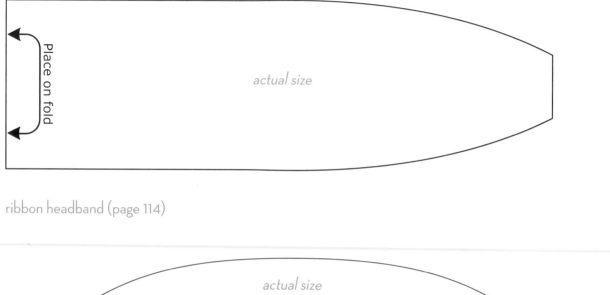

ribbon headband (page 114)

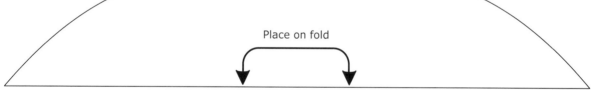

petal for cutout throw pillow (page 140) and custom ottoman cover (page 201)

pencil for appliquéd journal (page 184)

Place on fold

enlarge 150%

enlarge to desired size

rocks for cairn reverse-
appliqué tee (page 180)

actual size;
adjust for
smaller hands

tree for feast day appliqué tablecloth (page 194)

star for little star mittens (page 174)

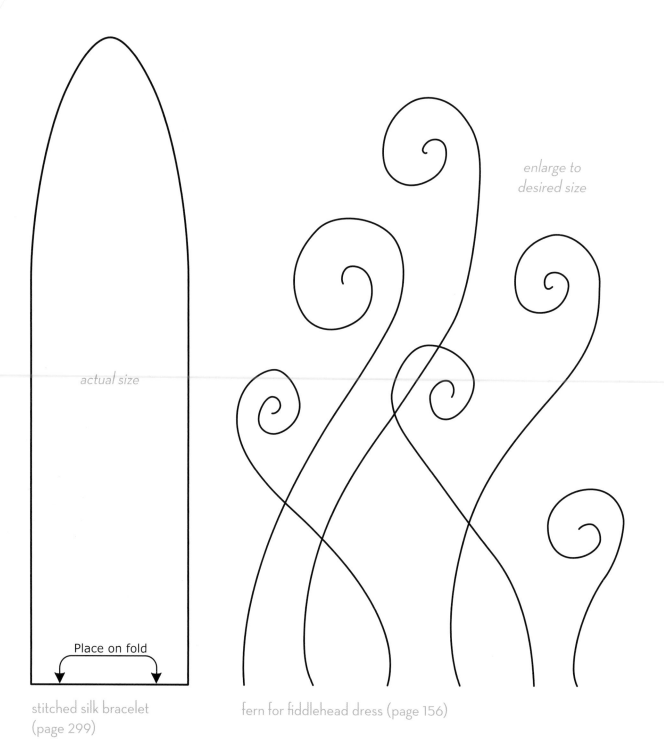

enlarge to
desired size

actual size

Place on fold

stitched silk bracelet
(page 299)

fern for fiddlehead dress (page 156)

*enlarge to
desired size*

*enlarge to
desired size*

*enlarge to
desired size*

bottles and apples for cider season table runner (page 186)

flowers for
sketched window sheers
(page 150)

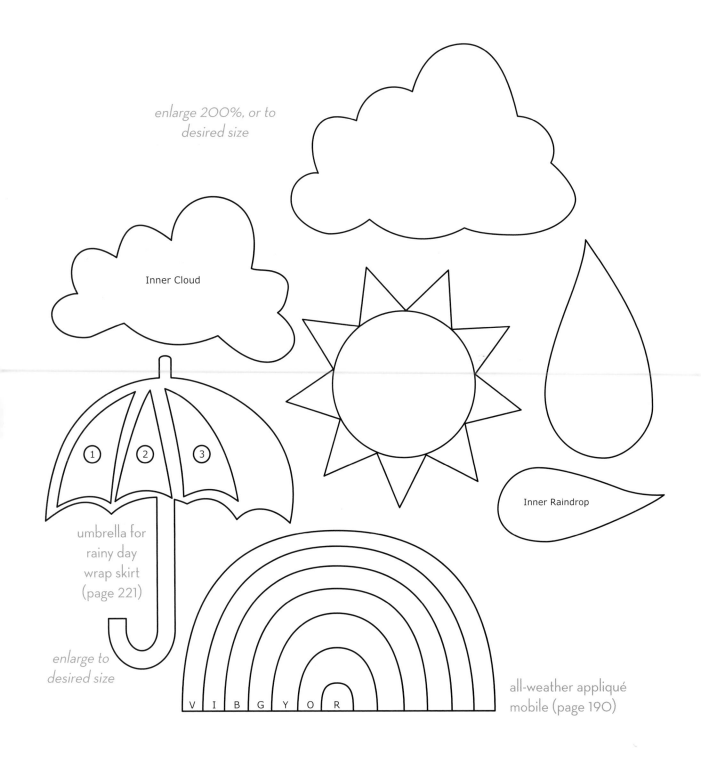

enlarge 200%, or to
desired size

Inner Cloud

① ② ③

umbrella for
rainy day
wrap skirt
(page 221)

Inner Raindrop

enlarge to
desired size

V I B G Y O R

all-weather appliqué
mobile (page 190)

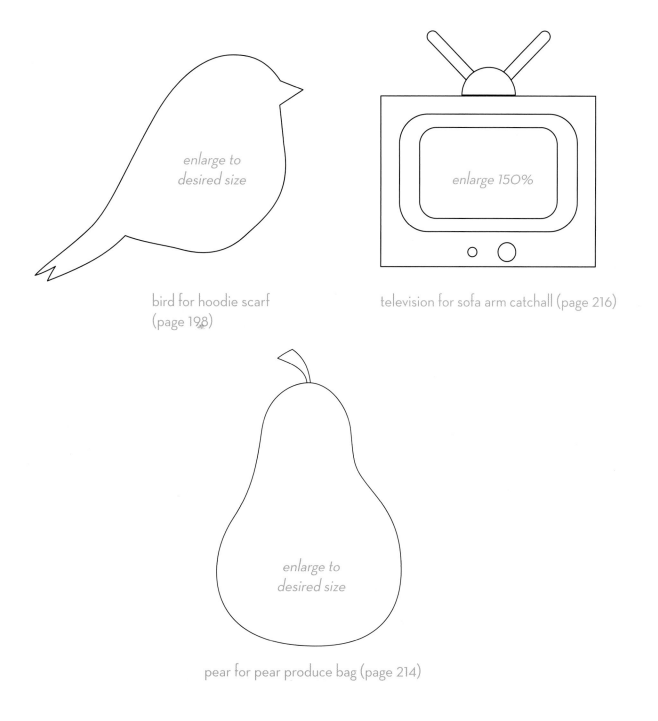

*enlarge to desired size*

*enlarge 150%*

bird for hoodie scarf
(page 198)

television for sofa arm catchall (page 216)

*enlarge to desired size*

pear for pear produce bag (page 214)

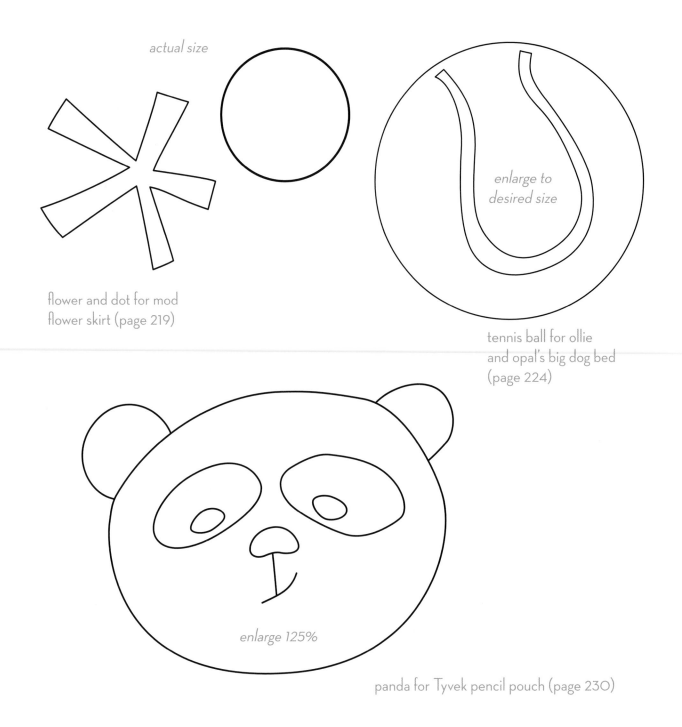

*actual size*

flower and dot for mod
flower skirt (page 219)

*enlarge to
desired size*

tennis ball for ollie
and opal's big dog bed
(page 224)

*enlarge 125%*

panda for Tyvek pencil pouch (page 230)

*actual size*

flowers for ponytail flower (page 282) and clever leather shoulder bag (page 255)

*enlarge to desired size*

flowers for reverse-appliqué skirt (page 188), modern stretch velvet skirt (page 192), and blossoming appliqué blanket (page 206)

enlarge 190%

umbrella for
rainy day wrap
skirt (page 221)

enlarge to
desired size

panel for four-panel hat (page 270)

enlarge to
desired size

swallow for birds in flight
headboard (page 162)

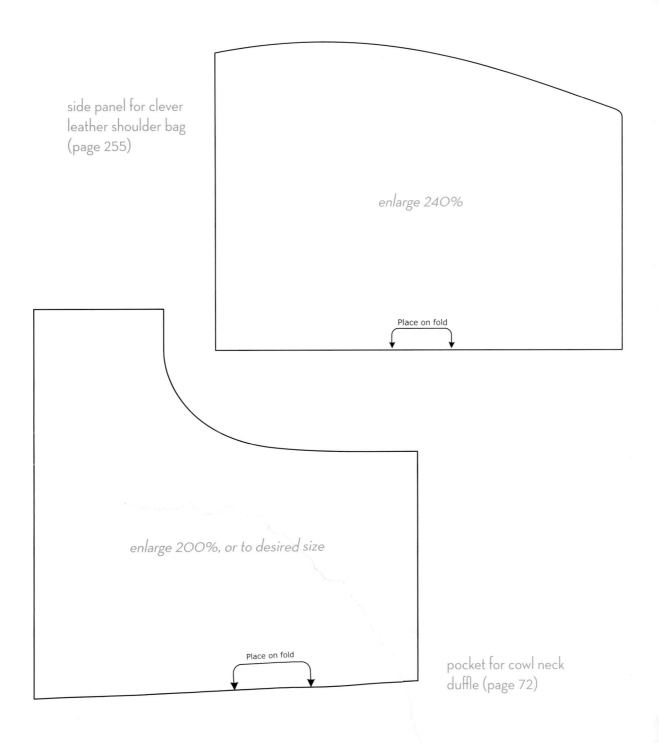

side panel for clever
leather shoulder bag
(page 255)

enlarge 240%

Place on fold

enlarge 200%, or to desired size

Place on fold

pocket for cowl neck
duffle (page 72)

# Our Favorite Sources for Fabric and Specialty Supplies

## Purl Soho

This is our favorite online fabric shop, hands down, but if you are ever in New York City, you **must** walk into their physical shop (but be prepared to covet and drop a few bucks). Joelle curates an amazing collection of fabrics from simple and fine to patterned gems from the likes of Kokka and Liberty of London. Purl is also our go-to source for wool felt. They were incredibly generous while we were making this book and donated as much fabric as we asked for — we *know!*

Visit them at www.purlsoho.com.

## Knit Fabrics

There are many places to visit online for jersey fabrics, including Etsy and eBay (these shops come and go, but we especially like High End Fabrics on eBay). You can also find perfectly great knits, if you shop with a discriminating eye, at large chain fabric stores.

## Trim and Fold Over Elastic

We have bought a lot of beautifully colorful fold over elastic at Etsy. Just go to the "supplies" section and type in "fold over elastic" in the search box. We love buying from these small businesses. You can find a lot of ribbon and other trims on Etsy, as well.

## Ribbon

For every color in the rainbow of velvet ribbon (which we just love so much), head on over to M&J Trimming at www.mjtrim.com (or visit their incredible physical store in New York City). They are big and will have whatever color ribbon you need, and offer a lot of other trims, too.

# Acknowledgments

Storey Publishing is the perfect home base for this book; it's been such a pleasure to collaborate with the amazing, encouraging people who work there. Our profound thanks to Deborah Balmuth for showing no hesitation and for kindly asking if we'd be interested in upping our 30 projects to 101; to Alethea Morrison for her brilliant artistic direction; to Carolyn Eckert for her clear and awesome vision for the book, the fun photo shoot and to the gods of fate who made it clear that she was destined to be our designer; to Alexandra Grablewski, our crazy-talented photographer, who could make even a dung ball look good with her gorgeous use of light; and to Beth Baumgartel for being such a positive and hard-working copy editor — you made it so painless!

We would also like to thank Alison Fargis for her thoughtful guidance; Cindy Littlefield for a crucial jump-start when we needed it most; and Sally Weaver, Bill Milne, and Ann Lewis for generous donations of talent and great taste when this project was first coming to life.

## From Nicole

My creative life does not exist in a vacuum, and I am blessed with a great number of people who have inspired and motivated me to realize many things. Honestly, I don't think this book would have happened without them. First, my dear friend Catherine Newman, who has not only opened many doors for me but has lovingly shoved me through them. Her creativity and never ending ideas have been deeply inspiring — not to mention her humor; my friend Tanya Rapinchuk for being able to do absolutely anything she wants to do — you blow me away and I strive to follow in your do-it-all footsteps; my sister Andrea Blum for her artful life — everything she touches becomes beautiful; my sweet pals, Maddie DelVicario and Kathleen Traphagen, for simply being talented, funny, loving, present and for caring for my kids when I was in the thick of it; my mom, Jackie Blum, for being the most supportive mom a girl could have; and, of course, my amazing family — Jonathan, my gorgeous, crazy-smart, visionary man; my wildly creative daughter, Ava, who will do whatever she sets her mind and heart to; and Harry, my darling and funny boy who makes and makes stuff.

And, there is no forgetting my talented coauthor, Debra, here. This book was her idea. What a good idea. Thank you!

## From Debra

When my family and I moved to western Massachusetts almost seven years ago, I found myself suddenly surrounded by astoundingly talented women; they inspired me to try my hand at capturing that creative energy in the pages of a book. Heartfelt thanks to all of you, and especially to Kandy Littrell, Kimberly Stoney, Caitlin Bosco, Katie Craig, and Margot Glass. Special thanks also to Scott Moyer and Joe Regal for publishing-biz guidance and to Emily Takoudes for spurring me to get my ideas out into the world. I am also so grateful for my treasured pals Deborah Lewis Legge and Kahane Corn Cooperman, who dazzle me and motivate me and whose incredible spirits guide me even when we are far apart. Heartfelt thanks to my father, Mark, and my mother, Reba, for being there always, and for showing me what sheer will and smarts can accomplish; and special and deepest gratitude to John, my captivating fellow wayfarer and love of my life, and Joe, my wondrous, brave, fun-seeking son — I'm so indebted to both of you for your love, patience, and tireless boosterism. You make every day possible. And finally, major thanks to Nicole, whose beautiful designs and joyful approach to life give this book its heart and soul.

# Index

Page numbers in *italics* indicate illustrations.

## A

a-line skirts, *27*, 46-48, *46*, *47*, *48*
all-weather appliqué mobile, 190-91, *191*, *306*, *307*
apple template, *305*
appliqué, 170-207
    all-weather mobile, 190-91, *191*, *306*, *307*
    big-dot duvet cover, 204-5, *204*, *205*
    blossoming blanket, 206-7, *206*, *207*, *309*
    cairn reverse-appliqué t-shirt, 180-81, *180*, *181*, *303*
    cider season table runner, 186-87, *186*, *187*, *305*
    custom ottoman cover, 201-3, *201*, *202*, *203*
    eyeglass case, 176-77, *176*
    feast day tablecloth, 194-97, *195*, *196*, *197*, *303*
    four-panel hat, 270-71, *270*, *271*, *310*
    hoodie scarf, 198-200, *198*, *199*, *200*, *307*
    little star mittens, 174-75, *174*, *175*, *303*
    modern stretch velvet skirt, 192-93, *192*, *193*, *309*
    reverse-appliqué skirt, 188-89, *188*, *189*
    ribbon-appliqué embellished hoodie, 182-83, *182*, *183*, *309*
    stacked dot scarf, 178-79, *178*, *179*
appliquéd journal, 184-85, *184*, *185*, *302*
armies, blanket-stitched, 246-47, *246*, *247*
art kit, travel, 153-55, *153*, *154*, *155*

## B

backtacking, 18
bamboo/modal jersey, 13, 221, 276

bath mat, reversible loopy, 264-65, *264*, *265*
beaded cuff, 287, *287*
belt, reversible graphic, 248-49, *248*, *249*
bias-cut, 15
bias strips, 20, *20*
bias tape, 19
big-dot duvet cover, 204-5, *204*, *205*
binding, 19-21, *20*, *21*
binding loops, 61, *61*
birds in flight headboard, 162-65, *163*, *164*, *165*, *310*
bird template, *310*
blankets
    blossoming appliqué, 206-7, *206*, *207*, *309*
    line-quilted, 117-19, *117*, *118*, *119*
    upcycling, 244
blanket-stitched armies, 246-47, *246*, *247*
bloomer's, girl's, 252-54, *252*, *253*, *254*
blossoming appliqué blanket, 206-7, *206*, *207*, *309*
bobbins, 17
bonnet, wild thing newborn, 294-95, *294*, *295*
bookmark, leather, 286, *286*
border-stitched linen place mats, 116, *116*
bottle template, *305*
boxes, nesting, 126-27, *127*
bracelet, stitched silk, 299, *299*, *304*
bustle skirt, 48, 90-92, *90*, *91*, *92*
bust measurements, 26, *26*

## C

cairn reverse-appliqué t-shirt, 180-81, *180*, *181*, *303*

canvas, 15
    all-weather appliqué mobile, 190
    custom ottoman cover, 201
    fabric photo frame, 122
    jute edged throw rug, 94
    log lugger, 292
    mail organizer, 238
    nesting boxes, 126
    personalized project folder, 111
    sofa arm catchall, 217
    travel art kit, 153
    wall art, 149
canvas loose-leaf paper, 284-85, *284*, *285*
cap sleeves, 42, *43*
card and envelope, custom-stitched, 240-41, *240*, *241*
cardboard, 228, 232-33, *233*
cardigans
    meandering, 108-9, *108*, *109*
    sweet thing newborn, 296-98, *296*, *297*, *298*
    ugly sweater turned pretty, 272-73, *272*, *273*
catchall, sofa arm, 216-18, *216*, *218*, *307*
chalk, 18
cider season table runner, 186-87, *186*, *187*, *305*
clever leather shoulder bag, 255-59, *255*, *257*, *258*, *259*, *309*, *311*
clipping, 18, *19*
coloring book wrap skirt, 50, 144-45, *144*, *145*
colors, solid, 13
compass, 18
cork trivet, 229, *229*
corners, 18, *19*, 21, *21*

cotton fabric, woven. *See* canvas; woven cotton fabrics
cotton jersey knit fabrics, 12–13
  keyhole t-shirt, 101
  layered hemline skirt, 88
  linen skirt wavy hemline, 131
  pretty pillowcase, 107
  reverse-appliqué skirt, 188
  stacked dot scarf, 178
  stretch-panel skirt, 54
  super-jersey neckerchief, 113
  tubular sundress, 158
  two-panel a-line skirts, 46–48
cowl neck duffle, 36, 72–74, *72, 73, 74*
cross grain, 14, *14*
cuff, beaded, 287, *287*
curtains
  sketched window sheers, 150–52, *150, 151, 152, 305*
  upcycling, 244
curves, 18, *19*
custom-stitched card and envelope, 240–41, *240, 241*
cutout throw pillow, 140–43, *141, 143, 302*
cutting mats, 18

**D**

decorative stitches, 104–6, *104–5, 106*
  border-stitched linen place mats, 116, *116*
  cider season table runner, 187, *187*
  custom-stitched card and envelope, 240–41, *240, 241*
  fabric photo frame, 122–23, *123*
  linen skirt wavy hemline, 130–31, *130, 131*
  line-quilted blankets, 117–19, *117, 118, 119*
  meandering cardigan, 108–9, *108, 109*
  nesting boxes, 126–27, *127*
  personalized project folder, 110–12, *110–11, 112*
  pretty pillowcase, 107, *107*
  stitched lamp shade, 124–25, *125*
  super-jersey lingerie bag, 120–21, *120, 121*
  super-jersey neckerchief, 113, *113*
  swishy sundress, 128–29, *128, 129*
  *See also* free-motion stitching
dish cover, potluck, 166–67, *166, 167*
dog bed, Ollie and Opal's big, 224–25, *224, 225, 308*
doodled scarf, 136–37, *136, 137*
doodling with thread, 134
  *See also* free-motion stitching
double-fold binding, 20
double-fold hems, 19
dresses
  fiddlehead, 36, 156–57, *157, 304*
  four-panel garment, 38, *38–45, 39, 40, 41, 45*
  measurements for, 26, *26*
  ruffled dressy, 40, 78–83, *78, 79, 81, 82, 83*
  shirred empire waist, 36, 75–77, *75, 76, 77*
  two-panel garment, 34–37, *35, 37*
  two-tee, 40, 262–63, *262, 263*
  *See also* sundresses
dress shirt wrap skirt, 50, 266–67, *267*
duck cloth, 15
duvet cover, big-dot, 204–5, *204, 205*

**E**

edgestitching, 128, *128*
elastic, fold over, 19
embroidery, 84, 87, *87*
  *See also* decorative stitches
empire waist
  shirred, 36, 75–77, *75, 76, 77*
  swishy sundress, 128–29, *128, 129*
exposed seam tunic, 40, 86–87, *86, 87*
eyeglass case, 176–77, *176*

**F**

fabric markers, vanishing-ink, 18
fabric photo frame, 122–23, *123*
fabrics
  preparation of, 11, 12, 14, 15
  right vs. wrong side of, 15
  selection of, 11
  types of, 12–15
feast day appliqué tablecloth, 194–97, *195, 196, 197, 303*
feather stitch, *22*
felt, 15, 140
felted sweaters, 244
  blanket-stitched armies, 246
  four-panel hat, 271
  lettuce-edged neck warmer, 268
  ugly sweater turned pretty cardigan, 272
  wool jumper, 250
fiddlehead dress, 36, 156–57, *157, 304*
flare, 26, *27*
fleece, 198
floor cushion, vintage tablecloth, 260–61, *261*
flower templates, *305, 309*

fold over elastic, 19
four-panel garment, 38–45, *39, 40, 41, 45*
    exposed seam tunic, 87
    ruffled dressy dress, 78
four-panel hat, 270–71, *270, 271, 310*
free-motion stitching, 17, 132–69
    birds in flight headboard, 162–65, *163,*
        *164, 165*
    coloring book wrap skirt, 144–45, *144,*
        *145*
    cutout throw pillow, 140–43, *141, 143*
    doodled scarf, 136–37, *136, 137*
    fiddlehead dress, 156–57, *157*
    happy home memo board, 168–69,
        *168, 169*
    line art lunchbox, 146–47, *147*
    pebble tee, 138–39, *138, 139*
    potluck dish cover, 166–67, *166, 167*
    sketched window sheers, 150–52, *150,*
        *151, 152*
    travel art kit, 153–55, *153, 154, 155*
    tubular sundress, 158–61, *158, 159,*
        *160, 161*
    wall art, 148–49, *148*
freezer paper, 209, 210
fused plastic wallet, 236–37, *236*
fusible web, 173

## G

gift tags, sewn cardboard, 232–33, *233*
gracefully gathered neckline shirt, 36,
    68–69, *68, 69*
grainline, 14, *14, 15*
guest towels, modern, 288–89, *289*
guest-worthy hanger, 278–79, *278*

## H

hanger, guest-worthy, 278–79, *278*
happy home memo board, 168–69, *168,*
    *169*
hat, four-panel, 270–71, *270, 271, 310*
headband, ribbon, 114–15, *114, 115, 302*
headboard, birds in flight, 162–65, *163,*
    *164, 165, 310*
hems, double-fold, 19
home-decor weight fabric
    birds in flight headboard, 162
    custom ottoman cover, 201
    feast day appliqué tablecloth, 194
    jute edged throw rug, 94
    ribbon trimmed tote, 99
hoodie, ribbon-appliqué embellished,
    182–83, *182, 183*
hoodie scarf, 198–200, *198, 199, 200, 307*

## I

interlock knits, 12, 14
irons and ironing boards, 18

## J

jersey knit fabrics, 12–13
    bustle skirt, 90
    exposed seam tunic, 87
    fiddlehead dress, 156
    four-panel garment, 38
    gracefully gathered neckline shirt, 68
    mod flower skirt, 219
    pebble tee, 139
    pleated neckline top, 71
    ruched tunic, 67
    ruffled ribbon sundress, 63
    ruffled wrap, 96
    swishy sundress, 128
    two-panel garments, 34–37, *34, 35,*
        *36, 37*
    *See also* cotton jersey knit fabrics
journal, appliquéd, 184–85, *184, 185, 302*

jumpers, wool, 36, 250–51, *250, 251*
jute edged throw rug, 93–95, *93, 94, 95*

## K

keyhole t-shirt, 36, 101–3, *101, 102, 103*
knit fabrics, 12–15, *14,* 20
    *See also* jersey knit fabrics
knit stitch, *22*
kraft paper, 18, 29

## L

lamp shade, stitched, 124–25, *125*
layered hemline skirt, 48, 88–89, *88, 89*
leafy ruffle tunic, 36, 84–85, *84, 85*
leather bookmark, 286, *286*
leather shoulder bag, 255–59, *255, 257,*
    *258, 259, 309, 311*
lettuce-edged neck warmer, 268–69,
    *268, 269*
line art lunchbox napkins, 146–47, *147*
linen
    border-stitched linen place mats, 116
    cider season table runner, 187
    fabric photo frame, 122
    guest towels, 288
    monogrammed shaving pouch, 212
    wall art, 149
linen skirt wavy hemline, 130–31, *130, 131*
linen votive, 290–91, *291*
line-quilted blankets, 117–19, *117, 118, 119*
lingerie bag, super-jersey, 120–21, *120, 121*
little star mittens, 174–75, *174, 175, 303*
log lugger, 292–93, *293*
Lycra, 13

## M

mail organizer, 238–39, *239*
meandering cardigan, 108–9, *108, 109*

measurements, 24–26, *26*, *27*
memo board, happy home, 168–69, *168*, *169*
mitered corners, 21, *21*
mittens, little star, 174–75, *174*, *175*, *303*
mobile, all-weather appliqué, 190–91, *191*, *306*, *307*
modern stretch velvet skirt, 48, 192–93, *192*, *193*, *309*
mod flower skirt, 48, 219–20, *219*, *220*, *308*
monogrammed shaving pouch, 212–13, *213*

N
napkins, line art lunchbox, 146–47, *147*
neckerchief, super-jersey, 113, *113*
necklace, pretty pendant, 300–301, *300*, *301*
necklines, 31, *31*
    cowl, 72–74, *72*, *73*, *74*
    gracefully gathered, 36, 68, *68*
    pleated, 36, 70–71, *70*, *71*
    ribbons for, 63
neck warmer, lettuce-edged, 268–69, *268*, *269*
needles, sewing machine, 17
nesting boxes, 126–27, *127*
notching, 18, *19*

O
oilcloth, 167
Ollie and Opal's big dog bed, 224–25, *224*, *225*, *308*
onesie, modern, 280–81, *280*, *281*
ottoman cover, custom, 201–3, *201*, *202*, *203*, *302*
overcast stitch, *22*

P
panda template, *308*

paper, 228
paper, canvas loose-leaf, 284–85, *284*, *285*
patterns, making your own, 27–30, *28*, *29*, *30*, *31*
pear produce bag, 214–15, *215*, *307*
pebble design, 136, *136*, 138, *139*, *139*
pebble tee, 36, 138–39, *138*, *139*
pencil pouch, tyvek, 230–31, *230*, *308*
personalized project folder, 110–12, *110–12*, *112*
petal template, 140
photo frame, fabric, 122–23, *123*
pillowcases, 107, *107*
pillows, cutout throw, 140–43, *141*, *143*, *302*
pins, 18
pique fabric, 63
place mats, border-stitched linen, 116, *116*
pleated neckline top, 36, 70–71, *70*, *71*
pockets, 74, *74*
ponytail flower, 282–83, *282*, *283*, *309*
pot holders, vintage, 245, *245*
potluck dish cover, 166–67, *166*, *167*
preshrinking, 12
presser feet, 17, 134, *135*
pretty pendant necklace, 300–301, *300*, *301*
print fabrics, 13
produce bag, pear, 214–15, *215*, *307*
project folder, personalized, 110–12, *110–11*, *112*

Q
quilting presser foot, 17

R
rainy day wrap skirt, 50, 221–23, *221*, *222*, *223*, *310*
raw-edge appliqué, 172, *172*
raw-edge binding, 20
rayon, jersey knit, 13

reusing fabrics. *See* upcycling
reverse-appliqué, 173, *173*
reverse-appliqué skirt, 48, 188–89, *188*, *189*, *309*
reversible graphic belt, 248–49, *248*, *249*
reversible loopy bath mat, 264–65, *264*, *265*
ribbon-appliqué embellished hoodie, 182–83, *182*, *183*
ribbon headband, 114–15, *114*, *115*, *302*
ribbons, 60, 63
ribbon trimmed tote, 98–100, *98*, *100*
rib knits, 14
rotary cutters, 18
ruched tunic, 36, 65–67, *65*, *66*, *67*
ruffled dressy dress, 40, 78–83, *78*, *79*, *81*, *82*, *83*
ruffled ribbon sundress, 36, 62–64, *62*, *63*, *64*
ruffled wrap, 96–97, *97*
ruffles, how to make, 60–61, *60*, 82–83
rugs, jute edged throw, 93–95, *93*, *94*, *95*

S
scarf
    doodled, 136–37, *136*, *137*
    hoodie, 198–200, *198*, *199*, *200*, *307*
    stacked dot, 178–79, *178*, *179*
scissors, 18
scoop neck, 31
seam rippers, 18
sewing machines, 16–17
sewing techniques, 18–21, *19*
sewn cardboard gift tags, 232–33, *233*
shaving pouch, monogrammed, 212–13, *213*
shawl, simple jersey, 276, *276*
sheets, 244
shirred empire waist dress, 36, 75–77, *75*, *76*, *77*
shirring, 128, *129*

shirts
    four-panel garment, 38
    gracefully gathered neckline, 36,
        68–69, *68*, *69*
    measurements for, 26, *26*
    patterns for, 27–31, *28*, *29*, *30*, *31*
    pleated neckline, 36, 70–71, *70*, *71*
    two-panel garment for, 34
    *See also* t-shirts; tunics
short sleeves, 42, *43*
shoulder bag, clever leather, 255–59, *255*,
        *257*, *258*, *259*, *309*, *311*
silk jersey fabrics, 13, 78, 299
simple jersey shawl, 276, *276*
sketched window sheers, 150–52, *150*,
        *151*, *152*, *305*
sketching with thread, 134–35
    *See also* free-motion stitching
skirt flare, 26, *27*
skirt length, 26, *26*
skirts
    a-line, *27*, 46–48, *46*, *47*, *48*
    bustle, 48, 90–92, *90*, *91*, *92*
    layered hemline, 48, 88–89, *88*, *89*
    linen with wavy hemline, 130–31, *130*,
        *131*
    modern stretch velvet, 48, 192–93, *192*,
        *193*, *309*
    mod flower, 48, 219–20, *219*, *220*, *308*
    reverse-appliqué, 48, 188–89, *188*,
        *189*, *309*
    stretch-panel, 54–57, *54*, *55*, *56*, *57*
    two-panel, 46–48, *46*, *47*, *48*
    *See also* wrap skirts
sleeves
    how to make, 42–44, *42*, *43*, *44*
    length of, 26, *26*
    patterns for, 28, *28*, 30, *30*
smocking stitch, *22*
sofa arm catchall, 216–18, *216*, *218*, *307*

solid colors, fabric, 13
stabilizers, 134
stacked dot scarf, 178–79, *178*, *179*
star template, *303*
stenciling, 208–25
    mod flower skirt, 219–20, *219*, *220*, *308*
    monogrammed shaving pouch, 212–13,
        *213*
    Ollie and Opal's big dog bed, 224–25,
        *224*, *225*, *308*
    pear produce bag, 214–15, *215*, *307*
    rainy day wrap skirt, 221–23, *221*, *222*,
        *223*, *310*
    sofa arm catchall, 216–18, *216*, *218*, *307*
stitched-edge appliqué, 172, *172*
stitched lamp shade, 124–25, *125*
stitched silk bracelet, 299, *299*, *304*
stitches, 13, *22*
    *See also* decorative stitches
straight grain, 14, *14*
straight stitch, *22*, 106, 135
stretch direction, 14, *14*
stretch-panel skirt, 54–57, *54*, *55*, *56*, *57*
stretch stitches, 13, 135
sundresses
    ruffled ribbon, 36, 62–64, *62*, *63*, *64*
    swishy, 36, 40, 128–29, *128*, *129*
    tubular, 158–61, *158*, *159*, *160*, *161*
super-jersey lingerie bag, 120–21, *120*, *121*
super-jersey neckerchief, 113, *113*
sweaters. *See* felted sweaters
sweet thing newborn cardigan, 296–98,
        *296*, *297*, *298*
swishy sundress, 36, 40, 128–29, *128*, *129*

T

tablecloths
    feast day appliqué, 194–97, *195*, *196*,
        *197*, *303*

upcycling, 244
    vintage tablecloth floor cushion,
        260–61, *261*
table runner, cider season, 186–87, *186*,
        *187*, *305*
tape measures, 18
television template, *307*
templates, 302–11
three-panel wrap skirt, 49–53, *49*, *51*, *52*,
        *53*, 145
throw pillow, cutout, 140–43, *141*, *143*,
        *302*
throw rug, jute edged, 93–95, *93*, *94*, *95*
tissue case, vintage hankie, 277
tools, 16–18
torsos, patterns for, 29, *29*, 31, *31*
totes, ribbon trimmed, 98–100, *98*, *100*
travel art kit, 153–55, *153*, *154*, *155*
tree template, *303*
tricot stitch, *22*
trimming, 18, *19*
trivet, cork, 229, *229*
t-shirts
    for appliqué, 179
    cairn reverse-appliqué, 180–81, *180*,
        *181*, *303*
    for girl's bloomer's, 253
    keyhole, 36, 101–3, *101*, *102*, *103*
    for meandering cardigans, 108–9, *108*,
        *109*
    for pattern pieces, 27–30
    pebble tee, 36, 138–39, *138*, *139*
    for super-jersey lingerie bags, 121
    two-tee dress, 262–63, *262*, *263*
    upcycling, 244
tubular sundress, 158–61, *158*, *159*, *160*, *161*
tunics
    cowl neck duffle, 36, 72–74, *72*, *73*, *74*
    exposed seam, 40, 86–87, *86*, *87*
    four-panel garment for, 38

leafy ruffle, 36, 84–85, *84*, *85*
measurements for, 26, *26*
ruched, 36, 65–67, *65*, *66*, *67*
two-panel garment for, 34
two-panel garments, 34–37, *34*, *35*, *36*, *37*
 cowl neck duffle, 72
 fiddlehead dress, 156
 gracefully gathered neckline shirt, 68
 keyhole t-shirt, 101
 leafy ruffle tunic, 84
 pebble tee, 139
 pleated neckline top, 71
 ruched tunic, *67*
 ruffled ribbon sundress, 63
 shirred empire waist dress, 75
 swishy sundress, 128
 tubular sundress, 158
two-panel skirt, 46–48, *46*, *47*, *48*
 bustle skirt, 90
 layered hemline skirt, 88
 modern stretch velvet skirt, 193
 mod flower skirt, 219
 reverse-appliqué skirt, 188
two-tee dress, 40, 262–63, *262*, *263*
tyvek pencil pouch, 230–31, *230*, *308*

## U

ugly sweater turned pretty cardigan, 272–73, *272*, *273*
umbrella template, *310*
upcycling, 23, 242–73

## V

vanishing-ink fabric markers, 18
velvet, 114, 193
vintage hankie tissue case, 277
vintage pot holders, 245, *245*

vintage tablecloth floor cushion, 260–61, *261*
v-neck, 31
voile, 151
votive, linen, 290–91, *291*

## W

waist measurements, 26, *26*
wall art, 148–49, *148*
wallet, fused plastic, 236–37, *236*
wavy lines, 106, *106*
wild thing newborn bonnet, 294–95, *294*, *295*
wind spinner, 234–35, *234*, *235*
wool felt, 15, 140, 174, 177
 *See also* felted sweaters
wool jersey fabrics, 13
 doodled scarf, 136
 keyhole t-shirt, 101
 leafy ruffle tunic, 84
 reverse-appliqué skirt, 188
 shirred empire waist dress, 75
 stacked dot scarf, 178
 super-jersey neckerchief, 113
wool jumpers, 36, 250–51, *250*, *251*
woven cotton fabrics, 13, 14–15
 appliquéd journal, 184
 coloring book wrap skirt, 145
 cutout throw pillow, 140
 line art lunchbox, 146
 pretty pillowcase, 107, *107*
 stitched lamp shade, 124
 stretch-panel skirt, 54
 three-panel wrap skirt, 49
woven fabrics, 12, 13, 14–15
 binding for, 19–21, *20*
 grainline of, 14, *14*, 15
 preparation of, 14
wrap skirts

coloring book, 50, 144–45, *144*, *145*
dress shirt, 50, 266–67, *267*
rainy day, 50, 221–23, *221*, *222*, *223*, *310*
three-panel, 49–53, *49*, *51*, *52*, *53*, 145
wraps, ruffled, 96–97, *97*
writing with thread, 135
 *See also* free-motion stitching

## Z

zigzag stitch, 13, *22*

# Other Storey Titles You Will Enjoy

**One-Yard Wonders**
by Rebecca Yaker and
Patricia Hoskins.
101 hip, contemporary projects, from
baby items and plush toys to pet
beds and stylish bags, each made
from just a single yard of fabric.
304 pages. Hardcover with
concealed wire-o and patterns.
ISBN 978-1-60342-449-3.

**Fabric-by-Fabric
One-Yard Wonders**
by Rebecca Yaker and
Patricia Hoskins.
101 more beautiful, stylish, and
fun projects that use a diverse
range of fabrics.
416 pages. Hardcover with
concealed wire-o and patterns.
ISBN 978-1-60342-586-5.

**Mend It Better**
by Kristin M. Roach.
Creative, attractive, and easy
patching, darning, and stitching,
both by hand and machine.
224 pages. Padded hardcover.
ISBN 978-1-60342-564-3.

**Sew What! Bags**
by Lexie Barnes.
Totes, messenger bags, drawstring
sacks, and handbags — 18 pattern-
free projects that can be customized
into all shapes and sizes.
152 pages. Hardcover with concealed
wire-o. ISBN 978-1-60342-092-1.

**Sew What! Skirts**
by Francesca DenHartog &
Carole Ann Camp.
A fast, straightforward method of
sewing a variety of inspired skirts
that fit your body perfectly, without
relying on store-bought patterns.
128 pages. Hardcover with concealed
wire-o. ISBN 978-1-58017-625-5.

**The Sweater Chop Shop**
by Crispina ffrench.
One-of-a-kind clothing and
home dec items from recycled
wool sweaters.
176 pages. Paper.
ISBN 978-1-60342-155-3.

These and other books from Storey Publishing are available
wherever quality books are sold or by calling 1-800-441-5700.

Visit us at *www.storey.com*.